Be Epic!

Joe Fo

More Praise for
Content Inc.

"Instead of throwing money away and sucking up to A-listers, now there is a better way to promote your business. It's called content marketing, and this book is a great way to master this new technique."

—Guy Kawasaki, Chief Evangelist of Canva
and author of *The Art of the Start 2.0*

"How do you take the maximum amount of risk out of starting a business? Joe Pulizzi shows us. Fascinate your audience, then turn them into loyal fans. *Content Inc.* shows you how. Use it as your road map to start-up success."

—Sally Hogshead, *New York Times* and
Wall Street Journal bestselling author,
How the World Sees You

"*Content Inc.* is the most personal of Joe Pulizzi's books to date. The glimpse it provides into the minds of today's content marketing leaders should serve as inspiration to anyone who wants to build their own company, career niche, or energized brand. You cannot put this book down without feeling motivated to go change your own future for the better."

—Jeffrey K. Rohrs, CMO, Yext and author,
*Audience: Marketing in the Age of
Subscribers, Fans & Followers*

"The approach to business taught all over the world is to create a product and then spend a bunch of money to market and sell it. Joe outlines a radically new way to succeed in business: Develop your *audience first* by creating content that draws people in and then watch your business (and products) sell themselves!"

—David Meerman Scott,
bestselling author of 10 books including
The New Rules of Marketing and PR
and *The New Rules of Sales and Service*

"The digital age has fundamentally reshaped the cost curve for entrepreneurs. The key challenge now is no longer access to capital, it is access to audience. Joe vividly describes the formula for developing a purpose-driven business that connects with an engaged and loyal audience around content. With brand, voice, and audience, building and monetizing a business is easy."

—Julie Fleischer, Sr. Director,
Data + Content + Media, Kraft Foods

"Today, anyone, anywhere with a passion and a focus on a content niche can build a multimillion-dollar platform and business. I did it and so can you. Just follow Joe's plan and his *Content Inc.* model and you can make it happen."

—John Lee Dumas, Founder,
EntrepreneurOnFire

CONTENT INC.

CONTENT INC.

HOW ENTREPRENEURS USE CONTENT
TO BUILD MASSIVE AUDIENCES AND CREATE
RADICALLY SUCCESSFUL BUSINESSES

JOE PULIZZI

New York   Chicago   San Francisco   Athens   London   Madrid
Mexico City   Milan   New Delhi   Singapore   Sydney   Toronto

1 2 3 4 5 6 7 8 9 0   DOC/DOC   1 2 1 0 9 8 7 6 5

ISBN   978-1-259-58965-2
MHID   1-259-58965-X

e-ISBN   978-1-259-58966-9
e-MHID   1-259-58966-8

Library of Congress Cataloging-in-Publication Data
Pulizzi, Joe.
   Content Inc. : how entrepreneurs use content to build massive audiences and create radically successful businesses / Joe Pulizzi. — 1 Edition.
      pages cm
   ISBN 978-1-259-58965-2 (hardback : alk. paper) — ISBN 1-259-58965-X (alk. paper) 1. Target marketing. 2. Social media—Computer network resources. 3. Customer relations—Management. I. Title.
   HF5415.127.P8498 2015
   658.8'72—dc23   2015021346

McGraw-Hill Education books are available at special quantity discounts to use as premiums and sales promotions or for use in corporate training programs. To contact a representative, please visit the Contact Us pages at www.mhprofessional.com.

*To all those crazy people in the world
who have risked it all to start a business.
This book is for you.*

Contents

CONTENTS

PART 8
NEXT-LEVEL CONTENT INC.

CHAPTER 23

PUTTING IT ALL TOGETHER   269

CHAPTER 24

JOIN THE MOVEMENT   283

Foreword

By all reasonable accounts, I had just thrown my life away.

Up until this point, I had done it all the "right" way. Excelled my first year of law school and graded on to law review. Clerked for great firms my second and third years.

And yet I had just quit my big law firm job only four years after graduation. Even worse, I had done it so I could "write on the Internet."

Try explaining that one to your mom.

Now, most unhappy attorneys are afflicted with the desire to write. But you don't quit your job to do it. And when it came to the Internet in 1998, you had to write a business plan to succeed, not *content*.

After all, the firm I quit was the one that took Michael Dell from dorm room to billionaire. I had access to connections, but I didn't seem to want them.

In hindsight, perhaps I *was* a little crazy. The writing life was for me, I thought, but I didn't want to be a cog in the machine of Hollywood films or New York publishing.

Every evening after work for four tedious years, I had been staring at a computer screen, exploring the Internet. All those people, all over the world—there had to be a way to make a living from reaching them with my words.

What I was actually setting out to do was to start a business. And yet I had never taken a business class, never read a marketing book, never once thought of myself as an entrepreneur.

I wanted to build an audience and find a way to make a living from it. Fortunately, my cluelessness was an asset, because the Internet turned a lot of conventional wisdom on its head.

At the time, e-mail newsletters were the vehicles for content publishing, before blogs took over. I started out creating witty pop culture e-zines with the hope of selling advertising.

As far as attracting an audience goes, I succeeded. Tens of thousands signed up, and one of my titles got coverage from *Entertainment Weekly*, *Sight and Sound Magazine*, and my then hometown *Austin Chronicle*.

What I didn't get, however, was revenue. Online advertising is a tough game today, but in 1998 for a newbie like me, it seemed impossible.

My problem, I came to realize, was that I didn't have a product or service to sell. Then I realized that I *did* have something to sell, and trust me . . . I needed the money.

My law license was still active. So in 1999 I started yet another e-mail newsletter, this one focused on legal issues related to the Internet. I was hoping to pick up enough client work to survive while I figured out the other business model.

It took off. I was soon turning away clients, picking and choosing the best work, securing the best retainers. I was amazed . . . but more importantly, *I was hooked*.

Through the process of starting one company that failed, and one firm that didn't, I discovered something important—I loved starting businesses. Rather than a traditional writer, I was an *entrepreneur who could write*, and that's served me well.

That's because content is what people want online, and marketing and advertising are what people easily avoid. I knew how to create the former, and that's how I attracted and held the attention that led to revenue, profits, and success.

The practice of law was still no fun, so I set my sights on the lucrative real estate industry, which was clueless about the things I knew about online content and marketing. Between 2001 and 2005—despite being completely unknown and with little more than several content-rich websites—I started and ran two virtual real estate brokerages.

I was now making more money than if I had remained an attorney at that big, prestigious law firm. I was actually making more than many of the senior partners. More importantly, I was convinced that relevant content designed to build an audience of prospects was the way to succeed when starting a new business.

In 2005, I decided I wanted more. I had no passion for real estate—I just had to prove to myself that I could succeed outside of law. With that out of the way, I truly believed that my journey as an entrepreneur had just begun.

In December 2005, I registered the domain name copyblogger.com. The idea was to teach people the unique intersection of content and copywriting skills I had used to start three successful service businesses. On January 9, 2006, the site launched.

What *Copyblogger* was (and is) about is called *content marketing*. I figured the terminology part out thanks to a guy named Joe Pulizzi, the author of the book you now hold in your hands. More on him in just a bit.

Back to 2006. *Copyblogger* takes off—despite the fact that I'm again completely unknown in the field—because people were frustrated with typical blogging and online copywriting advice. I merged the two topics together and advocated the heresy (at the time) that you should sell products and services with content instead of relying on advertising.

Here's a short summary of what happened next:

Between 2007 and 2009, I launched a new start-up off *Copyblogger* every year, mostly software, each of which achieved seven figures in revenue in a year or less. In 2010, I merged several of those companies together to form Copyblogger Media in order to execute on a grander vision.

In 2014, Copyblogger Media introduced a complete SaaS system for content marketers and online entrepreneurs. We also hit $10 million in revenue.

Did I mention that we never took venture capital, didn't advertise, and were profitable every year? That's all thanks to the audience I started building in 2006.

Now, I'm not the only one with a story like this. Many start-up businesses have grown out of audience-first approaches, specifically from the blogging world. But the start-up community generally failed to take notice.

That changed a bit with the inclusion of a case study about Copyblogger Media in the *New York Times* bestseller *The Lean Entrepreneur*, by Brant Cooper and Patrick Vlaskovits. That's when my concept of the "minimum viable audience" reached well beyond the *Copyblogger* world.

An MVA is the point when your audience starts growing itself through social sharing and word of mouth. Even better, it's also when you start getting the feedback that tells you what product or service your audience actually wants to buy.

A case study on a single page in *The Lean Entrepreneur* was certainly eye-opening to many fledgling entrepreneurs. But the book you're holding right now is more like a master class that provides a six-step process for creating successful companies like the seven I've started so far (without all my early missteps and mistakes).

This is exactly what an entrepreneur like you needs to develop a content strategy that builds a winning company. And you don't have to be a writer; but you do have to think like a media producer.

It goes without saying that I would have killed to have *Content, Inc.* in 1998 when I was starting out. So be prepared to be enlightened. And who better to deliver the goods than the guy who's been talking about content marketing since 2001?

They call Joe Pulizzi the "godfather of content marketing" for good reason. He started his own multimillion-dollar company using the same content-intensive and audience-first approach he advocates here.

As I mentioned, Joe was the one who convinced me to adopt the term *content marketing* in 2008, just as he's convinced marketing departments across the world to craft content strategies to market smarter. He's an amazing industry evangelist and an even better human being.

There's no better time than now to get started, and *Content Inc.* is the perfect starting point. Just in case you're worried that the tactics and strategies you're about to discover won't work in the here and now, let me share this with you.

In January 2015, exactly nine years after *Copyblogger* debuted, I launched a simple e-mail newsletter called *Further*. It's a personal development publication, which means I've once again entered a field where I'm completely unknown.

Although the project is young and has no definitive business model, it's already achieved a minimum viable audience. That allows me to start evolving it and discovering what the audience wants—and that's where the fun and profit begin.

This one could be my biggest yet. The path to yours begins here.

Brian Clark
CEO, Copyblogger Media
Boulder, Colorado

Introduction

> The reasonable man adapts himself to the world: the unreasonable
> man persists in trying to adapt the world to himself.
> Therefore all progress depends on the unreasonable man.
> GEORGE BERNARD SHAW

I left a six-figure executive publishing position in 2007 to start a business. Even though I had been thinking about leaving my job for a while, and I had a product in mind to sell, the product wasn't going to be ready anytime soon.

So I had no job and no product to sell (and no income). It wasn't a good position to be in with two small children (ages three and five at the time) and a mortgage to pay. The web developer I was working with didn't believe we could get the online offering ready for at least nine months. Ouch.

What to do? Without a product to pitch, I focused all my attention on building an audience. In a few weeks, the blog was up and running.

Three to five times a week, I was creating and distributing helpful information targeted to marketers in large companies—the audience I wanted to reach eventually with my new product. A few months later, I was starting to build a small, loyal following.

Fast-forward to the present day. Our company, Content Marketing Institute, has been named to the Inc. 500 fastest-growing private companies list for three years running, becoming the fastest-growing business media organization in North America. We have consistently grown our revenues at 50 percent per year for the last four years. In 2015, we'll top $10 million in revenues.

Through a lovely accident, I stumbled on a powerful way to build a business in the digital age—and now believe there is no better way to go to market. By focusing on building an audience *first* and defining products and services *second*, an entrepreneur can change the rules of the game and significantly increase the odds of financial and personal success.

Let me repeat that: I believe the absolute best way to start a business today is *not* by launching a product, but by creating a system to attract and build an audience. Once a loyal audience is built, one that loves you and the information you send, you can, most likely, sell your audience anything you want. This model is called Content Inc.

But did I develop a method that is difficult to replicate, or are there other entrepreneurs and start-ups that used a similar strategy?

The True Story of David and Goliath

The challenges facing every entrepreneur who dreams of success can be summed up in one of two interpretations of the biblical story of David and Goliath.

Growing up in the Catholic school system, I heard the David versus Goliath story often. David is the ultimate underdog; Goliath, the Philistine giant, the most powerful warrior on the planet. David, a young boy, doesn't have a chance to defeat such a powerful and skilled warrior.

But through David's faith in God, *a handful of smooth rocks*, and perhaps a small miracle, David defeated Goliath.

Jack Wellman from the *Christian Crier* asserts that "Goliath had everything going for him. He had every advantage possible. He had great ability and he was trained, equipped, experienced, battle tested, and battle hardened, and he was completely fearless. He was totally confident but it could also be said that he was overconfident." He was also about 6 feet 9 inches tall.

And then here comes David, small and totally outmatched. Just a boy, David won because he had supreme confidence in the Lord, who was with him, and the giant lost the seemingly unlosable battle.

> *Reaching into his bag and taking out a stone, he slung it and struck the Philistine on the forehead. The stone sank into his forehead, and he fell facedown on the ground.*
>
> *So David triumphed over the Philistine with a sling and a stone; without a sword in his hand he struck down the Philistine and killed him.*
>
> *David ran and stood over him. He took hold of the Philistine's sword and drew it from the sheath. After he killed him, he cut off his head with the sword.*
>
> *When the Philistines saw that their hero was dead, they turned and ran. (1 Samuel 17)*

David beat Goliath because of his faith in God. Of course, David had confidence in victory because the Lord was with him. But perhaps there is another way to interpret this story . . .

Goliath: The Underdog

Malcolm Gladwell gave me a new perspective on this story in his book *David and Goliath: Underdogs, Misfits, and the Art of Battling Giants*. Gladwell's version makes perfect sense to my entrepreneurial spirit.

According to Gladwell, Goliath was indeed a giant, who was also extremely slow to move. Add to that, he was wearing 100 pounds of armor. Some medical experts believe Goliath was suffering from acromegaly, a hormone imbalance that causes a human to grow to extraordinary size. If that was the case, his vision was most likely impaired as well.

How about David? Yes, David was small in stature, but he was an accomplished "slinger" and could target and strike large beasts from great distances. Light on his feet, David could move unsuspected on a target and still win an attack from far away.

The biblical interpretation tells us that David, the underdog, was shown favor by the Lord, which helped him defeat Goliath, the heavy favorite. Actually, Goliath had no chance to win. *God favored David by helping him discern a better strategy.* The fight was over before it ever began.

Changing the Game

David won because he played an entirely different game than Goliath did. If David would have fought Goliath as tradition demanded, one warrior in hand-to-hand combat against another, he would have lost.

And this is what happens to almost every entrepreneur dreaming up an idea that will make him or her successful. Entrepreneurs, whether bootstrapped or funded, have no resources compared with those of the large enterprises they are competing with.

ENTREPRENEURS ARE GETTING BAD ADVICE

According to the U.S. Small Business Administration, the first step in starting a business is to develop a business plan. The standard business plan includes things like "defining what you are selling" and "creating a sales and marketing plan." Of course it does. I'm sure if you search the thousands of different business plans on the web, they all look pretty much the same. Every start-up essentially plays the game by the same rules.

Even Peter Thiel, cofounder of PayPal and the first outside investor in Facebook, focuses all the attention in his book *Zero to One* on developing an amazing product unlike the world has ever seen. While I believe Thiel offers some excellent advice to entrepreneurs, the premise is the same as all the other expert advice out there: create a product first. Find the problem, and then solve the problem with an exceptional product or service.

But the results aren't exceptional . . . at all. According to the U.S. Census Bureau, the majority of businesses fail in their first five years. And every other statistic out there on start-up failure actually says it's probably a lot worse than that.

Why do people go to market with their business in the same way? Is humanity so devoid of creativity that we've accepted that there is only one way to start and grow a business?

CAN CONTENT INC. BE REPLICATED?

Brian Clark, founder of Copyblogger Media, shares his story in both the Foreword of this book and throughout as a case study. Brian, a recovering attorney, had some amazing ideas about how businesses should market online. Unfortunately (or maybe I should say fortunately), he didn't have a product to sell.

For one year and seven months, Brian developed amazing content on a consistent basis to a targeted audience. He defined his ultimate mission as:

To create media assets that depended on the permission to contact my audience, not the permission of a media gatekeeper.

Or shorthand: Become the expert resource that attracts the right audience without having to buy advertising on someone else's platform.

And Brian did just that. Today, Copyblogger Media is one of the fastest-growing SaaS (software as a service) companies on the planet.

In our research for Content Inc., we've been able to uncover countless entrepreneurs in varied industries using a similar philosophy. In other words, Brian and I are not alone. And the better news? The Content Inc. model can be replicated (but more on that in a second).

THE CONTENT INC. FUTURE IS NOW

In the future, thousands of businesses around the globe will be leveraging a Content Inc. go-to-market strategy. Why? Because having a singular focus on audience, and building a loyal audience directly, gives you the best understanding of what products ultimately make the most sense to sell.

Content Inc. tells us that there is a better way and a better model that leads to a better life for entrepreneurs and business owners. You have the opportunity to be like David, who looks like an underdog to the Goliaths of the world, but the truth is that you've simply uncovered a better business strategy than all the rest.

THE CONTENT INC. MODEL

In our experience working with hundreds of businesses, and the dozens of interviews associated with this book, we've found that there are six distinct steps to the Content Inc. model (see Figure I.1).

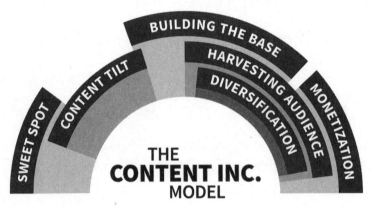

Figure I.1

1. The Sweet Spot

Simply put, the entrepreneur needs to uncover a content area that the business model will be based around. To make this happen, we need to identify a "sweet spot" that will attract an audience over time. This sweet spot is the intersection of a knowledge or skill set (something the entrepreneur or business has a competency in) and a passion area (something the entrepreneur or business feels is of great value to him or her personally or to society at large).

For example, Andy Schneider has built an entire business around his celebrity persona, the Chicken Whisperer. Andy's knowledge area is backyard poultry. To put it mildly, Andy knows more about raising chickens in a backyard than just about anyone else on the planet. At the same time, Andy has a passion for teaching. Andy loves helping his friends with their backyard chicken-raising whenever he can.

2. Content Tilt

Once the sweet spot is identified, the entrepreneur needs to determine the "tilt," or the differentiation factor, to find an area of little to no competition.

Claus Pilgaard is one of the most well-known celebrity figures in Denmark, all because of the extraordinary way he talks about chili peppers. Claus's YouTube videos have garnered millions of views, including one where Claus conducts the Danish National Chamber Orchestra playing "Tango Jalousie" while eating the world's hottest chili peppers. That video alone (http://cmi.media/CI-ChiliKlaus) has seen more than 3 million views (note that this is more than half the population of Denmark).

Claus's sweet spot was the intersection of his skill at performance art and his passion for chili peppers. But Claus realized there was an abundance of content and experts around the "heat" behind chili peppers, but a content gap around the taste of peppers. As he explains in an interview:

> I was actually sitting there in this little summer house getting a little bored and I had my camera with me and thought, "What if you talked about chili peppers in the same way as you were told about raising wine?" You talk about all the different kinds of tastes, not about the alcohol but what it tastes like. Is it coffee, or is it food? What is it? So instead of telling about how hot these peppers were, I was getting around the peppers and talking about the different varieties. And then my body started to tell another story [while eating the peppers]. Maybe that's why they [the videos] became so popular.

Claus always had a passion for chili peppers, but it wasn't until he started telling a different story around "taste" that the business model grew legs. The "tasting" addition to the sweet spot (what we call the "tilt") is what made the difference.

3. Building the Base

Once the sweet spot is found and the tilt occurs, a platform is chosen and a content base is constructed. This is exactly like building a house. Before we get into all the paint and fixtures and flooring options, we have to plan and install the foundation. This is done by consistently generating valuable content through one key channel (a blog, a podcast, YouTube, etc.).

Today, Content Marketing Institute (CMI) offers a print magazine, research papers, podcasts, ongoing workshops, and more . . . but for the first four years, it was just a blog. The blog became the core channel that initially drew in the original audience. The blog originally started as just me, blogging approximately three times per week. In 2010, we opened up the blog to additional contributors at five times per week. In 2011, the blog went daily, even on weekends.

Not until success was found in the blog (the platform) did CMI diversify to other channels.

4. Harvesting Audience

After the platform is chosen and the content base is built, the opportunity presents itself to increase the audience and convert "one-time readers" into ongoing subscribers.

This is where we leverage social media as key distribution tools and take search engine optimization seriously. At this point, our job is not just to increase web traffic. By itself, web traffic is a meaningless metric. Our goal is to increase traffic to increase the opportunity to acquire an audience.

Here's how Michael Stelzner, CEO of Social Media Examiner, explains this step in the process:

> We were arguably late to the game, because by the time we launched SME [Social Media Examiner] there were thousands of other blogs that were dedicated to social, but I saw that as marketplace justification more than anything else. But I didn't doubt once I began, because I knew how to track metrics; I knew what mattered. I knew email acquisition was the key metric and I had decided that we weren't going to promote (meaning "sell") anything until we had at least

10,000 email subscribers. And we got to that number so quickly that I knew we were really onto something.

. . . last year we had 15 million unique people visit SME. We have 340,000 people that we email every single day. We currently publish 8–10 original articles every single week.

The critical acknowledgment for this area: while there are many metrics to analyze content success, the number one metric is the subscriber. It's almost impossible to monetize and grow your audience without first getting the reader to take action and actually "subscribe" to your content.

5. Diversification

Once the model has built a strong, loyal, and growing audience, it's time to diversify from the main content stream. Think of the model like an octopus, with each content channel being one of the eight arms. How many of those arms can we wrap our readers in to keep them close to us (and coming back for more)?

ESPN, originally started as a sports-only cable television station in 1979, began with a $9,000 investment by Bill and Scott Rasmussen. Now, almost 40 years later, ESPN is the world's most profitable media brand with operating earnings of more than $4 billion according to Forbes.com.

For 13 years, ESPN directed its attention on only one channel for 100 percent of its audience-building focus—cable television. Then, starting in 1992, the floodgates opened on diversification, first with the launch of ESPN radio. Then ESPN.com (originally called ESPN SportsZone) launched in 1995, followed three years later by *ESPN the Magazine.*

Today, ESPN has a property in almost every channel available on the planet, from Twitter to podcasts to documentaries. Even though the channels were limited in the 1980s and 1990s (compared with today), ESPN didn't diversify until the core platform (cable television) was successful.

6. Monetization

It's time. You've identified your sweet spot. You've "tilted" to find an area of content noncompetition. You've selected the platform and built the base. You've started to build subscribers, and you've even begun to launch content on additional platforms. Now is when the model monetizes against the platform.

By this time, you are armed with enough subscriber information (both qualitative and quantitative) that a multitude of opportunities will present themselves to generate revenue. This could be consulting or software or events or more.

Rand Fishkin, CEO of Moz (originally called SEOMoz), started his blog on search engine optimization insights back in 2004. In less than five years, Moz had over 100,000 e-mail subscribers.

Rand originally monetized the audience through consulting services, but in 2007, Moz launched a beta subscription service for software tools and reports. By 2009, Moz closed the consulting business entirely and focused on selling software to its audience. Figure I.2 shows the results.

The best part? Rand's success looks amazingly unusual, but it isn't. The more I've researched this, the more I've found that these are typ-

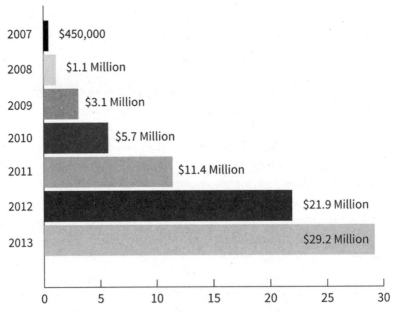

Figure I.2 Rand Fishkin has grown Moz from a struggling consulting practice to a fast-growing, $30 million enterprise.

ical numbers for a Content Inc.–based business. The key is following the six steps as outlined above and being patient enough for the model to work.

THE AUDIENCE FOR THIS BOOK

Forty years ago, Harvard Business School professor Howard Stephenson defined entrepreneurship in this manner:

> *Entrepreneurship is the pursuit of opportunity without regard to resources currently controlled.*

Before starting the research for this book, I believed that the term *entrepreneur* was relegated to start-ups. According to the above definition, this is an incorrect presumption. As Eric Reis contends in *The Lean Startup*, when you look at the entrepreneur in this way, it should be "regardless of company size, sector, or stage of development."

At the same time, Reis explains that "a startup is a human institution designed to create a new product or service under conditions of extreme uncertainty." This combined look at the core definitions of *entrepreneurship* and *start-up* plays into Reis's argument, that neither one means that these terms are owned solely by new companies.

From this perspective, and leveraging a Content Inc. methodology, we have:

1. **A pure start-up.** You are creating a new organization, launching a content-first model. You are using funding from various sources to keep the lights on until you discover your revenue-generation product or service. An example is Brian Clark and copyblogger.com.
2. **A start-up inside a large organization.** You've received buy-in to develop an audience around a current customer segment. Your goal is to build an engaged audience around a content niche. Once that's complete, you'll look to monetize the platform into new or current product sales, or perhaps use it to keep customers more loyal. This is where most enterprises are with content marketing. They believe that if they launch a content platform, it will help their current business, but they are not 100 percent sure how it will unfold or what the ultimate benefits might be.

3. **A stalled business.** You currently have a number of products and services you sell, but you are not happy with your growth. You believe that building an audience around content can lead to new opportunities for the business. An example of this is LEGO. Years ago LEGO's growth stalled, so it took a fresh look at its audience and platforms. Today, LEGO is a vibrant, growing company. Much of this credit goes to the multitude of content platforms the company was able to build.

The majority of examples in *Content Inc.* revolve around the creation of a new or young organization, one that is developing processes around building a new audience that becomes loyal and engaged through content creation and distribution. Even so, I believe this book is relevant for any of the three "states of business" above.

HOW THIS BOOK IS ORGANIZED

Years ago my friend Henry and I were talking about how long a blog post should be in terms of number of words. His response was priceless. Henry said slyly, "A blog post is like a miniskirt . . . it needs to be long enough to cover the essentials but short enough to keep it interesting."

And that's exactly what you'll find in each chapter of *Content Inc.* Some chapters will be long, because I feel depth is needed in those areas. Some will be short. Needless to say, this book has been heavily edited to keep subjects interesting and relevant to you.

In addition, I've included key themes, action steps, and resources at the end of most chapters. One of my big pet peeves of nonfiction books is having to always go to the back of the book for resources. So, problem solved . . . we just put them at the back of the chapter.

And finally . . .

This book is not a personal memoir, but I will be sharing all the secrets about how we built our business using the strategies in *Content Inc.* I'll also be sharing multiple case studies, like Brian's and many others, to show that the Content Inc. methodology is not a one-hit wonder. Any entrepreneur in any industry can, by following a few important steps, develop a successful business by focusing on building audience first and product second.

Thank *you* for taking the time to make this journey with me.

If today were the last day of your life,
would you want to do what you are about to do today?
STEVE JOBS

CONTENT INC. INSIGHTS

- The majority of start-ups around the world begin their journey in exactly the same way as every other company. Why are we doing this since the majority of start-ups fail? The formula needs to change.
- I fell into a happy accident with the Content Inc. model. And I wasn't alone. The great news is that, by reverse engineering my success model and dozens of others like it, there is a systematic way to create a Content Inc. business that works.
- Whether you are a solo start-up or an innovative group within a large enterprise, Content Inc. can and will work with patience and the right content plan.

Resources

Malcolm Gladwell, *David and Goliath: Underdogs, Misfits, and the Art of Battling Giants,* Little, Brown and Company, 2013.

Peter Thiel, *Zero to One: Notes on Startups, or How to Build the Future,* Crown Business, 2014.

Scott Shane, "Failure Is a Constant in Entrepreneurship," NewYorkTimes.com, accessed April 7, 2015, http://boss.blogs.nytimes.com/2009/07/15/failure -is-a-constant-in-entrepreneurship/.

Jack Wellman, "David and Goliath Bible Story," Patheos.com, accessed April 7, 2015, http://www.patheos.com/blogs/christiancrier/2014/04/15/david-and -goliath-bible-story-lesson-summary-and-study/#ixzz3H9qKZLbb.

Holy Bible, New International Version, Grand Rapids: Zondervan Publishing House, 1984, 1 Samuel 17.

Eric Schurenburg, "What's an Entrepreneur? The Best Answer Ever," Inc.com, accessed April 7, 2015, http://www.inc.com/eric-schurenberg/the-best -definition-of-entepreneurship.html.

Eric Reis, *The Lean Startup,* Crown Business, 2011.

James Andrew Miller and Thom Shales, *Those Guys Have All the Fun: Inside the World of ESPN,* Little, Brown and Company, 2011.

"ESPN.com Facts," accessed April 7, 2015, http://espn.go.com/pr/espnfact.html.

Claus Pilgaard, interview by Clare McDermott, January 2015.

Andy Schneider, interview by Clare McDermott, December 2015.

Rand Fishkin, interview by Clare McDermott, January 2015.

Mike Stelzner, interview by Clare McDermott, January 2015.

Part 1

Starting the Journey

How wonderful it is that nobody need wait a single moment
before starting to improve the world.

ANNE FRANK

To be successful at launching the Content Inc. model, we need
to get our goals and plans in the right place. Let's get started!

Chapter 1

Beginning with the End in Mind

Goals allow you to control the direction of change in your favor.
BRIAN TRACY

I went through a fairly long period of not feeling successful, though in hindsight it's more accurate to say that I didn't really know what success was.

I graduated from Bowling Green State University (just south of Toledo, Ohio) with a degree in interpersonal communications. My major had been "undecided," until the beginning of my junior year. The only reason I chose interpersonal communications is that it was the only degree I could pursue that would allow me to graduate on time.

As I came close to graduation, I felt like sports marketing was something I'd be good at. I was lucky enough to get an internship with the Cleveland Cavaliers, the professional basketball team, after graduation. But after finding out that all the money went to the players (the operations team works *very* long hours for *very* little pay), I decided to go to graduate school.

With two weeks left before fall semester, someone dropped out of the teaching assistantship program at Penn State University, leaving an opening for yours truly. I taught four semesters of public speaking and ended up with a master's degree in communications.

Overeducated and underexperienced, I traveled to Cleveland, Ohio, to find a job. After sending out seemingly hundreds of résumés with no luck, I took the master's degree off my résumé and started to do temp work. After a few monthlong work engagements, I landed a full-time job at an insurance company working on internal communications projects.

Shortly after starting my new job, I read the book *Think and Grow Rich* by Napoleon Hill. It made a huge impact on how I defined success and what I really wanted to do with my life. Though I read the entire book, cover to cover, there was one powerful passage I felt particularly compelled to remember:

> *Opportunity has spread its wares before you. Step up to the front, select what you want, create your plan, put the plan into action, and follow through with persistence.*

It was then that I started to *set goals* for my life.

Next, I read *The 7 Habits of Highly Effective People* by Stephen Covey. The second habit listed is "Begin with the End in Mind," which means:

> *To begin each day, task, or project with a clear vision of your desired direction and destination, and then continue by flexing your proactive muscles to make things happen.*

It was then that I started to *write down my goals* for the first time.

After three years and a few promotions at the insurance company, I left for a new opportunity at Penton Media, the largest independent business-to-business media company in North America. It was there that I expanded on my education, learning the world of media communication, marketing communications, and corporate content creation. It was at Penton where I learned the power of listening to an audience and became familiar with the various business models that made media companies work.

In March 2007 I decided to leave Penton Media (where I was vice president of custom media) primarily because I didn't feel I had any real influence over the direction of the company (one of my written goals was to have influence at whatever job I was currently in). So I left and started what was to become the Content Marketing Institute.

In that same year, research conducted by Dr. Gail Matthews from Dominican University of California showed that people who wrote down their goals, shared with a friend, and sent weekly updates to that friend were on average *33 percent more successful* in accomplishing their stated goals than those who merely formulated goals.

So I started to share my goals with others; but more importantly, I reviewed those goals on a daily basis. That's right—every day I would read my goals, making sure I was staying on track.

A few years later, after reading the book *The 10X Rule* by Grant Cardone, I separated my goals into the following six categories:

- Financial goals
- Family goals
- Spiritual goals
- Mental goals
- Physical goals
- Philanthropic goals

The difference in the direction my life took from that point on is beyond remarkable to me.

TWO ACTIONS AND THEIR IMPACT
ON A CONTENT INC. APPROACH

I've been blessed with more than my fair share of fortune for many years, but in thinking back, I've found that those two daily behaviors I mentioned have likely made all the difference: *writing down my goals* and *consistently reviewing those goals.*

Why am I telling you this, and what does it have to do with content marketing and this book? Well, in this case, everything.

Every year, Content Marketing Institute and MarketingProfs release an annual benchmark study on the state of content marketing in North America, the United Kingdom, and Australia (see http://cmi.media/CI-research for the full study).

Upon getting the initial results of the latest study, we looked deep into the data to see if we could determine what differentiates the great content marketers (those who state they are effective with content marketing) from everyone else. While many characteristics came to the surface, we only found two critical differentiators. Great content marketers do two things differently from the rest

- They document their content marketing strategy in some way (written, electronic, etc.) (see Figure 1.1).
- They review and consistently refer to the plan on a regular basis.

So, of all the characteristics we looked at, these two actions made the most difference in determining content marketing success. It seems

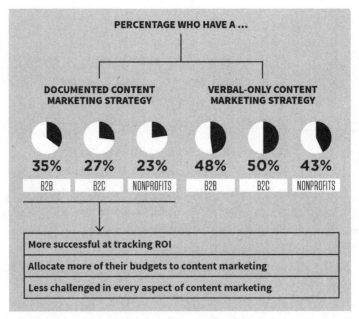

Figure 1.1 Elite content marketing organizations have a habit of writing down their plans and documenting their strategy.

Source: Content Marketing Institute/MarketingProfs

so simple, but the fact is that few marketers are doing these two things consistently.

From a personal perspective, these are the same two actions that made all the difference in my life's successes, both personally and professionally.

DO THIS FIRST

Yes, this book is filled with actionable items on how to develop and execute your own Content Inc. initiative; but without setting direction for your life, what good will it do?

I've seen so many smart entrepreneurs start with a business idea they think will change the world, only to fail many months later by not having their priorities straight.

Your work begins now. Before you embark on this journey with me, you need to get your six goal areas in order. Here's how to do it. Under each area, list at least two actionable goals with specific numbers and timetables. It doesn't have to be perfect. The goals will change on an ongoing basis as you learn more about yourself. And most likely, if you are reading this book, those "career" goals may not be ready for show yet. No worries . . . you can fill certain areas in as you delve into the book.

Content Inc. Tip

Try using Evernote to keep track of your goals so you can keep them with you at all times, whether you are on your computer, tablet, or smartphone. If that doesn't feel right, just use a traditional Moleskine notebook and keep it with you at all times.

Content Inc. in Action

My Six Goal Areas

Financial

I own companies that I can control at a distance and have great people working for me.

1. _____
2. _____
3. _____

Family

I have healthy children who believe they can accomplish anything.

1. _____
2. _____
3. _____

Spiritual

I pray every evening with my family.

1. _____
2. _____
3. _____

Mental

I read one book per month on something non–business related.

1. _____
2. _____
3. _____

Physical

I run three times per week and compete in two half-marathons per year.

1. _____
2. _____
3. _____

Philanthropic

I have helped turn Cleveland, Ohio, into a vibrant city.

1. _____
2. _____
3. _____

What You Are Risking with a Content Inc. Approach

When I left my "real job" to start a business, countless friends and family members voiced their concerns.

"Are you sure you want to take that big a risk and leave a secure job?"

The question was understandable. I had a young family with two small kids. Heck, even my friends who were entrepreneurs and business owners questioned my move from a six-figure salary and solid benefit package.

The problem was, as "cushy" as some may have thought my position to be, I didn't have much say in how the company was run. I had virtually no control over what the company did or did not do. I'm not sure if my position was at risk, but my job seemed awfully risky, benefits and all.

What Can You Control?

If you've ever read any of Robert Kiyosaki's books (from *Rich Dad* series fame), you may see risk a bit differently than most. Here's an overview of Mr. Kiyosaki's thinking:

> *If you cannot make a phone call or send an e-mail that will directly influence how a company is run, then investing in that company is like gambling at the casino.*

I have investments in the stock market. I own stock in Facebook, Google, Electronic Arts, and others. But to be honest, since I cannot call the CEOs of these companies to influence change, these investments are risky to me personally. For whatever you think about investing in stocks, if you have no control over what decisions are made, you are just playing the odds that some companies, for whatever reason, may perform better over time and increase in value.

Is Starting a Business Riskier than Taking a Steady Job?

During a phone interview in early 2015, a reporter made the comment to me, "You really took a risk by leaving your job and launching a new concept."

My response was something like this:

Yes, at first it seemed like I was risking a lot. But in hindsight, I made the safest move possible. Over the time I've been an entrepreneur, many of my friends lost their jobs. A number of my well-respected and incredibly smart teacher friends sweated nights and weekends hoping their levy would pass so they could keep their jobs. Amazingly talented people I know who write, draw, construct, design, and more for other people have been struggling to find a "steady job" to support their families. But in taking control of as much of my life as possible, I believe my move was the least risky of all.

I honor and respect what many of my family members and friends do for a living. What they do helps so many people in many different ways. But I also worry about their livelihood.

While 2014 was an amazing year for many of my friends and colleagues, a good number of my "corporate friends" lost their jobs in downsizing and restructuring efforts.

Taking Control Back

Not everyone is cut out to be an entrepreneur or take a Content Inc. approach. It requires a unique combination of passion, vision, perseverance, patience, and blind belief in yourself to become a success. But I believe we have to start thinking differently about how the seemingly safe choices we make are actually incredibly risky. Some questions to consider:

- In your current situation, do you have enough control to help set the direction of the business? Will the CEO or business leader take a meeting from you and actually listen?
- What can you do in your current role to start to win over that influence?
- Are you investing in assets that you have some say in (e.g., real estate or investments in companies and individuals), or are you investing all your money into "good bets" (e.g., the stock market)?

> For whatever reason, we've been lulled into thinking that certain things are safe and certain things are risky. I believe the majority of human beings are living with blinders on to this fact. My hope is that you start to look at your current job, your career, and your investments a bit differently.
>
> So many things in life we have no control over . . . for those few things we do have control over, we need to grab it and run.

AS YOU BUILD . . .

As you move into building a Content Inc. model, there are two critical things to start thinking about. The first is what the legal entity for the business should be. In our U.S. examples, it seems the most popular legal model is the creation of an LLC (limited liability company) taxed as an S corporation (see a professional legal consultant for advice on your situation). The second is hiring a virtual assistant. If you are going to make Content Inc. work for you, you need to be focused on the business. Offloading calls and scheduling to someone else is not a "nice-to-have," but critical. Two resources to check out are Chris Ducker (http://cmi.media/CI-virtualstaff) and Jess Ostroff (http://cmi.media/CI-dontpanic), who both offer highly recommended virtual assistant services.

CONTENT INC. INSIGHTS

- Before you begin your Content Inc. journey, start with why. Why are you doing this? What do you want to achieve? Visualize who you really want to be.
- Write down and review your goals as often as you possibly can.
- Contemplate what you are really risking in your current position. Our view of risk is heavily shaped by what others think. Try to look at your situation objectively and determine if the Content Inc. risk is worth it.

Resources

Napoleon Hill, *Think and Grow Rich*, Ralston Society, 1937.

Grant Cardone, *The 10X Rule*, Wiley, 2011.

Stephen Covey, *The 7 Habits of Highly Effective People*, Free Press, 1989.

Dr. Gail Matthews, *Dominican University Goals Study*, 2007, http://www
.dominican.edu/academics/ahss/undergraduate-programs-1/psych/faculty/
fulltime/gailmatthews/researchsummary2.pdf.

Robert T. Kiyosaki, *Rich Dad, Poor Dad*, Plata Publishing, 2000.

Chapter 2

The Content Inc. Opportunity

Whatever you can do or dream you can, begin it.
Boldness has genius, power and magic in it!
JOHANN WOLFGANG VON GOETHE

I had the pleasure of meeting Jon Loomer in San Diego at Social Media Marketing World 2013. As fate had it, we just happened to sit next to each other during the opening keynote. During one of those uncomfortable icebreakers, Jon and I began to talk about our kids and hobbies, but I was really interested in his backstory.

Jon has had his share of struggles. After dealing with his son's battle with cancer (neuroblastoma) and being laid off from work two times in a two-and-a-half-year period, Jon was at a crossroads.

Then, in February 2012, Facebook rolled out its Timeline for Pages product. Jon was hooked immediately. He became interested in Facebook when he worked for NBA.com in 2007, and this recent Facebook move fanned that interest. So Jon went to his website, JonLoomer.com, and started to consistently create content about the Facebook product. Everything was educational, helpful, and remarkably detailed.

Almost immediately, Jon felt like something just clicked. That first year, Jon blogged on the subject of Facebook religiously (creating approximately 350 blog posts in that first year alone).

By 2015, Jon was getting over 400,000 page views per month and had 50,000 e-mail subscribers who asked to receive his information every week. If you ask anyone about who is the leading expert in advanced Facebook marketing, Jon's name almost always comes up first.

And the best part . . . Jon has developed a remarkably substantial, growing business—all while still coaching his son every year in baseball.

What Jon has accomplished would have been impossible 20 years ago. Today, this model (called Content Inc.) is absolutely possible. But more than that, I believe Jon, and the others you'll hear about in this book, has uncovered the least risky business-launch model on the market today.

Michael Stelzner, founder of Social Media Examiner, says it best:

It's hard work. I'm not going to lie. Anyone who tells you that it's really easy to build a content business is not telling you the truth. You have to accept the fact that this is going to be grueling, difficult, time consuming, and laborious work. But if you're willing to roll up your sleeves and get dirty, and are willing to constantly analyze what you're doing and scrap what doesn't work and continue what does work, and keep at it, you can be very, very successful.

WHAT CHANGED?

Before 1990, there were only eight channels available where a company could communicate with a consumer: at an event, by fax, through direct mail, by telephone, on television, through the radio, on a billboard, or in a print magazine or newsletter (see Figure 2.1). In 2015, there are literally hundreds of channels where consumers access content.

Before 1990, large media companies had the most power because they controlled the information channels . . . they controlled the audience. Now 25 years later that power has almost completely shifted to the consumer. This means that today anyone, anywhere, can be a publisher and build an audience. This is a major development in the communications market that impacts every business, large and small.

In my previous book, *Epic Content Marketing*, I detail five reasons for this power shift:

1. **No technology barriers.** In the past, the publishing process was complex and expensive. Traditionally, media companies spent hundreds of thousands of dollars on complex content management and production systems. Today, anyone can publish for free online in five minutes (seconds?) or less. At the same time, almost 2 billion consumers have smartphones (eMarketer) and 75 percent of U.S. households have Internet access (U.S. Census). *Simply put, anyone can publish, and anyone can receive content.*

2. **Talent availability.** When I started in the publishing business 15 years ago, it was often a challenge to find writers and other content creators of particular expertise. Two things have changed since then. First, credible journalists, writers, and producers are very willing to work with nonmedia companies. In the past, many content creators would balk at the idea of working with nonmedia companies, because it was often considered "lower" work. That stigma has since gone. Second, between Google, dozens of content marketplaces, and direct access through social media, content creators are significantly easier to find. *This means, any company of any size can get access to the best content creators on the planet* (if the company wishes to do so).

3. **Content acceptance.** Take a look at the current state of consumer behavior:
   - 61 percent of consumers say they feel better about a company that delivers custom content, and are more likely to buy from that company (Content Council).
   - People spend more than 50 percent of their time online looking at content (Nielsen).
   - 70 percent of consumers prefer getting to know a company via articles rather than ads (Content+).
   - 90 percent of consumers find custom content useful, and 78 percent believe that organizations providing custom content are interested in building good relationships with them (CMO Council).

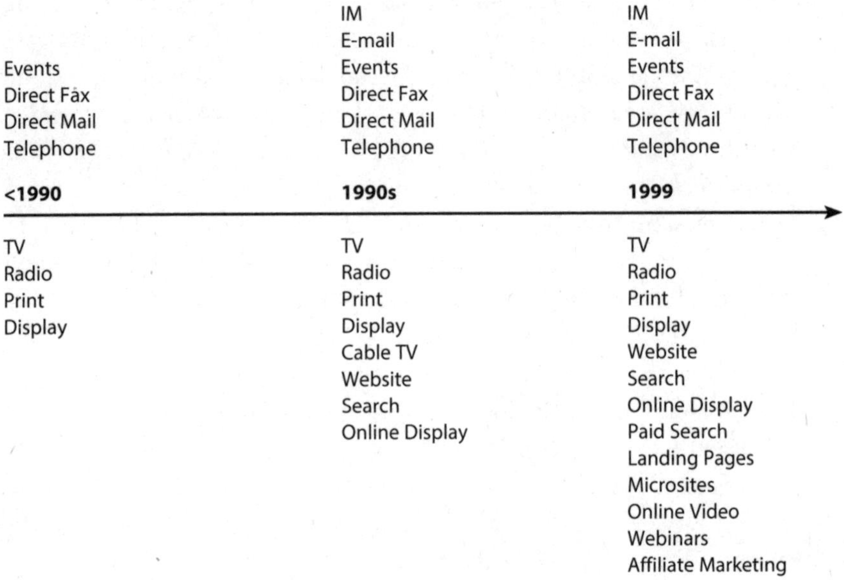

	IM	IM
	E-mail	E-mail
Events	Events	Events
Direct Fax	Direct Fax	Direct Fax
Direct Mail	Direct Mail	Direct Mail
Telephone	Telephone	Telephone
<1990	**1990s**	**1999**
TV	TV	TV
Radio	Radio	Radio
Print	Print	Print
Display	Display	Display
	Cable TV	Website
	Website	Search
	Search	Online Display
	Online Display	Paid Search
		Landing Pages
		Microsites
		Online Video
		Webinars
		Affiliate Marketing

Figure 2.1 Back in 1990, there were only eight channels to communicate with customers. Today there are hundreds.

Image source: Jeff Rohrs, Salesforce.com

	Snapchat/WeChat
	Apps/Push Notifications
	GroupTexting
	Social DM
	Voice Marketing
Mobile E-mail	Mobile Email
SMS	SMS + MMS
IM	IM
E-mail	Email
Events	Events
Direct Fax	Direct Fax
Direct Mail	Direct Mail
Telephone	Telephone
2000s	**2015**
TV	TV
Radio	Radio
Print	Print
Display	Display
Website	Website
Search	Search
Online Display	Online Display
Paid Search	Paid Search
Landing Pages	Landing Pages
Microsites	Microsites
Online Video	Online Video
Webinars	Webinars
Affiliate Marketing	Affiliate Marketing
Blogs	Blogs/RSS
RSS	Podcasts
Podcasts	Contextual
Contextual	Wikis
Wikis	Social Networks
Social Networks	Mobile Web
Mobile Web	Behaviorial
	Social Media and Ads
	Virtual Worlds
	In-Game Advertising
	Widgets
	Twitter
	Mobile Apps
	Geolocation
	Pinterest
	Vine
	Periscope/Meerkat

Figure 2.1 *Continued.*

The key here is that you don't have to be the *New York Times* or the leading trade magazine in your industry to get people to engage with your content. Readers are open to receiving and engaging in any content that will help them live better lives, get better jobs, or solve a particular task. *The point: You have as much opportunity to deliver amazingly helpful content as anyone else.*

4. **Social media.** Social media won't work without valuable, consistent, and compelling information creation and distribution. If any individual or company wants to be successful in social media, it needs to tell compelling stories first. Interesting and helpful stories spread, which means that much of the marketing of our content is assisted by other people. *Social media is useless without having the content to fuel it.*

5. **Google.** Every time Google updates its search algorithms, the most helpful and usable information rises to the top. While the system is not perfect, it's extremely democratic. *This means that even the smallest company that understands digital content creation and distribution can beat out a big media company with the right processes.*

Today anyone, anywhere, can publish books, develop media sites, and create feature-length movies, with each one having the ability to reach an audience directly. For example, writer-director Sean Baker released his latest movie, *Tangerine*, at the 2015 Sundance Festival to glowing critical review. The big deal? He filmed the entire movie using an iPhone 5S.

Disruption is happening everywhere, but nowhere is this more apparent than around content creation and distribution.

Entrepreneurs and small businesses need to be rejoicing. Today's availability of technology means that any business in any industry can develop an audience through consistent storytelling. No longer does the company with the biggest marketing budget win the most attention. Businesses are now rewarded on the substance of their message and on the audience they can attract through the consistent flow of information.

ENTER CONTENT INC.

In 2007, Lauren Luke began selling makeup products on eBay in an effort to subsidize her modest day job as a taxi dispatcher in Newcastle,

England. In an effort to improve her eBay sales, Lauren began creating practical makeup application videos and distributed them on YouTube. Five years, and 135 million views, later, Lauren had built a bigger audience than Estée Lauder on YouTube.

How did Lauren do it? How did Jon Loomer make success happen? Did the stars align in each of these cases, or is there something about how they launched and positioned their businesses that we can learn from and replicate? Did they just happen to find a model that is *not* capital intensive in any way and in which the core asset is derived from selling knowledge?

Over two years and countless interviews, we've been able to deconstruct and then reengineer the Content Inc. model. As we noted in the Introduction, we've identified a series of steps each entrepreneur took, which together helped us create a new and viable business model for start-ups (see Figure 2.2):

- **The sweet spot.** Mixing a knowledge area or skill with a passion area.
- **The content tilt.** Looking at the traditional content niche defined as slightly off-center, to create a true differentiation area.
- **Building the base.** Consistent publishing in one core channel.
- **Harvesting audience.** Converting the publishing activity to the asset of subscribers.

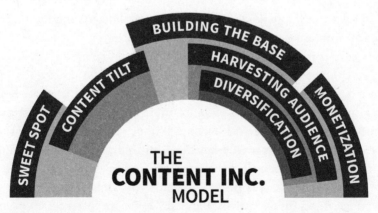

Figure 2.2   The Content Inc. model.

- **Diversification.** At the proper time, expanding the publishing process to additional channels.
- **Monetization.** Monetizing the audience through the selection of products or services that will be the source of revenue and profit for the business.

Outside of a slight variation here and there with our model companies, these six steps define the Content Inc. model. In the next few chapters, we'll open up the kimono on each one of these areas so that you too can launch and execute a Content Inc. model.

A THOUGHT ON WHY

Don Schultz, the father of integrated marketing and author of *Integrated Marketing Communications*, discusses the idea that any company, anywhere in the world, can copy everything about what you as a company do . . . except for one thing—how you communicate. The way we communicate with our prospects and customers is the one remaining way we can actually *be* different.

In their book, *Experiences: The 7th Era of Marketing*, Robert Rose and Carla Johnson build on Schultz's commentary by adding that it is content, and the experiences that customers have with our content, that is the ultimate differentiator.

This is why entrepreneurs that follow a Content Inc. strategy have a strategic advantage over other companies. The entire business model is dedicated to developing content experiences and building an audience, and not to pitching products in any way.

NO PRODUCT? THAT'S GOOD!

Sometimes having product offerings hurts a Content Inc. model. Take the print magazine industry, for example. For years, print magazine publishers were so protective over keeping print advertising dollars that they were ignoring the audience's need for digital. Print magazine providers that didn't listen to this change are no longer with us.

When all your focus is on an audience you know deeply, instead of a product, good things usually happen. When we listen intently to our audience, we are automatically led to new product opportunities. The challenge is that sometimes we don't know when the model will take shape—and why patience with the Content Inc. model is key. As Chris Brogan, founder of *Owner* magazine, states, audiences are eager for their lives to be changed in some way. Focusing on that gives Content Inc. the advantage.

Content Inc. Learnings from Napoleon Hill

Napoleon Hill's classic, *Think and Grow Rich*, was first published in 1937. Now, in the book's 78th anniversary year, Napoleon Hill's lessons are still extremely relevant and valuable, especially today.

Desire

Whatever the mind can conceive and believe, it can achieve.

You can talk about all the things Content Inc. businesses should do to attract and retain customers—content strategy, content planning, content organization, content integration, etc.—but desire is numero uno. Everywhere I speak I hear the objection that most businesses simply do not have the desire to be *the* informational resource for their customers and prospects—these businesses don't want it enough. They talk of content creation as a chore, not as a core service to customers that is necessary for the company's survival.

Faith

Faith is the "eternal elixir" which gives life, power,
and action to the impulse of thought!

Wanting it is one thing, but actually believing you can be *the* informational expert for your industry is another. When we first started Junta42 in 2007 (which ultimately pivoted to Content Marketing Institute in 2010), we firmly believed that we would be the informational resource for our industry. It was unquestioned. It was only a matter of time, energy, and persistence.

Rarely do you see this kind of faith with nonmedia companies. When I worked at Penton Media (a business media company) and met with the chief editors for our brands, they believed without question that their brand was the leading provider of information in the space. It was a nonissue . . . it just was. That is exactly the kind of faith you need to be the expert in your field.

Specialized Knowledge

General knowledge, no matter how great in quantity
or variety it may be, is of but little use . . .

One of the biggest failures when it comes to content is a lack of specialization. I see heating and air-conditioning companies blogging about the town festival next week. I see manufacturing companies creating articles on human resources best practices. It hurts to see this.

To be the expert in your industry, you must first define your customers' pain points and the niche industry you will cover that will make a difference in your business and in your customers' lives. Get laser-focused. Think of yourself as the trade magazine for your industry. Cover that. Be the expert in that area. If you are a large enterprise, you will need separate content strategies, not a broad one that makes no impact on anybody.

Imagination

It has been said that man can create anything
which he can imagine.

As Napoleon Hill says, ideas are the products of the imagination. For a Content Inc. approach to work, you need to embrace not just being a factory for content, but an idea factory. Just as news organizations cover the "news of the day," you need to cover the news as it relates to your content niche (more on that later). Take the content that you have and think creatively about storytelling concepts—visual, textual, and audio—in new and compelling ways.

Decision

Procrastination, the opposite of decision,
is a common enemy which must be conquered.

In his book, Napoleon Hill profiled hundreds of the most successful people in the world. Every one of them had the habit of reaching decisions promptly and of changing these decisions slowly, if and when they were changed. Unsuccessful people, the book says, have a habit, without exception, of reaching decisions, if at all, very slowly and of changing these decisions quickly and often.

This first, successful type of mentality is the one you need to bring to your Content Inc. endeavor.

Persistence

Will-power and desire, when properly combined,
make an irresistible pair.

Without a doubt, the biggest reason content marketing fails is because it stops. I've seen business after business start a blog or e-newsletter or white paper program or podcast series and stop after a few months. Content marketing is a war of attrition. It's a process. Success does not happen overnight. You must commit for the long haul if you want to be successful.

Before you dive into the rest of the book, I want to give you a serious warning . . . there is quite a bit of risk involved with unleashing the Content Inc. model. Some things to consider:

- **Patience.** The model takes time to work. Many of the case studies discussed in this book didn't blossom for a year or two or more. The payoff is big, but it may take a while to get there.
- **Lack of funds.** Content Inc. is not an immediate "get-rich-quick" scheme. You are building a valuable asset. While you are doing that,

revenue may be hard to come by. Lower your expenses and get lean so you can make it to the finish line.

- **Against the grain.** Content Inc. is a philosophy that most experts would vehemently disagree with. You are doing something that almost no one would ever think of doing.
- **Going small to go big.** Many fail because they don't pick a content niche that's small enough. They are afraid the niche will be too small to monetize. I've never found that to be the case. Most failures occur because the entrepreneur goes too broad and not narrow enough.

Now that you've been warned, get ready for the business model that will change your life. If you stick with it and can battle against the negativity, success is yours to have.

CONTENT INC. INSIGHTS

- Developing a successful Content Inc. model will take time, but it is not nearly as risky as developing a traditional business model.
- Once you develop a relationship with a loyal audience, you can create products and services and ultimately sell whatever you want.
- If done right, you'll have an advantage by employing a Content Inc. model because you'll understand your future customers' needs (and informational pain points) better than almost anyone else.

Resources

Jon Loomer, interview by Clare McDermott, January 2015.

"2 Billion Consumers Worldwide to Get Smart(phones) by 2016," eMarketer .com, accessed April 18, 2015, http://www.emarketer.com/Article/2-Billion -Consumers-Worldwide-Smartphones-by-2016/1011694.

"Census Bureau's American Community Survey Provides New State and Local Income, Poverty, Health Insurance Statistics," census.gov, accessed April 18, 2015, http://www.census.gov/newsroom/press-releases/2014/cb14-170 .html.

"Sundance: Sean Baker on Filming 'Tangerine' and 'Making the Most' of an iPhone," Variety.com, accessed April 18, 2015, http://variety.com/video/ sundance-sean-baker-on-filming-tangerine-and-making-the-most-of-an -iphone/.

"AOL and Nielsen Content Sharing Study," SlideShare.net, accessed April 18, 2015, http://www.slideshare.net/duckofdoom/aol-nielsen-content-sharing -study.

Don Schultz and Heidi Schultz, *IMC—The Next Generation*, McGraw-Hill Professional, 2003.

Robert Rose and Carla Johnson, *Experiences: The 7th Era of Marketing*, Content Marketing Institute, 2015.

Part 2

The Sweet Spot

The essence of strategy is choosing what not to do.
MICHAEL PORTER

Every successful content creator has a sweet spot. Now it's your turn to find yours.

Chapter 3

Knowledge
or Skill + Passion

Your work is to discover your work
and then with all your heart to give yourself to it.
BUDDHA

Matthew Patrick grew up in the small city of Medina, just outside Cleveland, Ohio. For as long as he can remember, he's been passionate about gaming, from growing up with a Mario-themed bedroom to late nights with friends playing Dungeons & Dragons. During high school when most boys in his class went out for sports, Matthew joined show choir, played the viola in orchestra, and took part in every stage show the school offered.

Yes, Matthew loved performing, but he was also a genius, scoring a perfect 1600 on his SAT on his way to a college degree in neuroscience. Instead of going to fraternity parties on weekends at college, Matthew hosted "Friday Fondue" nights playing Zelda (a popular video game).

After college, Matthew had his sights set on acting and moved to New York, where he toured with various shows. For two years, Matthew took whatever role was available—and saw about as much success as the average starving actor in New York. To put it lightly, times were tough. Theater wasn't the life Matthew was hoping for.

By 2011, Matthew gave up his dream of becoming an actor and decided to go after a "real" job. Unfortunately, acting and directing were not skills that innovative enterprises were hiring for. Over the next two years, Matthew sent out countless résumés. During that time he was unemployed, and worse yet, his confidence had bottomed out. Not one person opened a door to give Matthew the shot he seemingly deserved.

Matthew pulled himself up by his bootstraps and decided to create a résumé booster that companies simply couldn't ignore. He believed that if he could show companies that he knew how to create an audience and that he understood the inner workings of new media, enterprises would see value in those skills.

While watching an online program on learning through gaming, the idea of creating Game Theory videos was born. *Game Theory* became a weekly YouTube video series that combined Matthew's passion for gaming and video games with his skill set of math and analytics (see Figure 3.1).

After 56 episodes over a one-year time frame, Matthew had an audience of 500,000 YouTube subscribers interested in his take on how math works in gaming. For example, his episode "How PewDiePie [an online video celebrity] Conquered YouTube" generated more than 5

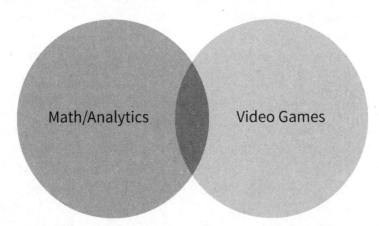

Figure 3.1 Matthew Patrick combined his passion for video games with his knowledge expertise in math and analytics to develop his sweet spot.

million views. His episode "Why the Official Zelda Timeline Is Wrong" saw more than 4 million downloads.

Today, Matthew Patrick's Game Theory brand has well over 4 million subscribers. Matthew has been hired directly by some of the biggest YouTube stars on the planet to help them attract more viewers. Even the mighty YouTube itself hired MatPat (his online name) to consult directly to help YouTube retain and grow its audience numbers.

THE SWEET SPOT

Start where you are. Use what you have. Do what you can.

ARTHUR ASHE

The Content Inc. model is dependent on first identifying the sweet spot. Simply put, the sweet spot is the intersection of a knowledge or skill area and a passion point (see Figure 3.2).

Let's take a look at a variety of sweet spots among other Content Inc. entrepreneurs.

Claus Pilgaard (Branded as Chili Klaus)

As we said in the Introduction, Claus grew up a musician. He was admitted to the Royal Academy of Music, where he graduated in 1996.

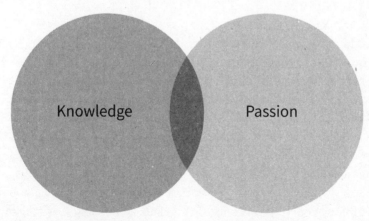

Figure 3.2 The sweet spot.

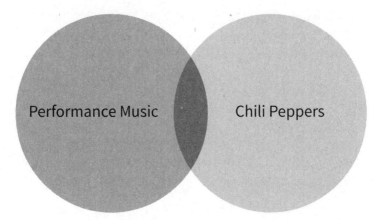

Figure 3.3 Claus Pilgaard's skill in performance music and his passion for chili peppers created a powerful sweet spot.

He became a music director for several reviews in Denmark, going by the name of "Klaus Wunderhits," and even appeared on a local variety show called *Varieté 007*.

Claus had always been an amazing musician, but it wasn't until he found his sweet spot, in combination with chili peppers, that Claus became a Danish phenomenon (see Figure 3.3).

Michelle Phan

At an early age, Michelle Phan found that she was an artist. Simply put, she could draw with the best of them. Michelle's childhood was fraught with turmoil. Her family moved dozens of times while she was a child, and abuse was something she was unfortunately familiar with.

Drawing on her face (makeup) became a release for Michelle. She believed that makeup could make everyone superheroes, where they could escape and defeat evil, even against all odds. In 2005, Michelle started a blog combining her skill in art and drawing and her passion for makeup (see Figure 3.4).

Today, Michelle's makeup tutorials have been seen over a billion (yes, billion) times. Now one of YouTube's top stars, Michelle has expanded her empire to include a book (released in 2014) and a full cosmetic line called "em," produced by L'Oreal.

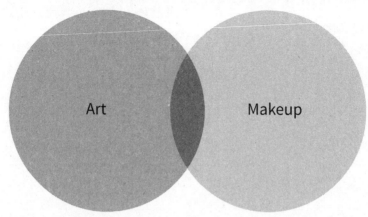

Figure 3.4   Michelle Phan is a highly skilled artist. Her love of makeup mixed with her skill in art has made the difference.

Andy Schneider (Branded as the Chicken Whisperer)

Andy Schneider is the backyard poultry king and has become the go-to resource for anything and everything chickens. As Andy began to raise chickens in his Atlanta-area backyard, he began to sell them to his friends directly and then on Craigslist. There were many who were interested in raising their own chickens, but they needed a lot of education to just get started. So Andy formed a "meetup" in Atlanta to answer questions from those interested in backyard poultry (see Figure 3.5).

According to Andy, "All these people are from the Atlanta metro area; we could meet once a month, have a great time, break bread in the meeting room in the backroom of a restaurant, and share our experiences and learn. So I got online and found a great resource, Meetup.com, very popular, millions of meetups all around the country for people who have hobbies."

That club met several times a month, and as the club grew, local media started to notice. The local CBS affiliate did an interview with Andy, which was picked up by Atlanta's major newspaper, the *Atlanta Journal Constitution*. From there, Andy grew the Chicken Whisperer platform into a book, a magazine (with over 60,000 subscribers), and a radio show, which has now run for over five years with more than 20,000 weekly subscribers. He also travels around the country doing

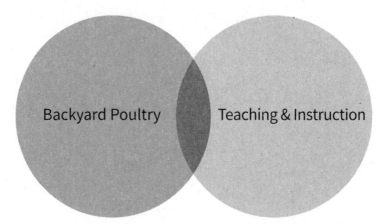

Figure 3.5 Andy Schneider's sweet spot mixes his knowledge of backyard poultry with his passion for teaching.

road shows, exclusively sponsored by Kalmbach Feeds, his major financial supporter.

FINDING YOUR SKILL OR KNOWLEDGE AREA

In looking at various Content Inc. subjects, the model can work by identifying either an exceptional knowledge area or a unique skill. What do we mean by *knowledge? Knowledge is information acquired about a particular subject through study or observation.*

Joseph Kalinowski, our creative director at Content Marketing Institute, has knowledge (by the definition above) in a number of areas including the band KISS, the Pittsburgh Steelers, Star Wars action figures, and Jack Daniels. In any one of these topics, Joseph would destroy the average person with his knowledge in that area.

In addition to his knowledge areas, Joseph is also a skilled graphic designer. *Skill* is defined by dictionary.com as "the ability to do something well" or an area that a person has "expertise or competence" in. *Simply put, skill is knowledge used properly.*

If Joseph were going to employ a Content Inc. strategy and look to build an audience in a specific market or demographic area, he could choose from the number of knowledge areas he has, *or* he could look to his skill in graphic design.

Where to Start?

If you are an individual, begin by listing those areas in which you have a large skill set or knowledge area in something versus the average person. This is brainstorming time, so more is better at this point.

Knowledge Areas   **Special Skills**

_____   _____

_____   _____

_____   _____

_____   _____

_____   _____

_____   _____

If you completed the exercise correctly, you should have vastly more knowledge areas than skill areas.

Here's how mine turned out.

Knowledge Areas   **Special Skills**

Musicals   Public speaking

Billy Joel songs   Nonfiction writing

The color orange   Building publishing models

Cleveland sports teams   Teaching

80s baseball cards

Maybe your situation is closer to that of the Indium Corporation. Indium, a global manufacturing company headquartered in upstate New York, develops and manufactures materials used primarily in the electronics assembly industry. At its core, the company develops soldering materials to keep electronic components from coming apart.

Rick Short, Indium's director of marketing communications, knew that Indium employees had more knowledge about industrial soldering equipment than just about any other company in the world. This makes sense . . . soldering is the knowledge area where Indium manufactures most of its products.

At the same time, the Indium culture is that of sharing knowledge . . . of a rising tide lifting all ships. The company had subject-matter experts that were willing to share, as well as a marketing team that was excited about sharing knowledge via social media (a rarity for a manufacturing company, especially in 2005; see Figure 3.6).

That platform chosen for this sweet spot was a blog. Today Indium has over 70 blogs and 21 bloggers. Since the first blog was begun in 2005, Indium has generated more leads at just 25 percent of its previous marketing investment.

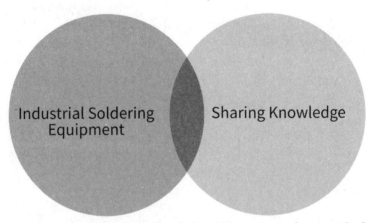

Figure 3.6 Indium's sweet spot has helped the company become the leading informational expert on soldering for engineers.

UNLEASHING YOUR PASSION

Steve Jobs's commencement speech, given in 2005, has been watched over 10 million times. In it, he gives the following advice: "You've got to find what you love. . . . [T]he only way to do great work is to love what you do. If you haven't found it yet, keep looking, and don't settle."

Cal Newport, author of the book *So Good They Can't Ignore You*, believes that if Steve Jobs had taken his own advice, Apple Computer would have never happened. Newport states that "if a young Steve Jobs had taken his own advice and decided to only pursue work he loved, we would probably find him today as one of the Los Altos Zen Center's most popular teachers."

Walter Issacson, who authored the Jobs biography, sees it differently. Jobs's passion was not for Zen Buddhism specifically; it was for simplicity. Everything in Steve Jobs's life revolved around the simple, which extended into Apple's core design construct. As Jobs noted: "The way we're running the company, the product design, the advertising, it all comes down to this: Let's make it simple. Really simple."

Apple was fueled by Steve Jobs's passion for simplicity. And as Charles Schwab is quoted, "A person can succeed at almost anything for which they have unlimited enthusiasm."

This is exactly what we find in the Content Inc. model. Skill is one thing, but the passion is the energy behind what makes the model successful. It's why for months, and in many cases years, entrepreneurs create their content, ultimately waiting for the payoff.

Simply put, for Content Inc. to work, you need to get up every day loving the right side of that sweet spot, or the work doesn't get done. Matthew Patrick has a passion and love for video games. Andy Schneider loves being the teacher. Claus Pilgaard has a passion for chili peppers that most people simply do not understand. Michelle Phan gets up in the morning every day, ready to cover herself in makeup. Rick Short at Indium had the insight to understand the company's passion for sharing knowledge.

All these "passions" made it possible for the work to be done. With Content Inc., passion is the fuel that makes the engine go. All the skill in the world won't make your content engine go without passion.

Can Content Inc. Work Without Passion?

Jay Baer is CEO of marketing consulting firm Convince & Convert, as well as the *New York Times* bestselling author of *Youtility*. The following is taken from an interview with Jay on Content Inc. and passion:

> *Content for which you do not have a passion is really hard to get good at. If you don't love the content you're creating, it is unlikely to be good enough to have an impact. And that's why most of the people who you would consider to be disproportionately good at content have a true love, either for content marketing as a discipline, or a true love for the subject matter that they're creating content about.*
>
> *Marcus Sheridan [former CEO of River Pools & Spas] is effective not because he's the greatest writer in the world, but because he really wants to educate people about swimming pools. Joe [Pulizzi] is effective because he really wants to evangelize about content marketing. It's not that he has some disproportionately extraordinary writing techniques. That's the part that we don't talk about very much because we want everybody to believe that all you have to do is want to create content and follow the instructions in the books that we write and everybody can do it; and yeah, everybody can do it, but they can't do it great because they may not have the same level of passion.*
>
> *And if you do have that passion and you have that burning desire to educate or teach about whatever subject lights you up, that content can be good enough, can be infused with passion to the degree that you can build a business out of it like never before. Ten years ago you couldn't ever do . . . say . . . publish your own newspaper . . . how's that going to work? But today you can just say, I'm going to make a YouTube video every day about Japanese whiskey; and if you keep your nose to the grindstone, eventually you can be the Japanese whiskey guy and you can take ads, you can give speeches and all of those things that can happen.*

AN ALTERNATIVE VIEW OF THE SWEET SPOT

If you are an established company with an existing product base, finding the sweet spot between knowledge or skill and passion may not come naturally. In my last book, *Epic Content Marketing*, I offer an alternative sweet spot model that may work in replacement (see Figure 3.7).

Why is this model important? Your business might have a knowledge area that may not be relevant to customers. For example, there are a number of General Electric executives that are knowledgeable in business strategy. GE's internal training programs are some of the most famous ever developed by a corporation. That said, that knowledge may not translate into solving a customer issue or pain point. So GE's knowledge of business strategy may not work in the sweet spot model, depending on the customers GE is targeting with a Content Inc. initiative.

Doug Kessler, cofounder of content agency Velocity Partners, believes the sweet spot is three-dimensional: it's important to know the exact size, shape, and depth.

- "Size—your sweet spot should be a focused area; as tight a focus as possible without leaving stuff out."

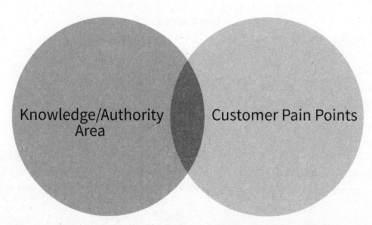

Figure 3.7 Leveraging passion in a larger organization is often a challenge. In these cases, replace passion with a customer pain point area.

- "Shape—you need to know exactly where your expertise reaches and where it stops." Just because you have knowledge of certain areas doesn't mean that authority naturally extends to other areas.
- "Depth—your expertise goes as deeply as it needs to go; you don't have to pretend it goes deeper."

I've found that this sweet spot example gains more traction in a larger enterprise environment, and I've seen both types of sweet spots work in different situations. Find the one that works best for you.

CONTENT INC. INSIGHTS

- The Content Inc. model begins with the sweet spot, the intersection of your knowledge or skill area and your passion. While it's possible to develop a sweet spot without a passion point, it's the passion that gives us our drive to continue until we build a successful Content Inc. model.
- While we have many knowledge and skill areas, we have much fewer passions. Life is too short to work on something every day that we are not passionate about, so you may want to start with you passions first.
- If your company is already established, consider replacing your passion area with a customer pain point to develop your sweet spot.

Resources

Matthew Patrick, "Draw My Life: Game Theory, MatPat and You," YouTube.com, accessed April 19, 2015, https://www.youtube.com/watch?v=8mkuIP_i3js.

Matthew Patrick, interview by Clare McDermott, February 2015.

Andy Schneider, interview by Clare McDermott, January 2015.

Michelle Phan, "Draw My Life: Michelle Phan," YouTube.com, accessed April 19, 2015, https://www.youtube.com/watch?v=05KqZEqQJ40.

Bruce Johnston, "How Indium Figured Out Their Social Media Marketing Content," Practicalsmm.com, accessed April 19, 2015, http://practicalsmm.com/2012/06/25/how-indium-corporation-figured-out-their-social-media-marketing-content/.

CRSA, Inc., "B2B Social Media Case Study Guide: Indium (Manufacturing)," SlideShare.net, accessed April 19, 2015, http://www.slideshare.net/csrollyson/b2b-social-business-case-study-indium.

The Apple History Channel, "Steve Jobs Stanford Commencement Speech," YouTube.com, accessed April 19, 2015, https://www.youtube.com/watch ?v=D1R-jKKp3NA.

Cal Newport, "Do like Steve Jobs Did: Don't Follow Your Passion," FastCompany.com, accessed April 19, 2015, http://www.fastcompany.com/ 3001441/do-steve-jobs-did-dont-follow-your-passion.

Walter Isaacson, "How Steve Jobs' Love of Simplicity Fueled a Design Revolution," Smithsonianmag.com, accessed April 19, 2015, http://www .smithsonianmag.com/arts-culture/how-steve-jobs-love-of-simplicity -fueled-a-design-revolution-23868877/?no-ist.

Jay Baer, interview by Clare McDermott, January 2015.

"Difference Between Knowledge and Skill," Differencebetween.net, accessed April 19, 2015, http://www.differencebetween.net/language/difference -between-knowledge-and-skill/.

Doug Kessler, "B2B Content Marketing: Finding Your Sweet Spot," Econsultancy .com, accessed April 19, 2015, https://econsultancy.com/blog/9279-b2b -content-marketing-finding-your-sweet-spot.

Chapter 4

Adding Audience to Your Sweet Spot

My sweet spot is figuring out how to make
a product that people love
and how to refine it to make them love it more.
All the rest is business noise.

NOLAN BUSHNELL

In early 2014, I had the opportunity to participate in a workshop for a number of enterprise marketers in Toronto, Canada. In one particular conversation at the workshop, the blog manager for a billion-dollar technology company told me she was having problems with her blog. She had been adding more and more daily content to the blog and at the same time was seeing stagnant website traffic and far fewer subscribers and conversions.

My first question was this: "Who is the audience for your blog?"

She answered: "We target 18 different audiences on the blog."

"I found your problem."

WHO'S THE WHO?

The sweet spot is a place where a combination of factors
results in a maximum response for a given amount of effort.
WIKIPEDIA

Countless businesses fail with their Content Inc. model because they stop after identifying the intersection of their knowledge area or skill and their passion. To this point, it's all about us. It's sharing what we know.

Who cares? Probably not very many people.

In order to complete the sweet spot formula, we need to identify the "who." Who is the audience for your content? Remember, for the Content Inc. model to work, we need to figure out how we can build the engine that positions us as the leading informational expert in our particular market niche. We want to define our audience as specifically as possible.

Ask the following questions:

1. Who is he or she? How does this person live an average day?
2. What's the person's need? This is not "Why does the person need our product or service?" but "What are his or her informational needs and pain points as they relate to the stories we will tell?"
3. Why will this person care about us, our products, our services? It's the information provided to him or her that will make that person care or garner attention.

Your idea of the "who" doesn't have to be perfect, but it needs to be detailed enough so that you can clearly visualize this person in your head as you develop content.

Doug Kessler, cofounder of the UK agency Velocity Partners, said the sweet spot is "the thing your company knows better than—or at least as well as—anyone else in the world." Understanding the "who" gives you the context you need to make this happen.

Marcus Sheridan from River Pools & Spas became the worldwide leader in information about fiberglass pools for those homeowners interested in purchasing a pool. If Marcus were targeting, let's say, manufacturers of fiberglass pools, the content would be vastly different. It's the "who" that gives the content the context it needs to be successful.

The Story of River Pools & Spas

In late 2009, River Pools & Spas, a 20-employee installer of fiberglass pools in the Virginia and Maryland area, was in trouble. Homeowners were not running out and buying fiberglass pools during the Great Recession. Worse yet, customers who had actually planned on buying a pool were calling up River Pools to request their deposits back, which, in some cases, ran around $50,000 or more.

For multiple weeks, River Pools overdrew its checking account. Not only was it becoming difficult to pay employees, but the company was looking at possibly closing up shop for good.

Marcus Sheridan, CEO of River Pools & Spas, believed that the only way to survive was to steal market share from the competition, and that meant thinking differently about how the company went to market.

At the beginning of this process, River Pools did just over $4 million in annual revenues and spent approximately $250,000 a year on marketing. There were four competitors in the Virginia area that had greater market share than River.

Two years later in 2011, River Pools & Spas sold more fiberglass pools than any other fiberglass pools installer in North America. The company also decreased its marketing spend from $250,000 to around $40,000, while at the same time winning 15 percent more bids and cutting its sales cycle in half. The average pool builder lost 50 to 75 percent in sales during the time that River Pools increased sales to more than $5 million.

Needless to say, River Pools & Spas stayed open for business.

How did Marcus do it? He wrote down every conceivable customer question and answered it on his blog. Today, from search engine results to social media sharing, Marcus and River Pools & Spas are the leading information provider in the world on the subject of fiberglass pools.

The Rest of the Story

River's story has been shared around the world. It's a fairly popular Content Inc. example. But here's something you probably don't know. River Pools is now a national, even an international, force because of its content creation. Marcus was being called upon by companies all over the world to install pools and was even asked to fly in to oversee an installation. Unfortunately, River Pools only serviced companies in a very small area and could not take advantage of the additional demand.

Enter manufacturing. River Pools made the decision to begin manufacturing its own fiberglass pools. This came about directly because of its content exposure. River Pools & Spas is now positioning itself as the leading installer *and* manufacturer of fiberglass pools, taking the business in a completely unexpected direction.

Once you develop an audience around your content, the opportunities to sell additional products is almost endless. River Pools & Spas is an example of Content Inc. in action.

MAKING IT REAL

As we add in our audience group, we've added a new dimension to our sweet spot (Figure 4.1).

Let's go back to our friend the Chicken Whisperer. Andy Schneider's original sweet spot was a knowledge area of backyard poultry and a passion for teaching and instruction.

Now let's add the audience to make our sweet spot come to life (Figure 4.2).

Now we have enough information to capture the sweet spot in a single sentence. This is very similar to how media companies start to construct an editorial mission statement (more on this in Chapter 6).

Andy Schneider's mission statement might have looked something like this:

Helping suburban homeowners answer all their possible questions regarding raising chickens at home.

PUTTING IT ALL TOGETHER

Now that you've seen a visual example of the sweet spot, let's start adding some dimension to your model. Here's a useful template you can use to begin to construct the initial stages of your strategy.

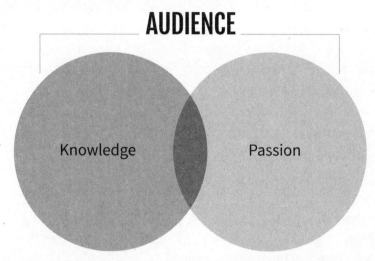

Figure 4.1 By adding your specific audience to the mix, now the sweet spot truly becomes meaningful.

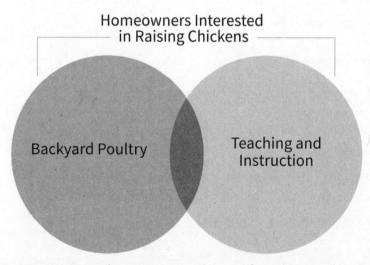

Figure 4.2 Wrapping the sweet spot with a specific audience will bring your sweet spot to life.

Mission: _____

_____

Key Audience: (Be as specific as possible.) _____

_____

Sample Titles/Functions:_____

_____

Why This Group Is Important: (This is a critical first step to thinking about the purchase power these people have. You'll learn more about this in Chapter 22 on monetization.)

_____

_____

_____

Sample Topic Areas:_____

_____

_____

Here are examples of what a completed form looks like for Content Marketing Institute. We have three different audiences that we target with our content. Note that when we began our Content Inc. model in 2007, we only focused on one audience. We added the second audience group in 2014 and the third group in 2015.

Content Marketing Institute

Mission: Advance the practice of content marketing.

Key Audience: Content marketing practitioners. CMI helps the people who are planning and executing the content marketing strategy in their large enterprise organizations.

Sample Titles/Functions: Content marketing director, content marketing manager, manager of digital strategy, vice president marketing, digital marketing manager, public relations manager/director, director of social media, communications directors.

Why This Group Is Important: The majority of marketing in organizations still involves paid media. CMI believes that, over the next decade, the majority of marketing will be content coming directly from brands instead of advertising or sponsorship on outside properties. Enterprises today are completely unequipped to handle this transformation and need vast amounts of education and training on the strategies and tactics of content marketing.

Sample Topic Areas: Building a strategy; building an audience; operationalizing the process (including getting executive buy-in and continually justifying and communicating progress); content creation; content promotion and distribution; measurement and ROI.

Intelligent Content

Mission: Educate, motivate, and prepare enterprise content practitioners to deliver the right content, at the right time, to the right audience, over the right channel, on any device, so that content (and those who plan, create, and deliver it) is valued by the audience and the business.

Key Audiences: Intelligent Content helps the people who need to understand the "plumbing behind the content."
- Content strategists who are charged with making content a scalable function within their enterprise organization
- Marketers who need to scale their content operations and make them more efficient

Sample Titles/Functions: Content strategists, user experience design, marketing change management, technical communicators, director of marketing, marketing technologists, digital content manager, digital marketing manager, manager marketing programs, marketing technology specialist roles.

Why This Group Is Important: Most content marketing programs involve an idea with one or possibly two outputs. In short, the program doesn't scale. Intelligent content means leveraging technology and processes so that:
- Content can be viewed as an asset in the organization
- The strategy is set up in such a way that content can be reused in multiple fashions with multiple outputs when the customers need it

The next generation of content marketing programs will need to become more intelligent in nature in order for marketing to take a leadership role in the overall organization.

Sample Topic Areas: Taxonomy, globalization, enterprise content management, personalization, responsive design, content engineering, content reuse, localization/translation, agile marketing processes, contextualization.

Content Inc.

Mission: Help entrepreneurs be content-driven instead of product- or service-driven and create media assets that depend on the permission to contact an audience, not the permission of a media gatekeeper.

Key Audience: Entrepreneurs, *growth* start-ups, small businesses that want to grow large.

Sample Titles: Founder, CEO, COO, owner, entrepreneur-in-residence, executive director

Why This Group Is Important: We believe the next generation of large enterprises needs to focus on building audiences instead of just releasing new products and services.

Sample Topic Areas: How to build your business around content from the ground up; making content marketing scalable for growth; how to build an audience; choosing the right content niche; how to value a subscriber; leveraging employees for marketing; staffing issues; business model selection.

In the movie *The Grand Budapest Hotel*, the job of the lobby boy was to know the clientele so well that he could anticipate their needs. That is your role now. Your job is to learn your audience so well that you'll be able to develop ongoing content that is so good, the people in your audience are not even aware they needed it in the first place.

If you are in need of an easy-to-use resource on building out who your audience really is, you'll find the CMI resource on audience personas (http://cmi.media/CI-personas) helpful.

CONTENT INC. INSIGHTS

- To be successful with our Content Inc. strategy, you have to become indispensable to your audience. That means creating a strategy that can actually position you as the leading informational or entertainment expert in your content area.
- The more audiences you target, the more likely you will fail. Focus on the most defined audience possible.
- As you get started, don't get bogged down focusing on more than one audience. Choose one audience and become the indispensable expert to that audience. Once that is successful, you can move on to other audiences.

Resource

The Grand Budapest Hotel, Fox Searchlight Pictures, released March 2014.

Part 3

The Content Tilt

You can't depend on your eyes when your imagination is out of focus.

MARK TWAIN

There is so much of the same content out there in the world. To succeed with Content Inc., you need to step out of the pack. Let's do this!

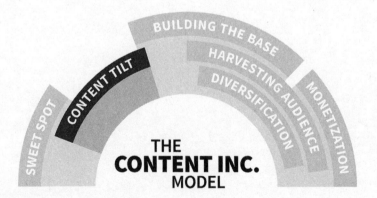

Chapter 5

Understanding the Power of the "Tilt"

When a trout rises to a fly, it does not swim
as much as tilt its fins and jet skyward.
JOSEPH MONNINGER

In the movie *The Matrix*, starring Keanu Reeves and Laurence Fishburne, Reeves's character (Neo) is tested to see whether he is "The One." While Neo is outside in the waiting area, a young protégé is holding up spoon after spoon, bending each one. As Neo sits beside the protégé, the young boy tells Neo that he has to look at the spoon in a different way . . . that the spoon actually does not exist at all.

Soon after, Neo was able to *tilt* his head to the side and slowly bend the spoon.

TELLING A DIFFERENT STORY

Peter Thiel, cofounder of PayPal (along with Tesla founder Elon Musk) and Facebook's first outside investor, believes that most businesses copy other businesses and thus fail. In his book *Zero to One*, Thiel tells businesses that they should "figure out something that nobody else is doing and look to create a monopoly in some area that's been underdeveloped. Find a problem nobody else is solving." Sadly, most companies are creating content and telling stories that are no different from anything else out there.

Just type "SEO e-book" into Google, and you'll get over 20 million results. There are a lot of businesses talking about the same things in the same way. Jay Baer believes that most businesses simply never go through the process of finding a content niche that they can own. In an interview with Jay, he tackles this concept:

> It's like, "Hey I like knitting, and I'm going to start a knitting blog." Really! There are 27 other knitting blogs. Why would anybody read yours? What is different? What is unique? What is interesting? Why would anyone stop reading the knitting blog that they've been reading for the last three years and read yours ever? And if you can't articulate that, you need to go back to the drawing board. And most people I find who haven't been doing this for a while just don't go through that competitive calculus, and it's dangerous.

There are hundreds of blogs on chili peppers that tell stories about the "heat" of the peppers. Claus Pilgaard found a way to tell a story that was radically different from that of his content competition . . . his messaging was around the "taste" of the peppers. Claus's content tilt made all the difference.

CONTENT TILTING

If Content Inc is going to work for you, your content must be different. It must fill a content hole that is not being filled by someone else. As Peter Thiel suggests, we must find a problem area that no one else is solving and exploit that area with content.

This is called "content tilting."

The word *tilt* has two primary definitions. The first is to cause to lean, incline, slope, or slant. If we tilt a glass or a table, we get to look at it from a different perspective. Neo, in *The Matrix*, tilted his head and saw the spoon differently and gained knowledge because of it.

The second definition of *tilt* is to aim or thrust, as you would tilt a lance in a joust. With this tilt, we look at the content niche in such a way that creates the opportunity for us to attack, and lead, and ultimately own the category.

While identifying the sweet spot is critical to the Content Inc. process, it's the content tilt that will separate you from everyone else in your market area. Andrew Davis, author of *Brandscaping*, calls this "the hook"—a simple twist on a familiar theme designed to entrap or ensnare your audience. Without "tilting" your content just enough to truly have a different story to tell, your content will fade into the rest of the clutter and be forgotten.

CASE STUDY: ANN REARDON

Sydney, Australia's Ann Reardon is the "baking queen of YouTube."

In 2011, after giving birth to her third son, Ann was looking for something to do during her night feedings, so she launched a recipe site called *How to Cook That*. "I wrote a recipe post every week and made some videos to complement the website. The videos were too big to upload to my website so I uploaded them to YouTube and started embedding them onto my site."

Before starting a family, Ann was a qualified food scientist and dietitian (her skill area). At the same time, she had a passion for teaching and working with children, so she changed careers and began working with youth in a poorer area of Western Australia.

"I absolutely loved it and have so many great memories," shares Ann. "But our budget was extremely tight so it was during this time that I taught myself to edit videos for the youth ministry, as well as self-catering for lots of events. Over time some of the young adults asked if I could teach them how to cook. A group would come over and we'd all bake and have a great time in my kitchen."

You may be thinking that recipe blogs and "how-to" baking on YouTube are nothing new, and you'd be right. What separates Ann is her content tilt.

Ann focuses her recipes and baking on seemingly impossible creations, such as desserts with five pounds of Snickers bars and a cake that, when sliced open, is a perfect replica of an Instagram logo.

"Many people start a YouTube channel and try to copy what has already been done but the horse has already bolted," Ann explains. "For every single breath you take, there is 8 hours of new video footage uploaded to YouTube, so I have to give viewers a good reason to come back and watch my channel."

In January 2012, Ann saw her 100th subscriber on YouTube and was thrilled. Exactly three years later, Ann has amassed more than 1 million subscribers and receives (believe it or not) more than 3,000 comments per week. In an average month, she'll see over 16 million views of her videos.

Along with the substantial revenues from her cut of YouTube advertising royalties, she has launched an app called "Surprise Cakes" and another app for photo sharing; and as well, she has a number of sponsored content opportunities with brands such as electrical appliance company Breville and kitchenware company World Kitchen.

Yes, Ann found her sweet spot, the combination of her knowledge of food and her passion for teaching, but it was her content tilt of seemingly impossible food creations that has made all the difference (Figure 5.1).

The Odd Struggle with Start-Ups and Content

Jay Acunzo, director of platform at NextView Ventures, a Boston-area early-stage venture capital company, works with a number of technology start-ups on the concept of content marketing. Oddly enough, while most tech start-ups want to create the best product in the world for their niche, they don't believe the same about their content.

In an interview, Jay notes:

> I say [to start-ups], do you think that your product, either now or in the future, is going to be the best solution to solving whatever problem you've identified in the market? Because that's really why tech founders start companies; they see a problem and they want to solve it better than what is in existence. So 100% of these founders say unequivocally yes, we're going to have a better product than our competitors.

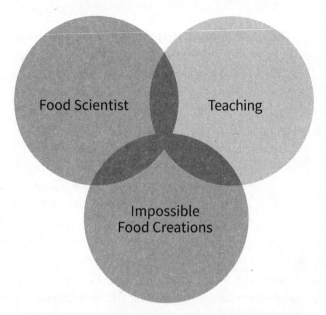

Figure 5.1 Ann Reardon's content tilt of "impossible food creations" is what separates her content from the thousands of other baking blogs.

So then I say, why is it true for your product but not your content? And for me it always comes back to mentality and skill set. They don't think about content in the way that [marketers] think about it. They think about it as a random collection of best practices that just get recycled. "So we've got to blog a lot . . . well everyone else is blogging so why should we blog?"

It's not about that. It's about can you solve the problem in a way that is unique? Your product does that, but your content should do that. Everybody is talking about theoretically how to do marketing and you're like "This is really hard; I'm going to build a product that is going to make marketing really, really simple and almost like plug and play." That's great! You're confident your product can do that, so if you're going to create content, don't just blog; do [something different].

> *They [start-ups] are so confident that they can do something different that no one has ever seen before with their product, and there is a lot of noise. A lot of people have done what they're doing before, but they're like no, I don't care; I'm going to do better. Yet when they come to the content, they're like no, I can't be different. I think it's mentality and skill set that is causing them to say that.*
>
> *. . . I think you just have to think much harder about choosing your niche and on what angle on the problem you're taking with your product . . . that has to come through with your content. And guess what, if you're content reflects the product and it's still not innovative enough, chances are that your product wasn't going to stick anyways, so you might want to revisit the actual thesis for the business. I'm always blown away by that. All these entrepreneurs are so confident that we can solve this problem better than anybody else with our product, and it should articulate that through the content too and they just don't think that way.*

SETTING THE "BEST OF BREED" GOAL

Those who succeed were—at one point or another in their lives—willing to put themselves in situations that were uncomfortable, whereas the unsuccessful seek comfort from all their decisions.
GRANT CARDONE, *THE 10X RULE*

Kevin Plank, CEO of Under Armour, now the number two sports apparel company in the world (behind Nike), states that if you don't have the business goal of being number one in your market, you'll never make it. When talking about his own organization, he says that every employee at Under Armour knows that the mission is to be the clear leader, no questions asked.

The same goes for your Content Inc. goals. Your ultimate objectives—those big hairy audacious goals (as named by Jim Collins of *Good to Great* fame) you worked on in Chapter 1—should make you cringe at least a little bit.

I *completely disagree* with marketing experts and consultants who say it's not necessary to be the leading information provider for your industry. I'm calling bull on that.

Yes, it is a bit audacious to go out on a limb and clearly state that your content should be an irreplaceable resource for your readers (and customers) . . . that you are indeed driving where the market is going from an information standpoint (like a media company). That said, be audacious!

If you are not striving to be the go-to resource for your industry niche, *you are settling for the comfortable*, whatever that means to you in goal-setting terms.

Simply put, you won't be successful with the Content Inc. approach if you settle.

WHAT IF YOUR CONTENT WERE GONE?

Let's say someone rounded up all your content and placed it in a box, like it never existed. *Would anyone miss it? Would you leave a gap in the marketplace?*

If the answer to this is no, *then we've got a problem, Houston*.

We want customers and prospects needing . . . no, *longing for* our content. It becomes part of their lives . . . their jobs.

Today, it's harder and harder to buy attention. You have to earn it. Earn it today, tomorrow, and five years from now by delivering the most impactful information your customers could ever ask for. Set the uncomfortable goals that will take your business to the next level.

Look at the goals you set in Chapter 1. If you are completely comfortable with them, you are settling for good enough. But good enough won't win the battle for customer attention. *Be great!*

FINDING YOUR CONTENT MARKETING HEDGEHOG

Let's go back to Jim Collins again and his fantastic book *Good to Great*. If you know anything about the book, you know about the hedgehog.

The hedgehog, in business, is that thing your business can be the best at . . . that combines your unique talents and passion into something you can make money doing.

In expanding on this topic for Content Inc., I believe we need to look at the hedgehog in four ways:

1. **What we cover.** In your niche, maybe you produce the best research, or the best how-to information, or the best investigative journalism.
2. **How we cover it.** This is channel specific. You possibly have a winning video series like *Game Theory* from Matthew Patrick or *How to Cook That* from Ann Reardon or an amazing podcast like *EntrepreneurOnFire* from John Lee Dumas.
3. **Why we cover it.** This is your higher purpose. To be a truly effective content marketer, you have to be creating and distributing content for the betterment of your reader-customer. Once you find that, then you can introduce a product. The matching of your customers' informational or entertainment needs and what you sell is the Content Inc. jackpot.
4. **Whom we cover it for.** Are there groups of people that are not getting the information they need to do their jobs better or live their lives to the fullest extent? Your hedgehog might be covering a piece of information for that niche group and then doing it better than anyone else.

CONTENT INC. INSIGHTS

- The sweet spot is not enough. In order for our Content Inc. model to succeed, we need to tilt our content in such a way that separates us from the competition.
- The majority of content developed every day is just like everything else out there. It does nothing for the reader or the producer. It doesn't matter the frequency of delivery or the channel you deliver the content through; if the content doesn't tell a different story, it will most likely be ignored.

Resources

The Matrix, Warner Brothers, released March 1999.

Peter Thiel, *Zero to One*, Crown Business, 2014.

Karsten Strauss, "YouTube Star Uses Sugar to Attract an Army of Followers," Forbes.com, accessed April 19, 2015, http://www.forbes.com/sites/

karstenstrauss/2014/08/29/youtube-star-uses-sugar-to-attract-an-army-of-followers/.

Breville Food Thinkers, "Cupcake Piñata Cookies," *How to Cook That*, by Ann Reardon and Breville, YouTube.com, accessed April 19, 2015. https://www.youtube.com/watch?v=D_nAfETePR8&list=UUrwSKj1SUAbS -HkfhZRhbSg.

David Reardon, e-mail interview with Joe Pulizzi, March 2015.

Sam Gutelle, "YouTube Millionaires: Ann Reardon Knows 'How to Cook That,'" Tubefilter.com, accessed April 19, 2015, http://www.tubefilter.com/ 2015/01/22/ann-reardon-how-to-cook-that-youtube-millionaires/.

CNBC, Squawk Box interview with Kevin Plank, February 5, 2015.

Jay Baer, interview by Clare McDermott, January 2015.

Jay Acunzo, interview by Clare McDermott, January 2015.

"Tilt: Definition," Dictionary.com, accessed April 19, 2015. http://dictionary .reference.com/browse/tilt.

Jim Collins, *Good to Great*, HarperCollins Publishers, 2001.

Chapter 6

Discovering Your Content Mission

Everything under the sun has been said . . .
you have to find a new way to say it.
HENRY WINKLER

Besides the underlying business model (how the money comes in), there is one thing that media companies do with their content planning that nonmedia companies do not do. Do you know what it is?

It's the editorial mission statement. Media companies start their strategies by developing an editorial mission statement that guides their content creation efforts and serves as a beacon for the overall business. I've launched over 30 media products in my career, from magazines to newsletters to events to webinar programs. In every one of those launches, the first few days were spent creating and fine-tuning the editorial mission. It is simply the first step in establishing a successful strategy.

Most businesses today have the opportunity to be publishers. The smart ones follow the basic strategies that media companies have used for years to successfully build their audiences.

YOUR CONTENT MISSION

A mission statement is a company's reason for existence. It's why the organization does what it does. For example, Southwest Airlines's mission statement is to democratize the travel experience. The mission statement for CVS is to be the easiest pharmacy retailer for customers to use. So, in simple terms, the mission statement answers the question, "Why do we exist?"

I cover the content marketing mission statement in most of my keynote presentations. It's critical to first set the tone for the idea of content marketing . . . or any marketing, for that matter. Marketing professionals, with both small and large businesses, get so fixated on channels such as blogs, Facebook, or Pinterest that they have no clue to the underlying reason of why they should use that channel in the first place. The "why" must come before the "what."

Your content tilt (Chapter 5) needs to be expressed in a way that you can communicate to your audience. It's a bold statement when you put your flag in the ground and tell your audience why you are different.

In *Epic Content Marketing*, I discuss three parts of the content mission statement:

- The core target audience
- The material that will be delivered to the audience
- The outcome for the audience

My favorite mission statement from a traditional media company is from *Inc.* magazine. You can find its mission on its About Us page:

Welcome to Inc.com, the place where entrepreneurs and business owners can find useful information, advice, insights, resources and inspiration for running and growing their businesses.

Inc.'s mission statement includes:

- The core target audience: Entrepreneurs and business owners.
- The material that will be delivered to the audience: Useful information, advice, insights, resources, and inspiration.
- The outcome for the audience: Running and growing their businesses.

Inc.'s mission statement is incredibly simple and includes no words that can be misunderstood. Simplicity is key for your content marketing mission statement.

Note that nowhere in the mission statement is *Inc.* talking about how it makes money. That's where most start-ups go wrong with their content creation . . . they always want to talk about what they are going to sell. If you do that, you'll never even get off the ground with your Content Inc. strategy.

CASE STUDY: DIGITAL PHOTOGRAPHY SCHOOL

Darren Rowse built two amazingly successful Content Inc. models. The first one, *ProBlogger*, focuses on small business blogging. The second, Digital Photography School, is one of the leading sources for beginning photographers on how to get the maximum out of their picture-taking skills.

But it didn't start out that way. Initially, Darren launched a camera review–type blog. As he explains:

Previous to ProBlogger I started a camera review blog that was my first commercial sort of blog and that had gotten to the point where it was full-time, but it wasn't a very satisfying blog to write. My readers would come for one day to research a certain camera and then disappear and never come back. So I always had this dissatisfaction with it that I wasn't actually building a community; I think that's what really feeds me, having ongoing readers. I always wanted a blog that was a bit more about helping people in a long-term way.

After this initial experiment didn't quite work, Darren came back to photography blogging, but changed his content tilt. Darren's "aha!" moment came with his focus on one particular audience.

"I guess one of the doubts I had along the way was around focus," says Darren. He recalls:

Very much early on it was about beginners, so it was very basic content and I had some doubts about whether I should start expanding into more intermediate level content, but I kind of stuck to that beginner stuff for the first two years and really built the audience there until my audience began to grow into the next level of content. So I didn't expand the expertise too early, which was good in hindsight.

That decision paid off, and Darren saw his total e-mail and social audience grow to well over a million subscribers.

Let's take a look at Digital Photography School's content mission. You can find it on the website's About Us page (http://cmi.media/CI-DPS).

Welcome to Digital Photography School—a website with simple tips to help digital camera owners get the most out of their cameras.

Let's dissect the mission statement:

- The core target audience: Digital camera owners.
- The material that will be delivered to the audience: Simple tips.
- The outcome for the audience: Get the most out of their cameras.

Darren expands on his mission by saying:

This "School" is not a formal one by any means. There are no classes, no teachers, no exams—rather it's a learning environment where I think out loud about what I know and where in our Forum we share what we're learning by showing our photos and ask and answer each other questions. Also, unlike most schools, the information here is free.

It's no wonder that beginning and intermediate photographers engage in Darren's site on a regular basis. Darren's content tilt, the reason why he separated himself, was his insight and ability to turn his focus on a beginner audience with helpful, consistent tips that his readers could use immediately. Long gone are Darren's days of reviewing cameras.

WANTS, NOT NEEDS

More and more, I find that the best Content Inc. programs revolve around aspirations, not needs. I've been guilty of telling marketers to "focus on customer pain points" since, well, forever. Focusing on pain points just gets you to the front door.

To get to the heart of your customers' needs, you have to focus on what they want to be and help them get where they really want to go.

What's in a Name?

In 2008 I sat in an American Business Media executive meeting and listened to Peter Hoyt speak. Peter is CEO of Hoyt Publishing, a family-owned media company. Hoyt stated that the name Hoyt Publishing limited many opportunities for the company, so the company changed its name to the In-Store Marketing Institute (renamed later as Point-of-Purchase Institute).

Upon making that change, Hoyt's revenues skyrocketed. "The institute really caught on and developed into something much bigger than I thought it would be," Hoyt said. "It has provided millions of dollars in new revenue and profit. Our net operating profit went from 7% in 2006 to 19% in 2008, and we keep reinvesting that yield to further serve the industry."

Hoyt's experiences were a direct reason why I changed our name to Content Marketing Institute. Not sexy by any means, but the name change positioned us as immediate experts. We also didn't have to spend time telling people what we did—they immediately knew.

The moral of the story? Sometimes taking a boring name that says exactly what you do is better than a brand that you have to put additional marketing into so people know exactly what your content mission is. The Chicken Whisperer, the *Game Theory* video series, and Digital Photography School all follow this model. And it works.

Instead of the basics like "saving money" and "lowering costs," let's raise the bar to things like "giving our customers more free time to live the lives they want to" or "being a person that can make a difference in the world."

It sounds corny, but it's so critical. To become that one resource that cuts through the clutter, the people in your audience need to believe that your content can *change their stars* (from the movie *A Knight's Tale*).

So, like Peter Thiel preaches, forget what your so-called competition is creating and distributing to your customers. You are better than that. Instead, become the content that your customers want to engage with over everything else. It's that kind of aspiration that will give you the vision to put a plan and team together that will truly make a difference.

In the kitchen of our house, there is a mission statement on the wall. I refer to it often. So do my two boys, now ages 12 and 14.

The mission statement is our family purpose. It's what we strive to be today and into the future. I believe that mission statement has been crucial to our family's success and happiness.

Here is what it says.

The Pulizzi Mission

As Pulizzis, we hold true the following with ongoing purpose and action:

We thank God every day for our blessings, even on days when we are challenged or face hardships.

We always share what we have with others, and help out whenever we can to whoever is in need.

We praise each other, as we are each blessed by God with unique talents.

We always finish what we start, always try even though we may be afraid, and always give the activity of the moment our full attention.

Short Version:

Thank God. Always Share. Say Nice Things. Give Our Best.

When the kids have questions about what they should and shouldn't do, my wife and I refer to the mission statement. And the best part? When visitors come into our house, the mission statement is noticed right away and almost always commented upon. It's one of those little things that make a difference.

CONTENT INC. INSIGHTS

- Once the content tilt is identified, we can begin to build our content mission. A sound mission includes who the specific audience is, what content we deliver to that audience, and what the audience outcome is.
- So many companies focus on what their competition is doing. With content, you compete with tens, even hundreds, of sources. Thus, it's pointless to focus on what the competition does. Focus on your audience.
- Sure, you can be successful focusing on informational needs, but take your program to the next level. If you can help people live better lives or get better jobs, you'll grab them emotionally and keep them as subscribers for life.

Resources

The Nerdist Podcast, Henry Winkler interview, December 15, 2014.

Digital Photography School, accessed April 19, 2015, http://digital-photography -school.com/.

A Knight's Tale, Columbia Pictures, released May 2001.

Marie Griffin, "The Idea That Transformed Hoyt Publishing," AdAge.com, accessed April 19, 2015, http://adage.com/article/btob/idea-transformed -hoyt-publishing/273350/.

Chapter 7

Ways to Unearth Your Content Tilt

I think being different, going against the grain
of society is the greatest thing in the world.
ELIJAH WOOD

To succeed with Content Inc., you need to create a platform that is the leading informational or entertainment resource around your content niche. This is not easy to do. Many entrepreneurs have ideas about what it is they want to create content around; they just don't go that extra mile to clearly differentiate themselves.

This chapter will help you do just that. Here are a number of strategies and tactics you can leverage to help identify your content tilt.

AMAZON.COM PRESS RELEASE METHOD

Ian McAllister, general manager for AmazonSmile, Amazon's charitable arm, states that before a new product is presented for development at Amazon, Jeff Bezos, Amazon's CEO, requires that a full press release be written as if the product were fully built and ready to launch.

"Iterating on a press release is a lot less expensive than iterating on the product itself (and quicker!)," says McAllister.

This type of approach is critical for visualizing our Content Inc. strategy and identifying what makes us stand out. It is our differentiating factor. Amanda MacArthur, managing editor for *Mequoda Daily*, details the critical parts of the Amazon press release method. In leveraging Amanda's words with a content marketing viewpoint, this is how to find your content tilt:

- **Heading**—*Name the content area in a way the reader will understand.*
- **Subheading**—*Describe who the market for the content is and what benefit they get.*
- **Summary**—*Give a summary of the content and the benefit.*
- **Problem**—*Describe the problem your content solves.*
- **Solution**—*Describe how your content elegantly solves the problem.*
- **Quote from You**—*A quote from a spokesperson in your company.*
- **How to Get Started**—*Describe how easy it is to get started.*
- **Customer Quote**—*Provide a quote from a hypothetical customer that describes how they experienced the benefit.*
- **Closing and Call to Action**—*Wrap it up and give pointers where the reader should go next.*

According to Fast Company, "The point is to help [Amazon employees] refine their ideas and distill their goals with the customer in mind." It can do the same for you and your Content Inc. strategy.

LEVERAGING GOOGLE TRENDS

Andrew Davis, author of *Brandscaping*, believes that Google Trends is the most important and most underutilized tool when it comes to locating your content niche. Davis, now a worldwide keynote speaker, includes a section in every one of his presentations on the power of Google Trends.

Google Trends is a free tool offered by Google that shows the search results and patterns of keywords worldwide or specific to regions. For example, if you type "kitchen blender" into Google Trends, you'll see that the searches peak every December in every year, conveniently right around the holidays and gift-giving season (Figure 7.1).

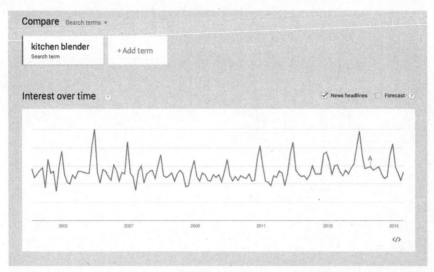

Figure 7.1   Search results on Google for "kitchen blender" peak every December.

Now let's go back to Jay Baer and his example (from Chapter 5) of someone starting a knitting blog: "I like knitting and I'm going to start a knitting blog. Really! There are 27 other knitting blogs. Why would anybody read yours? What is different? What is unique? What is interesting? Why would anyone stop reading the knitting blog that they've been reading for the last three years and read yours?"

Here's where Google Trends earns its stripes. If we do a Trends search for knitting, we find that overall searches (Figure 7.2) are actually down for that term (not a good sign).

But if we dig a bit deeper, we'll find gold. Moving down the page, as Figure 7.3 shows, you see a section called "Related searches." Here's where we find our tilt. Under the "Topics" area, we find that information around loom knitting (the product category) is up 300 percent in searches. If we look under the "Queries" section, we find that "loom knitting" is breaking out, as well as "knitting for beginners," "knitting a scarf," and "knitting stiches."

If we go back to Jay's example, instead of just focusing on knitting in general, the data might be telling us to focus on *innovative methods for using a knitting loom (for beginners).*

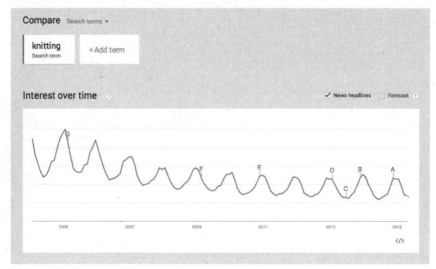

Figure 7.2 Search patterns via Google around the term *knitting* over time.

Topics				Queries			
	Top	**Rising**			**Top**	**Rising**	
Ravelry - Website		Breakout		loom knitting		+450%	
Loom - Product category		+300%		knitting for beginners		+190%	
Cardigan - Garment		+140%		knitting cast on		+120%	
Blanket		+130%		double knitting		+100%	
Stitch		+90%		circular knitting needles		+80%	
				baby knitting patterns		+70%	
				easy knitting patterns		+70%	

Figure 7.3 By scrolling to the bottom of a Google Trends search, you can discover related searches and breakout terms.

ASK YOUR POTENTIAL READERS

This is such low-hanging fruit that I almost didn't include it as a strategy. Asking your customers or potential readers seems like such a simple thing to do, but sadly it's rarely done.

I recently conducted a workshop for one of the largest manufacturing companies in the world. When I came to the section about building the content mission, senior marketers were asked if they ever surveyed or talked to their customers to identify content gaps or opportunities to tell different but needed stories. Unfortunately, each one of them said that the marketing team hadn't been employing any surveys or asking their audience what their pain points, needs, or wants were in any way.

Here is an opportunity to take advantage of what large enterprises don't do well—talk to your readers. Whether you ask potential readers (which could be your friends or family) face-to-face or you send out a survey (using a tool like SurveyMonkey) via e-mail, either or both ways should be part of your regular strategy. This is especially critical in the beginning stages as you are discovering your niche.

Setting Up Listening Posts

I started in the publishing industry in February 2000 at Penton Media. I learned what great storytelling was all about from my mentor, Jim McDermott. Jim constantly talked about the importance of "listening posts." Listening posts are all about getting as much feedback from a variety of sources as possible so you can find the truth.

Setting up listening posts is critical for all editors, journalists, reporters, and storytellers to make sure they truly know what is going on in the industry. For you, listening posts are critical so that you can identify your content tilt and make sure it's an opportunity for you to differentiate yourself. All of us need listening posts to truly discover our customers' needs. The following are all means of getting feedback from customers—in effect, functioning as listening posts.

1. **One-on-one conversations.** Adele Revella, one of the leading thinkers around audience personas, believes that nothing can replace talking to your customers or audience directly.
2. **Search of keywords.** Using tools such as Google Trends and search engine keyword alerts will allow you to track what customers are searching for and where they are hanging out on the web.

3. **Web analytics.** Dive into your web analytics. Finding out what content your readers are engaging in (and what they aren't) can make all the difference to your success.
4. **Social media listening.** Whether through LinkedIn groups or Twitter hashtags and keywords, you can easily find out what your customers are sharing, talking about, and struggling with in their lives and jobs.
5. **Customer surveys.** Survey tools like SurveyMonkey can easily be deployed to gather key insights into your customers' informational needs.

TESTING TILTS

Jay Acunzo from NextView Ventures employs a testing strategy every time he's considering a new content area. Recently, while gathering data for a target content area, he took small subsets of his database and sent out test content to different groups. For each one he measured the open rate, the click-through, the on-site engagement, and the unsubscribe rate. He did this for six weeks and, at the end of the process, identified a clear and overwhelming winner in a certain content subcategory.

Matthew Patrick, founder of *Game Theory*, whom we met in Chapter 3 and who has one of the most popular YouTube channels with over 4 million subscribers, found his niche through testing as well. According to Matthew, "I really started to approach the platform in a very experimental way. I would do A/B tests; I would run very small experiments with descriptions and things like that. And over time I was able to really get a sense of how users engage with this platform, but also how YouTube and their algorithms work to kind of sort videos and spread them across the system."

Once the data told Matthew what made a hit and what didn't, he built his model around that, which skyrocketed his Content Inc. model to success.

REPOSITION THE CONTENT AREA

The Content Marketing Institute was launched in April 2007. Even though I had used the term *content marketing* on and off for the previous six years, it was still new marketing terminology.

The dominant industry term at the time was *custom publishing*. From conversations with senior marketing practitioners (CMI's target audience), I could tell that that term was not something that resonated with them. But was there an opportunity for content marketing? Could changing the industry terminology be our content tilt?

I tinkered with the Google Trends tool and looked at a number of phrase variations. Here is what I found as it related to the dominant industry term (*custom publishing*) and an emerging term (*content marketing*).

- **Custom publishing.** If this were a stock for purchase, we at CMI definitely wouldn't want to own it. Every year people searched for this term less often. In addition, many of the articles referred, not to our idea of brands creating content, but to customized print books. This confusion was a problem.
- **Content marketing.** The term didn't even register on Google Trends. I began to think that if enough of the right content was created, a movement around the term could be started. With confusion around the other terms such as *branded content* and *custom content*, it was likely that the industry needed a new term around which to rally key thought leaders. In addition, without a clear leader in the "content marketing" group, CMI could move quickly and gain search market share if done correctly. As you can see in Figure 7.4, this strategy paid off.

So a combination of talking to our audience and using free tools like Google Trends helped CMI define its content niche and "tilt" around this name change.

HubSpot, the extremely successful marketing automation enterprise, employed the same strategy with the term *inbound marketing* (Figure 7.5). In 2006, HubSpot launched a blog around the concept and devel-

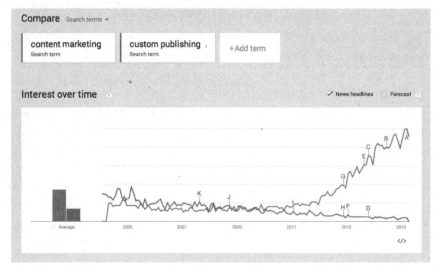

Figure 7.4 The terms *content marketing* and *custom publishing* have taken opposite paths, according to Google Trends.

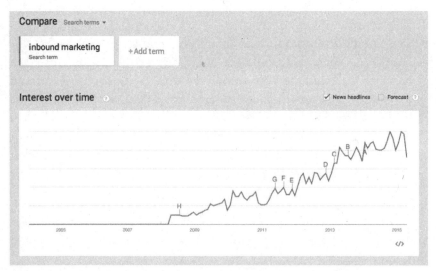

Figure 7.5 Content areas can be exploited with a name change and a lot of valuable content. The term *inbound marketing* is an example of this.

oped a book (called *Inbound Marketing*), a video series, and an event called Inbound. As you can see, the community gathered around this term and helped thrust HubSpot into a leadership position.

DOING THE WORK

I'm winding down this chapter with an invaluable lesson and quote from Ira Glass, the popular host and producer of *This American Life*. Glass stated the following on his show:

> *Put yourself on a deadline so that every week you will finish one story. It is only by going through a volume of work that you will close that gap, and your work will be as good as your ambitions. And I took longer to figure out how to do this than anyone I've ever met. It's gonna take awhile. It's normal to take awhile. You've just gotta fight your way through.*

Sometimes, to find your content tilt, you simply have to get started, do the work, and discover the opportunities. Jeff Bullas, the most popular social media strategist in Australia, started out his content platform by writing about celebrity news (his first post was about Jennifer Anniston). After months of creating content, Jeff found his groove specific to the emerging practice of social media. Jeff had to do the work to get to the content tilt.

The same situation happened with Jay Baer. Jay initially launched a blog primarily about e-mail marketing. In an interview, he said:

> *And I discovered in about 30 seconds that every time I wrote about email marketing I got 150 visits to the site, and every time I wrote about social media I got about 1000 visits to the site. And after that happened for a while I though, hum . . . I don't have a degree in statistics, but I see a trend here.*
>
> *So I said, we're going to write about social media until somebody tells us not to write about that, so I spent all my time writing about that. Then I had done a bunch of social media consulting in the past and said, well I guess if there's that much demand for this information then that's going to be the focus of the business, and it was.*

Jay would never have found this out if he had not put himself out there creating content. It's completely acceptable that you take your best shot (like Jay did) at a content tilt and start developing the platform. Maybe then you will find the Content Inc. niche that will drive your success.

- One of the most underutilized marketing tools on the planet is Google Trends. It is your job to leverage this tool to unearth your content tilt.
- If you focus on listening to customers first and selling second, it will open up amazing new opportunities to position your company.
- Sometimes to find your content tilt, you need to do the work. Perfection is unattainable with content, so if you have stalled your plans until you find the right tilt, the best prescription may be to just begin the creation process.

Resources

This American Life, produced by Ira Glass, WBEZ, 2014, http://www.this americanlife.org/.

Amanda MacArthur, "An Inspirational Press Release Template from Amazon," Mequoda.com, http://www.mequoda.com/articles/audience-development/ an-inspirational-press-release-template-from-amazon/.

Austin Carr, "The Real Story Behind Jeff Bezos's Fire Phone Debacle and What It Means for Amazon's Future," FastCompany.com, http://www.fast company.com/3039887/under-fire.

Jay Acunzo, interview by Clare McDermott, January 2015.

Adele Revella, *Buyer Personas*, John Wiley & Sons, 2015.

Jay Baer, interview by Clare McDermott, January 2015.

Todd Wheatland, "The Pivot: 4 Million People Glad Bullas Went Back to Tech," ContentMarketingInstitute.com, http://contentmarketinginstitute.com/ 2015/01/the-pivot-jeff-bullas/.

Part 4

Building the Base

It is not the beauty of a building you should look at;
it's the construction of the foundation that will stand the test of time.
DAVID ALLAN COE

You've found your sweet spot and identified your content tilt.
Now it's time to do the work.

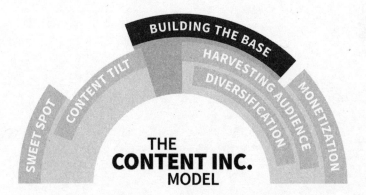

Chapter 8

Selecting Your Platform

Pilots have their names painted just beneath the canopy of their aircraft.
This gives the pilot a sense of ownership for his or her jet. What's more,
like cars, each aircraft has its own personality, so it's important for a pilot
to get to know and love his aircraft.

SIMON SINEK

If you've completed the work to this point, congratulations. Believe
it or not, the strategy behind the Content Inc. model is the hardest
part. Anyone, anywhere, with almost no resources can create a blog,
podcast, or YouTube series, but it takes research and thinking to build
an audience. That audience is what will ultimately power your entire
business model.

WHERE TO START?

As Michael Hyatt said in his book and blog, both entitled *Platform*,
your ideas and stories need a place to live if you are going to succeed.
According to Michael, "Without a platform—something that enables
you to get seen and heard—*you don't have a chance*. Having an awe-
some product, an outstanding service, or a compelling cause is no
longer enough."

The greatest media entities of all time selected one primary channel in which to build their platform:

- *Wall Street Journal*—Printed newspaper
- *Time*—Printed magazine
- TED Talks—In-person events
- ESPN—Cable television programming
- *Huffington Post*—Online magazine format
- *Rush Limbaugh*—Radio show

As you can see from the examples above, you have two choices to make when building your platform:

1. How will you tell your stories? Will it be through written word, through video, through audio, or in person?
2. Where will you tell your stories? What channel will you choose to distribute your content?

Mathew Patrick from *Game Theory* decided to create consistent videos and distribute them on YouTube.

Darren Rowse from Digital Photography School uses mostly articles with images, leveraging a website developed in WordPress.

John Lee Dumas from *EntrepreneurOnFire (EOF)* does a podcast every day; he distributes it mainly through iTunes, Stitcher, and SoundCloud and delivers show notes on a website.

BEFORE YOU START

In *Epic Content Marketing* I discuss six principles of content marketing that work. You need to remember these at all times during the process of building and executing your platform.

1. **Fill a need.** Your content should answer some unmet need of or question for your reader.
2. **Be consistent.** The great hallmark of a successful publisher is consistency. Whether you publish a monthly magazine or daily e-mail newsletter, the content needs to be delivered always on time and as expected. This is where so many Content Inc. strategies fall down.

3. **Be human.** Find what your voice is, and share it. If your company's story is all about humor, share that. If it's a bit sarcastic, that's okay too.

4. **Have a point of view.** This is not encyclopedia content. You are not giving a history report. Don't be afraid to take sides on matters that can position you and your company as an expert. One of the reasons Marcus Sheridan, and his company River Pools & Spas, has been successful is the emotion and bluntness Marcus relays in his content. People appreciate that.

5. **Avoid "sales speak."** When we at Content Marketing Institute create a piece of content that is solely about us rather than for an educational purpose, it only garners 25 percent of the regular amount of page views and social shares. Sometimes there are business reasons to do this, but the more you talk about yourself, the less people will value your content.

6. **Be best of breed.** Although you might not be able to reach it at the very beginning, the goal for your content ultimately is to be best of breed. This means that, for your content niche, what you are distributing is the very best of what is found and is available. If you expect your readers to spend time with your content, you must deliver them amazing value.

In all our Content Inc. case studies, these six elements are present. Be sure they are on your mind throughout your process of building your Content Inc. model.

CONTENT TYPES

According to the 2015 Content Marketing Institute/Marketing Profs Small Business Content Marketing Study, the most popular content types are as follows (in order of usage):

- Articles or blog posts
- Textual stories in e-newsletters
- Videos
- In-person events
- Reports or white papers

- Webinars/webcasts
- Books (print or digital)
- Printed magazines
- Audio programming
- Printed newsletters

The majority of Content Inc. success stories fall into these following content types:

- **Articles or blogs (or content-based websites).** CMI's main platform for building audience is by distributing content via a blog. Blogs started at three times per week and now run every day or multiple times per day.
- **E-newsletter programs.** As one example, Social Media Examiner delivers daily content via e-mail to over 300,000 business owners and marketers.
- **Videos.** Every week, Matthew Patrick (*Game Theory*) distributes a fresh video via YouTube.
- **Podcasts.** Every day, John Lee Dumas (*EOF*) presents a new podcast interview.

Companies utilizing Content Inc. strategies diversify their content channels into other properties once they attract a large enough audience. In the beginning, it's important to focus on creating amazing and relevant content with mostly one content channel (podcast, video, blog, etc.).

For detailed information on the specific pros and cons of each content type, download the complimentary *Content Marketing Playbook* at http://cmi.media/CI-playbook.

THE CONTENT CHANNEL

Now that you know how you are going to tell your story, you need to decide how you are going to deliver the content—the channel. Over the long term, you'll be distributing your content through a number of channels (see Part 5, "Harvesting Audience"), but right now you need to make a decision about the "core" channel.

You need to consider two major questions when making this decision:

- What channel offers the best opportunity to reach my target audience? (*Reach*)
- What channel gives me the most control over presenting my content and building my audience? (*Control*)

Let's look at the chart in Figure 8.1.

Brian Clark's *Copyblogger* has almost infinite control over its channel, a WordPress site that it owns. At the same time, *Copyblogger* needs to build a system to attract people to its content since its website doesn't reside within another ecosystem that can naturally bring it traffic.

On the other hand, *EntrepreneurOnFire* (podcast) and *GameTheory* (video) have a greater reach possibility than *Copyblogger* since they publish within an environment with a built-in audience. *EOF* publishes via iTunes, where there are millions of people who search for new podcasts every day. Same thing for *Game Theory*. Its target audience of teenagers is already on YouTube every day. As long as *Game Theory*

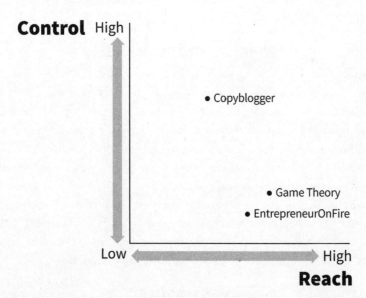

Figure 8.1 A blog like *Copyblogger* has more control but less reach than content programs like *Game Theory* and *EntrepreneurOnFire*.

continues to create compelling content that YouTube will deliver, it should grow an audience there.

The problem with *EOF* and *Game Theory* is that they are leveraging platforms that they have little or no control over. *Game Theory* has over 4 million subscribers. That's amazing, but technically *Game Theory* doesn't control those subscriber relationships; YouTube does. YouTube could decide tomorrow that it doesn't want *Game Theory* to have access to those people, or it might decide to publicize other content to Matthew Patrick's audience, like Jimmy Fallon, instead of *Game Theory*.

Consider the example of the duo SMOSH, the YouTube sensations who built an audience of 20 million subscribers on YouTube. Over the past couple of years, calls to action at the end of their video content were always to their owned website, Smosh.com, where they could sign up people for an e-mail subscription program that they had control over. The point here is if you choose a low-control channel as the main driver of your content distribution, be aware that at some point you'll want to convert the subscribers on that platform to your own subscribers (see Chapter 14).

BEWARE OF SOCIAL CHANNELS

Although social channels, such as Facebook and LinkedIn, are great places to build your digital footprint and followers, you ultimately have no control over what those companies do with your connections. Sure, LinkedIn lets your current connections see all the content you publish on LinkedIn, but LinkedIn could change its mind tomorrow. It has every right to do so as a private business, and you, a free member of the LinkedIn community, have no rights.

Social channels like Facebook, Twitter, LinkedIn, Pinterest, and Instagram and newer channels like Tumblr and Medium may all be solid considerations to build a platform depending on whom you are targeting, but it's important to understand the dangers.

THE SAFEST BET

Look at the fastest-growing media companies of today, such as BuzzFeed or Vice Media, or more mature new media platforms, such as the *Huffington Post*. You can even look at a traditional publisher like the *New York Times* or *Time* magazine. They are all very good at leveraging social channels and building an audience on those channels, but they *don't* build their main platform on social channels.

In every case, they build websites or print properties (both with subscribers) that they can own and control, and they leverage other channels to drive people back to the sites they own so they can convert passersby into an audience they can monetize.

PLATFORMS IN ACTION

Openview Venture Partners invests in growth-oriented technology companies. Back in 2009, Openview launched a content platform called Openview Labs (http://cmi.media/CI-openview), which delivers regular article content to attract subscribers to an e-newsletter offering (which now boasts over 36,000 subscribers . . . not bad for a venture capital company; see Figure 8.2).

Figure 8.2 Openview Venture Partners uses the content brand Openview Labs on a blog platform.

Kraft Foods, one of the leading collections of food brands in the world, owns KraftRecipes.com (http://cmi.media/CI-kraft). According to Julie Fleischer, Kraft Foods' senior director of Data + Content, KraftRecipes.com, Kraft employs 20 culinary professionals who work with Kraft products every day. There are currently 30,000 recipes on the company's website, where Kraft actually generates direct revenue from advertising on the site (Figure 8.3), as well as print advertising in its magazine, *Kraft Food & Family*.

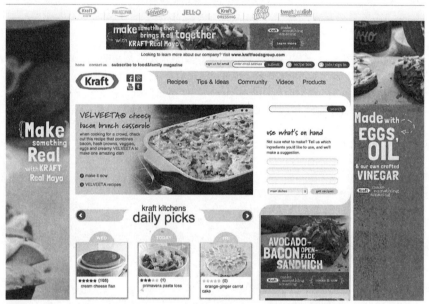

Figure 8.3   Kraft's content and recipe site KraftRecipes.com.

John Deere launched *The Furrow* magazine in 1895. It is still published today, produced in print and digital format in 14 different languages and distributed to 40 countries (http://cmi.media/CI-furrow). *The Furrow* has always focused on how farmers can learn the latest technology to grow their farms and businesses (Figure 8.4).

Figure 8.4   One of the oldest Content Inc. initiatives on the planet, *The Furrow* magazine from John Deere.

Got Tech?

What Should I Use to Build My Website?

Although there are a number of open-source (e.g., Joomla, Drupal) and closed-source (.NET) website publishing platforms, most Content Inc. businesses power their websites with WordPress. Approximately 75 million sites are powered by WordPress, which accounts for 19 percent of all websites on the planet. In addition, WordPress has a vibrant community, which means if you need to add a plug-in to your site, it's probably already been created.

What E-mail Platform Should I Use?

There are a number of excellent e-mail systems out there for small businesses. Consider Emma, MailChimp, or Aweber. Because e-mail subscribers are critical to your Content Inc. plan, it's smart to get started with a reputable e-mail provider sooner rather than later.

Hollywood celebrity Gwyneth Paltrow recently launched her own Content Inc. strategy, called Goop (http://cmi.media/CI-goop). Originally conceived in 2008 as a weekly e-newsletter on travel recommendations and shopping tips, Goop has evolved into a fully functioning media site with over 1 million subscribers (Figure 8.5).

Figure 8.5   Actress Gwyneth Paltrow is building a Content Inc. powerhouse at Goop.com.

CONTENT INC. INSIGHTS

- The greatest media brands of all time started the same way, delivering the same content type in the same content channel for years.
- When choosing the appropriate channel for your strategy, understand the risks of a social channel that you don't own. While the opportunity for gaining audience may be greater, ultimately the risk is much larger since you don't own that asset.
- In almost all cases, your blog platform strategy will work best in a WordPress platform. Before you launch, check out WordPress first.

Resources

Michael Hyatt, *Platform*, http://michaelhyatt.com/platform.

Michele Linn, "Kraft Foods: Tools to Create the Right Recipe for Your Content Marketing Plan," ContentMarketingInstitute.com, http://contentmarketing institute.com/2013/10/kraft-content-marketing/.

Craig Hodges, "How Kraft Owns the Recipe Business," KingContent.com.au, http://www.kingcontent.com.au/how-kraft-owns-the-recipe-business-five -lessons-from-julie-fleischer/.

Tom Ewer, "14 Surprising Statistics About WordPress Usage," ManageWP.com, https://managewp.com/14-surprising-statistics-about-wordpress-usage.

Chapter 9

Content Ideation

An idea that is not dangerous is unworthy of being called an idea at all.
OSCAR WILDE

Ann Handley, author of the book *Everybody Writes*, believes in the Content Inc. concept for two reasons, Handley says in an interview:

Number one . . . because it does put the needs of your audience first, in the sense that you see the audience as collaborative with your business . . . I like that audience centric point of view.

The second thing is that creating content isn't just for marketing. It's not just an external exercise designed to grow an audience; . . . the beauty of content is that it actually also grows the individual. So it grows the content creator at the same time. That means it almost forces you to evolve your thinking. When you're creating content and you're getting feedback from the audience it allows you to hone your vision, as well as embed your vision ultimately with whatever it is that you're creating.

Look at any leading informational resource on the web. The content that is first developed upon launch is always significantly different than it is now. Over time, the content evolved to better meet the needs of the audience, and at the same time the content creators began to find their own sweet spot (which sometimes takes time to find, as we've discussed).

> Finishing races is important, but racing is more important.
> DALE EARNHARDT

To get to a point of Content Inc. success, we need to do the work. Now that you've identified your sweet spot and determined what differentiates you and your content, coming up with consistently compelling content ideas may seem daunting. Putting in the work makes all the difference.

Most entrepreneurs fail at developing ideas for their content because they fail to plan. If you are at a point where you are sitting in front of the computer waiting for inspiration to strike, you're doing it wrong.

There is no one right way to develop ideas for your content projects, but you do need a process.

THE CONTENT AUDIT

Before you can determine what kind of content you need, you first need to figure out what you have. In addition, you need to determine whether what you have is any good at all or, better yet, whether you have some raw content that is still incredibly valuable that you can leverage throughout your Content Inc. strategy.

Why is this so critical? I've worked with dozens of companies that launched new e-books and white papers and hired freelancers and editors, only to find out midway through the process that much of the content initiative had already been created. Conducting even a simple content audit would have saved those companies time and money.

For a full overview of why and how to conduct a content audit, you'll find a handy resource at http://cmi.media/CI-audit.

50 QUESTIONS

One of the amazing things about Marcus Sheridan's success with River Pools & Spas is that he's never actually installed a fiberglass pool, even though the majority of the world believes he *is* the expert. His secret: "The ultimate content strategy is listening."

Marcus listens to customers, to employees, to podcasts . . . he's a consummate learner. Then he brainstorms for content ideas. "If you don't come up with at least 50 questions, you haven't tried hard enough," says Sheridan. "If you write two times per week, that's a whole year's worth of content."

Open a notebook and make a list of questions your audience would like to know about. At this point, there is no wrong answer. Don't stop and correct anything—just write questions. Finish your list of 50 questions and take a break. After a while, come back to the list to find the diamonds.

LEVERAGING FREEWRITING

Mark Levy (author of *Accidental Genius*) gave me a crash course in something called "freewriting." Freewriting, also called stream-of-consciousness writing, is a writing technique where the person writes for a set period of time without regard for spelling or even the topic. Mark uses this technique with his clients to unearth the raw content at the heart of the content creator.

Natalie Goldberg, author of *The True Secret of Writing*, outlines the rules of freewriting to include:

- *Give yourself a time limit. Write for a set period, and then stop.*
- *Keep your hand moving until the time is up. Do not pause to stare into space or to read what you've written. Write quickly but do not rush.*
- *Pay no attention to grammar, spelling, punctuation, neatness, or style. Nobody else needs to read what you produce.*
- *If you get off topic or run out of ideas, keep writing anyway. If necessary, write nonsense or whatever comes into your head, or simply scribble: do anything to keep the hand moving.*
- *If you feel bored or uncomfortable as you're writing, ask yourself what's bothering you, and write about that.*
- *When the time is up, look over what you've written, and mark passages that contain ideas or phrases that might be worth keeping or elaborating on in a subsequent freewriting session.*

HAVING FUN WITH GOOGLE ALERTS

Google Alerts is a free service (all you need is a Gmail account) that delivers web content to your inbox related to the words you are searching for. For example, if you are interested in content around the multiplayer game Minecraft, you could ask Google Alerts to send you a notification when Google finds a new page, say, on Minecraft tips or Minecraft releases.

You can receive alerts as they happen, every day, or every week. These articles can become new fodder for your content ideas.

Note: Also, don't forget that Google Trends rising or hot topics is a great resource for this as well.

TWITTER HASHTAGS

As with Google Alerts, your industry may have a number of hashtags that can be a beacon for new content. For example, there are multiple conversations on the web going on around "intelligent content." The hashtag for intelligent content is #IntelContent. By searching Twitter or setting up a dashboard with a Twitter management system such as Tweetdeck, you can monitor what is going on around the topic in social media. You can also use hashtags in Facebook and LinkedIn, but I've never found it as helpful as Twitter.

ANALYZE YOUR ANALYTICS

Jay Baer would never have found his content tilt of social media without analyzing his web traffic. After publishing a post about social media, he was seeing double and triple the traffic versus his former topic of e-mail marketing.

Make a habit of looking into your analytics on a weekly basis. Find out what people are most interested in and how they are finding your content. It may make sense to create more content around what's most important to your audience.

Note: While there are hundreds of analytics systems, Google Analytics is free and is relatively easy to install on your website.

EMPLOYEE DISCUSSIONS

So many employees are afraid to help you create content because they don't understand that much of the value is added in the editing process.

For your purposes, you want the "raw" content from them . . . the information that makes them subject-matter experts.

Relieve the members of your team of their worries by assuring them that the copy will be "polished up" during editing. Then get them rolling by offering the following tips:

- **Record it.** Just as in your 50 questions or freewriting exercise, just have them get it out. Get together for coffee with your employees and record the conversation. Simply talk with them about the challenges they are seeing. Before you know it, you'll have 20 content ideas.
- **Storyboard it out.** If the employees are having a tough time opening up, tell them to visualize what they want to say and write down key phrases or concepts onto sticky notes. They can even draw what they're thinking on sticky notes. This is an especially great way to organize thoughts for a longer piece.

ASK YOUR SOCIAL NETWORKS

Although it's important not to abuse this, asking your social networks can be helpful, especially if it's around a specific area. The reason why you are reading this book right now, and not reading about another topic, is because the idea for *Content Inc.* was far and away the most

---

Helpful Tech

A number of prolific bloggers use Evernote to track their content ideas. Evernote is an app that is used for journaling and that can sync with all your devices (smartphone, tablet, etc.). Joe Chernov, VP of content at HubSpot, uses Evernote to track new ideas and random thoughts and even write "in-progress" blogs.

Some people like to visually track content ideas, using mind-mapping software such as Mindjet. Newt Barrett, my coauthor on *Get Content Get Customers*, uses Mindjet to lay out each book chapter, in addition to the book table of contents and case study details.

Michael Hyatt raves about Scrivener. Scrivener is used mostly by screenwriters, but lately more and more bloggers have taken to the tool.

Figure 9.1 Gathering direct feedback from your connections via social media can sometimes be a blessing.

requested piece of information my social network asked for. (See Figure 9.1 to see the thank you note to my friends and followers on Facebook.)

READ A COMPLETELY IRRELEVANT BOOK

Every once in a while I dry up creatively. No matter what I do, I just can't get focused on a compelling topic. In this case of last resort, I pick up a book that is completely irrelevant to my content area. I've always found that my best content ideas pop into my head while I'm reading a good book. I highly recommend *Stranger in a Strange Land* by Robert Heinlein or classics like *To Kill a Mockingbird* or *The Hitchhiker's Guide to the Galaxy.*

> If you don't have time to read, you don't have time
> (or the tools) to write. Simple as that.
> STEPHEN KING

CONTENT INC. INSIGHTS

- Before you create any new content, be sure to analyze the raw content you already have available.
- Customer questions can be a gold mine for content ideas.
- Nothing works better to see what's working with your content than looking at actual content behavior. Make an appointment with your analytics program at least weekly to begin to determine what is catching fire.

Resources

Mark Levy, *Accidental Genius,* Berrett-Koehler Publishers, 2010.

Natalie Goldberg, *The True Secret of Writing,* Atria Books, 2013.

Bill Miltenberg, "To Save His Business, Marcus Sheridan Became a Pool Reporter," PRNews.com, http://www.prnewsonline.com/featured/2012/09/06/to-save -his-business-marcus-sheridan-became-a-pool-reporter/.

Stacey Roberts, "How to Consistently Come Up with Great Post Ideas for Your Blog," ProBlogger.net, http://www.problogger.net/archives/2014/02/03/ content-week-how-to-consistently-come-up-with-great-post-ideas-for-your -blog/.

Chapter 10

The Content Calendar

You can have it all. You can't just have it all at once.
OPRAH WINFREY

No matter how good we are at what we do or how many years we've been doing it, we all seek the elusive "better way" to accomplish our everyday tasks—new tools to explore, new techniques with which to experiment, new information to take into consideration. Innovations are constantly emerging to help people do what they do in less time, with less wasted effort, and with greater success. Reinvention is practically a commodity we trade these days to keep pushing our digitally enabled society forward.

Even the most steady and stalwart of tools in the content marketer's arsenal—the editorial (content) calendar—has transformed itself over the years, from a simple spreadsheet for tracking what we publish to an essential component for managing the entire life cycle of our organization's content marketing program.

All Content Inc. entrepreneurs have one thing in common—they keep and run their workflow through a content calendar. Let's get started.

THE BASICS

Start by gathering the Content Inc. strategy information on which you will be basing your content creation efforts. Your answers to the following questions will help you determine what you need to track in your calendar, as well as help you stay focused on your marketing goals as you plan your content creation.

- **Whom are you creating content for?** Keeping your target audience top of mind as you create your calendar will be essential for planning how to deliver on its needs through your content marketing.
- **Why are you creating content?** Your content marketing mission and goals will impact what you publish, where you publish, and how often, as well as how your team prioritizes, organizes, and categorizes, and tags its content creation efforts. For the most part, your content's success will be based on getting or keeping subscribers (see Chapter 14).
- **What resources do you have at your disposal?** Whether you have a dedicated team of writers and videographers, a stable of industry pros looking to share their insight, or just a handful of reluctant execs who will need some serious content creation hand-holding, the formats, frequency, and overall workflow you track in your calendar will likely depend on who is writing and where his or her expertise lies.
- **How can you stand out?** What unmet industry needs can be addressed with the content you create? What gaps exist in your current content creation efforts—or the efforts of your competitors? What industry events happen throughout the year to which you can tie your content for added exposure potential? Knowing where you can play a lead role in owning the audience's attention will help you fill your editorial calendar with impactful content that helps you meet your business goals.

SETTING UP THE CALENDAR

There are a number of paid and free calendaring tools that can help you set up your calendar. A few of these include:

- Trello
- Divvy HQ
- KaPost
- Central Desktop
- Workfront

However, it's perfectly fine to start out with a simple Excel spreadsheet or a shareable Google Sheet to track your content's progress through your editorial process.

Shanna Mallon, a writer for Straight North, offers some suggestions on a quick, easy way to build a content calendar that maps to your sales cycle. At the most fundamental level, we recommend that your editorial calendar include the following fields:

- The *date* the piece of content will be published
- The *topic* or *headline* of the content piece
- The *author* of the content
- The *owner* of the content—i.e., who is in charge of ensuring that the content makes it from ideation to publication and promotion
- The *current status* of the content (updated as it moves through your publishing cycle)

Depending on your company's content niche and mission, your team's workflow, the formats and platforms with which you plan to work, and the volume of content you will be creating, you may also want to track these elements to help you stay organized and on course over the long term:

- **The channels where your content will be published.** This can include only your owned channels (such as your blog, website, e-mail newsletters, etc.), or you can expand your tracking to include paid and social media channels, as well.
- **Content types.** Is it a blog post? A video? A podcast? An infographic? An original image? To get more mileage from the content you create, you might want to consider repurposing it into other formats at some point (see Chapter 13). So it's helpful to keep tabs on the types of assets you have on hand right from the start.
- **Visuals.** Speaking of assets, it's important that you don't overlook the appeal that visuals can lend to your content, in terms of both social sharing potential and overall brand recognition. Tracking the visual elements you include in your content efforts—such as cover images, logos, illustrations, charts—will make it easier to ensure that your work has a signature look and cohesive brand identity.

- **Topic categories.** This helps make your calendars more searchable when you are looking to see about which target topics you already created a lot of content—or which you haven't covered often enough.
- **Keywords and other metadata.** Metadata would include metadescriptions and SEO titles (if they differ from your headlines), which will help you keep your SEO efforts aligned with your content creation (more in Chapter 15).
- **URLs.** This info can be archived as an easy way to keep your online content audits updated or to link to older pieces of content in the new content you create.
- **Calls to action.** This helps you ensure that every piece of content you create is aligning with your company's marketing goals.
- **Audience outcome.** Perhaps my favorite part of the calendar, adding a reader outcome is important if you are working with multiple content creators. Listing the outcome means you are specific with what you want your audience to get out of your content. Is it to get a better job? Learn a specific task? Live a better life in some way? Having that listed will help any person or team creating the content understand the true purpose from the audience's point of view.

It may be helpful to have more than one editorial calendar—for example, you might have a master calendar where you can see everything at a glance and separate calendars for specific activities. The CMI editorial team uses a similar method: We created a spreadsheet with multiple tabs so that all the various editorial information we track can be found in one document.

Figure 10.1 shows our sample editorial calendar template, which you can download at http://cmi.media/CI-caltemplate and customize to your specific needs.

KEEPING YOUR CALENDAR FILLED AND FOCUSED

As we discussed in the previous chapter, content ideation is an ongoing and important process. As your content ideas become more refined, the place for them is your content calendar.

As you can see in the sample template in Figure 10.1, the CMI team also uses our calendar to track the topic ideas we want to try to cover

	Author	Headline	Status	Call to action	Category	Notes
Week of November 3						
Monday, November 3, 14						
Tuesday, November 4, 14						
Wednesday, November 5, 14						
Thursday, November 6, 14						
Friday, November 7, 14						
Saturday, November 8, 14						
Sunday, November 9, 14						
Week of November 10						
Monday, November 10, 14						
Tuesday, November 11, 14						
Wednesday, November 12, 14						
Thursday, November 13, 14						
Friday, November 14, 14						
Saturday, November 15, 14						
Sunday, November 16, 14						
Week of November 17						
Monday, November 17, 14						
Tuesday, November 18, 14						
Wednesday, November 19, 14						
Thursday, November 20, 14						
Friday, November 21, 14						
Saturday, November 22, 14						
Sunday, November 23, 14						
Week of November 24						
Monday, November 24, 14						
Tuesday, November 25, 14						
Wednesday, November 26, 14						
Thursday, November 27, 14						
Friday, November 28, 14						
Saturday, November 29, 14						

Figure 10.1   A simple example of an editorial calendar in Microsoft Excel.

in future content pieces (under the "Blog posts – Ideas" tab). Keeping a running list of ideas within our calendar spreadsheet makes it an easy reference tool when we need some topic inspiration or starter ideas for brainstorms.

Again, the fields you set up in your spreadsheet can vary by need, but at the very least we recommend that you track:

- The topic idea
- The owner of the idea
- The target keywords and categories to which the content would map (see Chapter 15)
- Who might be available and qualified to author the piece
- A time frame for when you will publish it

Michele Linn, CMI's VP of content, recommends adding additional tabs to your content calendar spreadsheet, including:

- Existing "brick" content (downloadable e-books or white papers used to attract subscribers) that can be used as a call to action in new content pieces
- Ideas for content that can be repurposed into multiple content pieces
- Content that can be compiled and curated

WORKING AHEAD

A common question from entrepreneurs pertains to timing. Exactly how far ahead do we have to plug in our editorial calendar?

While there is no "one right way" to do this, content teams will generally:

- Meet once per year to discuss the overall direction and editorial strategy. This gives you a general sense of your content direction as it aligns to your vision.
- Meet quarterly to compile the content themes for the upcoming quarter. This takes your general content and gets specific with weekly themes, contributors, and production schedules.
- Meet weekly to make changes as needed. This gives your team the opportunity to take advantage of fresh content that may need to find a home in the schedule or perhaps to take advantage of industry news (called real-time marketing).

The best editorial teams have a great idea of what they will publish over the next month—and know exactly what they will publish over the next two weeks. If you and your team are getting up not knowing what content will be produced, this will lead to lackluster content and process mistakes that will take a toll on your model.

CONTENT INC. INSIGHTS

- Without a content calendar, your strategy will not succeed.
- Although just one major editorial planning meeting a year may do, the content team should meet multiple times per month.
- Adding an "outcome" field to your content calendar will give content creators clarity about the ultimate mission of each content asset.

Chapter 11

Content Staffing

None of us is as smart as all of us.
KEN BLANCHARD

In almost every interview with entrepreneurs who employed a Content Inc. strategy, there was no team. It was just the lone entrepreneur trying to get a business started. This was certainly the case with me and Content Marketing Institute. The same with Brian Clark and Copyblogger Media. The same with the Chicken Whisperer and with Michelle Phan, the makeup millionaire.

But for the platform to work beyond a hobby-based business and blossom into a growth company, scalability is key. That means you need a team to get you to the next level.

CONTENT ROLES

"What staffing roles do we need to be successful with a Content Inc. approach?"

I hear this question all the time in companies of all sizes. It's a critical question, and one that is not easy to plan for . . . but plan we must.

While there is no perfect structure for a Content Inc. organization, and each one is different depending on the audience and the content niche, we need to think about filling certain roles now so that success is attainable.

Note: Don't think of the list below as new job titles, per se, but rather as the core competencies that need to be accounted for across the enterprise. As you'll see, many of these "roles" can be filled by multiple titles.

Chief Content Officer (aka Founder)

This is most likely you. This person is responsible for setting the overall editorial and content mission statement. As every staff member works to create and curate content, it is the CCO's responsibility to make sure that the stories remain consistent and make sense to the audience(s).

In addition, the CCO must understand how the stories translate into results that address the organization's business issues (driving new subscribers, keeping current subscribers, leading the way to revenue, etc.).

Sample titles: chief content officer, founder, owner, CEO, publisher

Managing Editor

Half storyteller and half project manager, the managing editor executes the content plan on behalf of the CCO. Whereas the CCO focuses on strategy (and some content), the managing editor's job is all execution, working with the roles below to make the stories come alive (including content scheduling).

Sample titles: managing editor, chief editor, project manager

Chief Listening Officer

The role of the CLO is to function as "air-traffic control" for social media and other content channels. This person is there to listen to the groups, maintain the conversation, and route (and/or notify) feedback to the team members who can engage in appropriate conversations (to you, to editorial, or perhaps to the sales team). This feedback mechanism is critical if the content is going to make a difference for your customers. The CLO also needs to keep tabs on how the content is performing on owned media sites (like a blog) and get that intelligence back to the CCO and managing editor.

Sample titles: social media manager, community manager

Director of Audience

This person is charged with monitoring the members of your audience, making sure all content creators are intimately familiar with their characteristics, their passion triggers, and the actions you want them to take. The director of audience is also responsible for building subscription assets (direct mail lists, e-mail lists, social media subscriptions) that can grow and be segmented as your content mission matures and expands.

Sample titles: audience development manager, circulation manager, subscription manager

Channel Master

Wherever your content is headed (social media, e-mail, mobile, print, in person, etc.), the channel master is responsible for getting the most out of each channel. What works best on SlideShare? When should you send your e-mails, and how frequently? What's the appropriate ratio of owned versus curated content your business should distribute on Twitter? Who is keeping track of mobile strategy and execution? Your team will look to the channel master for these and other answers.

Sample titles: managing editor, marketing director, social media manager, e-media manager

Chief Technologist

As marketing and information technology continue to merge, there will be a need for at least one individual (maybe more) whose sole purpose is to leverage the proper use of these technologies into the content marketing process. The person in this role will be responsible for your publishing systems (the plumbing) such as your website infrastructure and e-mail systems and how they integrate together.

Sample titles: e-media manager, IT manager, web services manager

Creative Director

The design and look of your content is more critical than ever, especially as visual social channels become an increasingly important method to attract and retain subscribers. The creative director is responsible for the overall look and feel of all your content, including the website, blog, images, photography, and every other piece of collateral you create.

Sample titles: creative director, graphic design manager

Influencer Relations

The role formerly known as media relations will evolve into that of a manager of influencers. This person's responsibilities include developing your "hit list" of influencers, maintaining direct relationships with them, and integrating them into your marketing process in the most impactful ways.

Sample titles: public relations manager, media manager, marketing director, communications manager

Freelancer and Agency Relations

As content demands continue to evolve (and increase), your organization's reliance on freelance talent and other external content vendors will grow as well. Organizations need to cultivate their own "expert" content teams and networks, and it is this person's job to negotiate rates and responsibilities so that all members of your team are united in their work on behalf of your Content Inc. program.

Sample titles: managing editor, project manager

Content Curation Director

As you begin to develop content assets, you'll have some amazing opportunities to repackage and repurpose your content (more on that in Chapter 13). The role of the content curation director is to continually look at all the content assets being developed by the organization and strategize ways to create new pieces of content from them.

Sample titles: social media director, content curation specialist, content director

Content Curation Case Study: Dwell

In 2014, I keynoted the Niche CEO Summit alongside some amazing publishers, including Michela O'Connor Abrams, president of Dwell Media. If you are not familiar with Dwell, it evolved from a small, niche print magazine focused on design to a fast-growing multimedia design brand.

Under Michela's leadership, the company became one of the top websites in the world, with nearly 300,000 paid magazine subscribers and with social media audience numbers that would make you blush (including over 500,000 followers on Twitter). Sure, the company has struggled, like all of us have, making changes in how it creates and distributes content. But it was one change that, Michela noted, made all the difference.

She Hired a Chief Content Curator

Content curation, for the most part, involves taking other people's content (let's call this OPC) and adding to it, enhancing it, and/or giving it a new context or perspective so that it evolves into a new piece of content. CMI played a role in this concept by defining content curation as:

> Content curation is a means by which we either supplement or promote our brand's point of view to our specific audiences within the context of how the "world" is talking about that particular topic.

While content curation with a focus on OPC is important, the content curation technique that took Dwell to the next level is focused on internal assets—that is, curating content that Dwell had already created.

Dwell tasked this content curation person with gaining a comprehensive and in-depth understanding of all the current content assets owned by the organization (i.e., no outside content gets factored in). Starting with a full-blown content audit, the curator who holds this position ultimately takes responsibility for:

- Understanding the content assets available to work with, including textual content, imagery, and audio content
- Effectively tagging, categorizing, and coordinating these materials into a data asset management system

- Working with the content marketing team on a clear channel plan
- Developing and executing a content curation strategy by using existing resources

Once the content is organized and there is a process in place for continual asset placement and management (including making sure those assets are easily findable), the curator can begin to fill needed gaps in the overall editorial calendar without having to spend money creating new content.

How does this work? Just a quick look at Dwell's Twitter feed shows example after example of stories and images culled from archived stories.

When content is tagged correctly and the curator can start to spot themes, new content packages emerge (such as the design images featuring "party pads," all coming from different issues over the past years—see Figure 11.1).

Michela believes that the secret (or now, not so secret) recipe to Dwell's recent success has been this newfound role.

Figure 11.1 Dwell has found that constantly repurposing image and blog content into social media collections has been successful.

HOW THE ROLES TRANSLATE INTO REAL PRODUCTION

At CMI, we have a number of people that make up the above roles, specifically:

- **Joe Pulizzi, founder.** I set the overall tone of the content. I continually look at how our subscribers are generating revenue for the organization. I also serve as the key spokesperson for the brand, which marketing leverages in a variety of ways.
  - *Role:* chief content officer (partial)
- **Michele Linn, vice president of content.** The content team reports to Michele. Michele's focus is on developing content that attracts or retains subscribers.
  - *Roles:* chief content officer (partial), managing editor
- **Cathy McPhillips, marketing director.** Cathy is responsible for distributing the content in all our available channels and analyzing the results. All our subscription goals also ultimately fall to Cathy.
  - *Roles:* channel master, director of audience
- **Joseph Kalinowski, creative director.** Joe oversees the visual direction of every piece of content that flows out of CMI.
  - *Role:* creative director
- **Monina Wagner, community manager.** Monina oversees all our social channels and listens to how the audience reacts to our content.
  - *Role:* chief listening officer
- **Laura Kozak, e-media manager.** Ultimately, any content that goes up on an owned web property (website, blog, event site) is Laura's domain.
  - *Role:* chief technologist (partial)
- **David Anthony, IT director.** David manages all our technology infrastructure, including hosting, marketing automation solutions, and website integrity.
  - *Role:* chief technologist (partial)
- **Lisa Dougherty, director of blog community and operations.** Lisa works with all our freelance writers and contributors, assisting them in their style and ensuring they meet deadlines.
  - *Role:* freelancer and agency relations

- **Amanda Subler, public relations and media manager.** Amanda works to get our content, such as our research, placed in media outlets and on blogger sites.
  - *Role:* influencer relations
- **Jodi Harris, editorial content manager.** Jodi's goal is to work with all our current content assets and build new e-books and reports that will drive new subscribers.
  - *Role:* content curation director

CMI also has a number of specialized roles that fill gaps in the process:

- Clare McDermott is chief editor of our magazine property, Chief Content Officer.
- Angela Vannucci, project director, oversees the production of the magazine and project-manages all our webinars.
- Robert Rose, chief strategy officer, serves as chief content officer for our property, Intelligent Content Conference, and oversees all our training and advisory.
- Marcia Riefer Johnston is managing editor, Intelligent Content. At CMI, we cover specialized areas of content targeting specific portions of our user base.
- Chuck Frey, director, online training, owns all our pieces of training material outside of blog posts.
- Pamela Muldoon, podcast director, produces all our podcasts.
- Lisa Murton Beets, our research director, owns every research report we do at CMI.
- For every piece of content we develop on the site, it is checked and proofed by two people, Yatri Roleston and Ann Gynn. We also check every piece of content so it aligns with our search engine optimization strategy.

OUTSOURCING YOUR CONTENT TO FREELANCERS

You may find that you need help developing ongoing content—or that you need additional content producers to keep up with the speed and quality of production.

How do you go about finding good external content contributors (sometimes called "stringers")? Should you look for a good writer

How Game Theory Operationalizes Content

Game Theory is a YouTube channel devoted to analytics and math behind different video game experiences. Founder Matthew Patrick, who started from nothing, has developed an audience of more than 4 million subscribers. Below, Matthew gives a detailed look at how he staffs his multiple business lines.

Game Theory operates two kinds of branches that nicely synergize with each other. There is the production component, which is all of the YouTube and creative processes. The biggest property is the Game Theorists, which currently employs around 13–16 people at this point. That includes freelance editors, writers, sales team, etc.

. . . on the production side, [there are] custom videos for video game brands, traditional advertisers and things like that, which live on the Game Theorists channel, that are promoting their product or talking about the service that they offer . . . I'm writing the copy, I'm the influence or talent in that and then we're always getting across their messaging points and driving the audience to convert sales.

So in addition to doing just our own standard videos, a good number of those are branded, either by video game companies coming in and asking for a piece of custom content or direct response companies, or just other brands asking for some kind of awareness campaign. That's the production side.

Then there is the consultancy wing. On the consultancy side we operate very much like a traditional consultancy. Our specialty is growing an organic audience in the media space with a specific emphasis around YouTube. And so right now our service offering really ranges the gamut based on what the client needs. We have everything from full one-day workshops where we will come into your company and basically take you and your team through YouTube 101 to 301; here is everything you need to know about content, what works on the platform, how to optimize your presence using very granular levels of optimizations, and moving forward how can you strategize for success.

> *And then there are also some longer-term projects. So we have people who are working almost in a full-time capacity with various companies acting as their content managers, as their channel managers.*
> *It's really been a spectrum, but that is all on the consultancy side. That's the fundamental principle, data-driven decision making to help grow an organic audience in the new media space.*

and teach him or her your business? Or should you hire someone who knows your industry and teach him or her to write? The following are a few tips to consider:

- **Remember that expertise is helpful, but it's not a deal killer.** Given the choice between a good writer who has a personality that closely matches your organization (but who is short on industry expertise) and an industry veteran who knows how to write but with whom you can't stand to be in the same room, go with the personality. Chemistry and personality are things that are entirely hard to change; research is a skill that can be taught—passion isn't.

  Looking for a marketer or writer or videographer is not the right approach. Even looking for a content strategist might not be. . . . I think what you really have to focus on is understanding the audience you're trying to attract with content and actually looking for people who understand the audience, who have domain knowledge and expertise that's beyond your product or your category, but understand the audience way better than you. (An interview with Andrew Davis, Brandscaping)

- **Hire right—copywriters, journalists, technical writers.** Because you've spent so much time on your strategy and your process, you should be very aware of what kind of writer you're looking for. Understand that copywriters work very differently and have very different sensibilities than journalists do. If you're looking for someone to write blog posts for you, a copywriter might not be your best bet.

On the other hand, if you're looking for someone to beef up your persuasive call to action for all the great white papers you're putting together, then a great copywriter may be exactly what you need.

- **Develop the right business relationship.** Understand the elements of your business relationship, and make them clear. For example, will there be one content item per week—and will your writer be paid a monthly fee? If so, how will you handle months that have 4½ weeks? Will there be an extra post that week? Given the size of your organization, you need to make clear the invoicing and payment terms—or understand what the writer needs. Also be clear on expectations. There should be no surprises such as blog posts suddenly becoming 1,000 words when they're supposed to be 750 . . . or content themes going wildly off topic.

Here are some of the things you'll need to communicate to your freelance writers:

- What content they will produce and where it falls on the content calendar. (Be very specific when drafts are due.)
- The goals for their specific contributions (both your goals and the outcome for the audience).
- What expertise or other third-party information they will need access to. (Will they be interviewing internal people, bringing in external information, or reworking your existing material?)
- Your budget (per piece, hourly, retainer, or barter).
- The number of revisions for each piece.

There are also a number of excellent services out there that can help you find the right content provider. Some to consider include:

- Scripted
- Zerys
- Upwork
- NewsCred
- Contently
- Writer Access

For a complete list and overview of content marketplace options, check out Robert Rose's full report at http://cmi.media/CI-collaboration.

BUDGETING FACTORS

In the near publishing past, freelancers used to get paid $1 per word. This still remains true for high-quality and unique content, like that for research reports and white papers. For article content, some services will price your content as low as 5 cents per word.

Word of warning: You usually get what you pay for. At CMI, we've found the most success in the retainer model—that is, working with a freelancer on a number of content assets over a period of time and then paying a monthly fee for the work. This arrangement is usually appreciated by both sides. The business can budget more easily with a set number, and the freelancer doesn't have to count words. After all, a piece of content should only be as long as it needs to be, so why set a limit? (A range should be just fine.)

Content Through Curation

BookBub, which offers users deals and notifications on bestselling books, realized that its best content creation plan was through external curation. Instead of creating original content, Bookbub launched with an e-mail newsletter almost exclusively made up of curated pieces of content from existing books. And it worked. Today, with millions of subscribers, Bookbub has become an amazing resource for those consumers who just love to read.

If you are thinking about curation software, consider services like Curata, PublishThis, Atomic Reach, and Percolate. For a complete list of providers, check out CMI's content curation toolkit at http://cmi.media/CI-curation.

TEST FIRST

With a large supply of writers in the workforce, there is no need to start with a long-term relationship. Test a writer out with a few stories, and see how that works. Ask yourself: Is the person's writing style to your expectations? Does he or she deliver on time? Is the person actively sharing the content via his or her own social network? (This is very important.)

Once the writer has met your expectations in these areas, then set out on a long-term deal. I've seen too many marketers and publishers get their "rock star" freelancers, only to kill the deal a few months later with neither party happy. Test the person out first so you don't waste your time.

TRY FLEECING THE MASTHEAD

Remember the masthead? It was that place where you found all the writers, editors, and circulation managers that worked at a print magazine. Today mastheads are harder to locate, but they still exist. And once found, they can be extremely useful to your model—you just need to know how to use them.

Opening up the leading trade magazine or visiting a website in your niche and finding the masthead is a gold mine for competent writers. These writers (many part-time) not only understand your customer base but can formulate relevant and original content in a skilled way.

Besides writers, the masthead also lists editors who can help turn your raw content into an engaging story.

The masthead also provides information on your audience. It shows circulation and the publishing roles responsible for circulation development, audience building, and subscriber generation. (Note: Another great place to get information about customer demographics is the publication's media kit.) This can help in targeting subscribers, building relationships, and ultimately getting people to buy from you.

Design needs? Check the masthead for that as well.

And the timing couldn't be better. At many media companies and trade publishers, the business models aren't working so well. Raises are harder to come by these days. That leaves the door wide open for you and your business.

BEFORE YOU HIRE

The majority of our CMI staff is built from contractors. These are people that want flexible hours, are looking for options for their life, and do not necessarily want to work 40 hours a week. What we've found is that there is amazing talent out there with individuals that are looking for this kind of flexibility.

When I started in the media business 15 years ago, we contracted with creative designers and freelance journalists from all over the world. We had to do this to find the best resources to complete a particular project.

A lot of owners want their employees doing all the content tasks without worrying about them working for other companies. They feel it is critical to building their company culture. This may work for some, but the cream of the crop in the media industry want more opportunity. A 1099 relationship works well in most cases. For our business, and in a few very important situations, we would not be able to hire the right talent without this type of flexibility.

CONTENT INC. INSIGHTS

- As a start-up, the majority of content roles must be completed by one or two people. As you grow, determine the more basic jobs at first and begin to outsource those, freeing you to focus on higher-value activities.
- Curating the content you've already created could be the key to keeping your budget under control.
- The most amazing writers and designers in your industry can be found by reviewing the mastheads of your industry trade publications.
- Before you hire, consider working with a freelance content contributor in a contractor relationship. It will save you much pain if it doesn't work out.

Chapter 12

The Collaborative Publishing Model

Alone we can do so little, together we can do so much.

HELEN KELLER

I went out to my friends that I had built relationships with. . . . And I decided to ask [them] if they would consider writing one article a month until they were bored.

So the five of us essentially each wrote one article a month. Then I got a volunteer . . . and she worked for free as my editor, behind the scenes, putting everything into WordPress.

. . . I'll tell you in the first couple of weeks the thing exploded. We had 10,000 e-mail subscribers literally in like 2½ months. (Michael Stelzner on founding the social media marketing education site Social Media Examiner, which now boasts over 350,000 subscribers.)

What do these companies have in common: Forbes, Content Marketing Institute, Social Media Examiner, Copyblogger Media, Moz, HubSpot, MarketingProfs, *Huffington Post*, and Mashable?

They all use a collaborative publishing model. Instead of having only a core set of writers and journalists employed by the brand (like traditional publishing has done), these brands reach out to their community to recruit and request relevant content to publish on their platform.

And they all are extremely successful businesses!

WHY CONSIDER COLLABORATIVE PUBLISHING?

Collaborative publishing, as a business model, is the idea that the entrepreneur or business actively recruits outside contributors to build a platform and an audience. Once the platform is built and sees some success, the opportunity exists to bring in thought leaders and community experts to fill content holes in your workflow.

Outside the benefit of covering content areas that may be difficult for you to do yourself or by paying freelancers, the biggest benefit to a collaborative model is the opportunity to attract a new audience to your content. Contributors have their own followers and subscribers, who, if things are done right, can be converted to become a part of your audience.

Many traditional media companies showcase "employed" talent only. They do not encourage members of the community to contribute to stories. This presents a clear opportunity for you.

The *Huffington Post* was founded in 2005 by a number of investors including Arianna Huffington, a spokesperson for the political left in the United States. In 2011 the *Huffington Post* sold for over $300 million to AOL and is one of the top 100 most popular sites in the world, according to Alexa.com.

The *Huffington Post* has hundreds of niche, targeted sites, where thousands of contributors around the world publish content for free, in exchange for the opportunity to be published. The *Huffington Post* employs a collaborative publishing model. Sure, it hires some amazing journalists, writers, and content producers, but much of what you see on the site is produced by thought leaders and active members of the community.

THE PROCESS

There are a number of ways to identify contributors to develop the collaborative model (we cover each of these in Chapter 16 on stealing audience), but the key to making the model work is as much about the process as it is the talent.

The first imperative is to set strict guidelines and expectations with your contributors. If you are lax about the content you allow on your site, you'll never be the leading informational expert in your niche.

Below is a sample e-mail that we send out to all our inquiring contributors:

Great to "meet" you Tim!

You'll find our full blog guidelines here (http://cmi.media/CI-guidelines), but I've summarized the top-line info below, for your convenience.

Our editorial mission is to provide expert-level insights and cutting-edge information that will help our readers advance the conversation around content marketing—as well as advance their skills to new levels of success. With this in mind, we look for posts that address the needs of experienced B2B and B2C content marketers who work at large organizations, and we ask that all submissions satisfy some specific requirements:

- Posts should be focused on advanced principles, techniques, tools, and processes that content marketers need to become familiar with to be successful. If you want to run any ideas by us, we're happy to let you know what may work.
- Rather than simply offering broad advice, posts should outline and explain how to execute on the key recommendations discussed.
- They should include relevant visuals whenever possible. Videos and other visual content are strongly encouraged.
- Where applicable, they should provide information or tools that readers can use, such as a template, a step-by-step process guide, or a checklist.
- We encourage the use of real-life examples and/or sample cases to help illustrate best practices and/or demonstrate how to make advice actionable.

Here is the list of key topics we cover:
- Strategy

- Operations, Teams, and Process
- Building Your Audience
- Content Creation
- Visual Content and Design
- Social Media
- SEO
- Content Distribution and Promotion
- Measurement and ROI
- Industry News and Trends

If you decide you'd like to contribute an article, kindly let me know an approximate timeframe so I can get you on the radar to follow up. By giving me a date, I promise I won't stalk you and you can adjust the date as needed as I realize priorities shift. If you have any questions or would like additional information on anything, please feel free to reach out. I look forward to working with you!

Have a great week!

Cheers,
Lisa

For an inside look at the entire CMI publishing process and how we execute the collaborative publishing model, please see Appendix B.

A REMINDER SYSTEM FOR CONTRIBUTORS

Once you have a set number of contributors, the process can get extremely complex. It's important to keep open communication with all your contributors. When you receive an inquiry to contribute to your site, follow these steps:

- **E-mail #1.** Send out confirmation of the submission receipt and what the contributor should expect around the general timing of the process.
- **E-mail #2.** Notify regarding approval or rejection of the post. If confirmed, there is typically a request for revisions.

- **E-mail #3.** Send a preview of the post. Once the article has been finalized and set up for production, your blog editor sends a preview of the post, as well as the likely publication date and any ideas on ways the writers can share the article with their own audience.
- **E-mail #4.** Notify the contributor of any blog comments. Once someone's first comment comes in, the blog editor or social media manager will forward that to the author and request that he or she engage and respond.
- **E-mail #5.** Send notification of top post. If the article is performing well, you'll want to let the contributor know and keep in contact with him or her. This means that the contributor is someone of value. You may want that person to develop another article at some point or to become a regular contributor.

CONTENT INC. INSIGHTS

- As you build out your channel, you'll need help to create content. While outsourcing for pay is always an option, building a collaborative publishing model should be considered.
- For collaboration to work, communication is key. Build a process before you reach out to contributors.
- Sometimes less is more. Start your collaborative publishing process with less of the right people first . . . then build out the program.

Resources

"The Huffington Post," Wikipedia, accessed April 28, 2015, http://en.wikipedia.org/wiki/The_Huffington_Post.

Top 500 Global Websites by Traffic, Alexa.com, accessed April 28, 2015, http://www.alexa.com/topsites/global;3.

Chapter 13

Planning for Repurposing

To repurpose an old thought, idea or memory
to a new purpose is the height of creativity.
STEVE SUPPLE

Robert Rose, CMI's chief strategy officer, teaches the marketers in all his master classes that "you're not creating a blog post, a video or a white paper . . . you are telling a story. That story can be told a myriad of ways to help extend your content marketing strategy."

Every content idea involves a story you are trying to tell. If you remember that the story can and should always be told in many different ways, you'll have a leg up on the competition.

In the fall of 2013, I committed to publishing my third book, *Epic Content Marketing*. Between my blogging schedule (I published original content once a week) and my speaking schedule (approximately two speeches per week), I was having trouble making the time. I needed 60,000 relevant words in six months.

Enter the "blog-to-book" strategy. I figured I needed about 25 chapters of about 2,000 words a chapter over the next 6 months to complete the book. And I had about 25 weeks until due date. So every week I wrote an article that would be published on either Content Marketing Institute or LinkedIn. Each article filled a hole in the book's table of contents and ultimately became part of the book.

In six months, the book was complete. I was able to fulfill two of my content creation obligations simply by planning ahead.

Most businesses simply don't think about repurposing ahead of time. They think, "I need a blog post or a white paper." They don't think in terms of the strategy Robert discusses above—of how one story idea can be told in dozens of different ways depending on the content needs of the organization.

CASE STUDY: *JAY TODAY*

Jay Baer publishes a three-minute video show called *Jay Today*. It covers Jay's ideas about business, social media, and marketing. Jay's team at Convince and Convert publishes a number of content pieces, including daily blog posts, research reports, podcasts, and more, but according to Jay, "*Jay Today* videos are among the strongest performers . . . and [have] become a lynchpin in our initiative to further atomize our content."

How does a three-minute video become the staple of a publishing empire? Because each *Jay Today* video becomes at least eight different pieces of useful content.

After each episode is complete, the company posts the show to five different places:

- Its YouTube channel
- iTunes as a video podcast
- iTunes as an audio podcast
- Its website
- Its Facebook page

The company also transcribes every episode using a service called Speechpad, which costs about $1 per audio minute for transcription.

If that's not enough, then Jay begins the process of atomization. He explains: "For each *Jay Today* episode that has been transcribed, my team and I rework the headline and copy three different ways, and post the video and written content as a blog post on LinkedIn, Medium, and on [our website], where I take the best episode of the prior week and rewrite it every Wednesday."

All in all, Jay's one video, encompassing all of three minutes in length, becomes:

- A video on YouTube
- A video on his Facebook page
- An iTunes episode
- A video iTunes episode
- An episode on his website
- A blog post (once per week)
- A post on LinkedIn
- A post on Medium
- A Google+ post
- 2 to 3 tweets
- 2 LinkedIn shares

Nothing about what Jay does is complex. The difference from what most businesses do is that what Jay does is planned—that there is purpose behind all the content creation.

Next time you have an idea for a blog post or a video, just remember that's not the case . . . you have an amazing story to tell. The next step is to come up with all the ways you can tell that story.

How to Get More from Content Inc. Through Repurposing

By Arnie Kuenn, CEO of Vertical Measures and Author of *Content Marketing Works*

Developing new materials for your content marketing requires a great deal of effort, from coming up with an idea and researching the topic to content creation and promotion. There are often multiple people involved in the process: copywriters, designers, SEO specialists, social media marketers, and others, which can make content marketing quite the investment. Fortunately, great content can be repurposed into something new and different, continually furthering your investment along the way.

The Benefits of Content Repurposing

Content repurposing requires altering a piece of content to make it fresh by changing the angle or switching up the format. Integrating repurposing into your strategy can lower costs, advance production, expand audience reach, and provide myriad additional benefits, including:

- **Expanding one idea into several content pieces.** For example, the topic of a popular blog post can be used for a slide show, a video, a free information guide, a white paper, a podcast . . . you get the idea. Repurposing allows you to leverage the research you conducted for one piece of original work across additional content projects.
- **Substantially cutting content creation time.** Certain elements that have already been created or curated—like images, quotes, or text—can be applied to new works.
- **Serving multiple different audiences.** Some people are visual learners, while others may prefer reading a document. Further, some people love to read in-depth research articles, while others wish to quickly skim blog posts to gain information. Content repurposing allows you to appeal to multiple audiences with different content preferences. For example, if you've created great video content, your script can be used as the basis of text documents, such as blog posts or downloadable PDFs. Similarly, statistics, facts, and figures can be illustrated through data visualization and delivered as infographics or charts.
- **Cross-promoting content.** Through repurposing efforts, you can cross-promote your great content pieces across multiple channels. For example, in a YouTube video description, you may link to a blog post, a slide show, and an infographic about the same topic, which sends traffic to your website or blog. This targeted traffic reinforces branding and increases the likelihood of attracting a subscriber.
- **Extending content's longevity.** With so much content being published every day, people are bound to miss a blog post or video once in a while. However, through repurposing, your audience may come across your content after it has been altered, through a different

channel. Additionally, repurposing evergreen content expands the life cycle even further, as it can remain relevant for years to come.

The Content Repurposing Process

Creating a repurposing plan at the beginning of your development will help you brainstorm and produce content efficiently, while keeping your repurposing process streamlined and in alignment with your other great content efforts.

Consider the following four steps:

1. **Take one story idea.** Begin to think of different ways in which the story can be told. In this initial phase, it is important to consider how one topic can be translated across multiple types of content. For example, if you have a store that sells sunglasses, your topic may be "sunglasses trends for 2016." Though broad, this topic can be the focal point of many content projects.

2. **Once you have a general topic, think of how it can be altered and applied across content types to appeal to numerous audiences.** In the sunglasses trends example, a few content pieces you can create might include:

   - Blog posts on women's or men's sunglasses trends for 2016
   - An infographic illustrating different styles of sunglasses predicted to be popular in 2016
   - A video interviewing your expert employees about 2016 sunglasses trends
   - A slide show featuring images and descriptions of the top sunglasses styles for 2016
   - An e-book on how to choose sunglasses for 2016 that fit your face and style

   And that's just the beginning. With a wide-ranging topic like sunglasses trends for 2016, it is easy to see how researching one concept can lead to multiple content pieces. Each piece has a different point of view and is transformed to appeal to a specific audience, but the core idea remains the same.

3. **Now that you have assembled a list of different takes on your core idea, start researching, keeping the first piece you want to create in mind.** Start with whatever piece makes the most sense. If you create a slide show, can you easily adapt it to create an infographic? Can a video script work as a blog post? The first piece of content you construct will take the most work up front, as it requires the greatest amount of research and development. However, know that when you've finished researching for your first content piece, you can undoubtedly apply your findings when creating additional content in the future.

4. **After you have created your first piece of content, repurpose your research and other elements from the project to make new works.** You may need to research more specific facets of your core idea as you go, but most of the grunt work should already be completed.

Key Content Types

There are a variety of content types you can utilize in content repurposing projects, and it's possible for one idea to be used across all media. Consider the following:

- **Blog posts.** Every content idea you have should be featured in a blog post, if not multiple posts. Most Content Inc. models have a blog, and with good reason—as small businesses with blogs generate 126 percent more leads (subscribers). Blog posts are a great place to start when creating content, especially if you have an active blog with lots of audience participation. You may be able to garner feedback about your core idea from readers, and audience participation may spark additional inspiration on how to take that idea further.
- **E-books and free guides.** You can create e-books and free guides by compiling all the blog posts you've written about a certain topic and adding additional components, such as a table of contents, images, more in-depth research, an index, etc. Often e-books and free guides are more detailed than blog posts and are considered high-value pieces. When offering a high-value piece, you may be able to collect

visitor information in exchange for access. For example, you may offer an e-book to people who sign up for your e-mail newsletter, or make a free guide available for those who enter basic visitor contact information.

- **Video.** Contrary to popular belief, you do not have to have a professional recording studio to produce a captivating video. A smartphone or everyday portable digital camera can record compelling video to be used in content repurposing projects. When thinking of video ideas, consider interviewing your employees or industry experts or creating a skit based on a facet of your core concept. Keep in mind that you can also produce a video without recording anything live—through moving graphics and voice-over audio.

- **Infographics.** Infographics are excellent vehicles for data, processes, and visual content. They can be used to explain a topic in a step-by-step fashion, showcase data in an interesting way, or illustrate a story. When a topic lends itself to visual interpretation, creating an infographic is the way to go.

- **Slide shows.** Slide shows are not just for presentations anymore. Creating a slide show can often challenge you to simplify an idea, as you don't want to create a text-heavy slide show. If someone wants to read a text document, he or she will seek out a blog post or free guide. Slide shows cater to visual learners, featuring images and short descriptions.

Get the Most Out of Your Content

In summary, content repurposing is a very efficient way to make the most of your great content creation efforts. Numerous content pieces can stem from just one main idea, each catering to a different audience in a unique way. The process of repurposing can save you time and money and extend your initial content marketing investment, making it a worthwhile strategy.

A FINAL REMINDER

Remember, just because you are repurposing the same content many different ways, you are not duplicating content. Every story you tell should be unique in its own way. That means if you are leveraging the same content asset in a blog post versus a Facebook post or YouTube video, each story needs to be told in a different way. Ann Handley calls this "reimagining" the content.

The worst thing you can do is take the same content and spam it out over all your channels. That will never work. Be sure to focus on which audience uses which channel and adapt your stories accordingly.

CONTENT INC. INSIGHTS

- Most repurposing isn't planned . . . it happens after the content is created. Smart businesses plan out the different content assets in advance.
- Remember, you are telling a story. That story can be told in many different ways.
- Planning for repurposing means that every content asset you create needs to be different in some way.

Resources

David Gould, "Content Repurposing: How to Lower Marketing Costs and Expand Audience Reach," VerticalMeasures.com, accessed April 28, 2015, http://www.verticalmeasures.com/content-marketing-2/content-repurposing-how-to-lower-marketing-costs-and-expand-audience-reach/.

Mike McGrail, "The Blogconomy: Blogging Stats [Infographic]," socialmedia today.com, accessed April 28, 2015, http://www.socialmediatoday.com/content/blogconomy-blogging-stats-infographic.

Jay Baer, "How to Make 8 Pieces of Content from 1 Piece of Content," convince andconvert.com, accessed April 28, 2015, http://www.convinceandconvert.com/content-marketing/how-to-make-8-pieces-of-content-from-1-piece-of-content/.

Part 5

Harvesting Audience

You can only build something massive by starting with something
small to effectively close the distance.

DANNY INY

You've chosen your platform and developed the assets and a
publishing schedule that attracts a niche audience. Now it's
time to create a system that builds the valuable subscriber base
for your company.

Chapter 14

The Metric That Drives the Model

I made mistakes in drama. I thought drama was when actors cried.
But drama is when the audience cries.

FRANK CAPRA

After Facebook's IPO in 2012, the stock dipped by over 50 percent, down to less than $20 per share. Since then, Facebook's value has more than quadrupled. The major reason, according to a *Fast Company* article, is a revision that Facebook made to its management and performance structure.

During the time Facebook's stock was struggling, Facebook's ad team had been responsible for revenue, while the product team was focused on user engagement. After months of lackluster results, and a clear lack of a unified team effort, Facebook decided to reward all its employees on their performance against a single metric: revenue. It was argued that "the enterprise would get a whole lot more ideas, and they would be better, more creative, more diverse."

And boy, did this change work. In November of that year, App Ads came out, representing a true collaboration between the ad team and the product team. It was a game changer and added over $1 billion in revenue.

THERE WILL BE ONE TO RULE THEM ALL

One Ring to rule them all, One Ring to find them;
One Ring to bring them all and in the darkness bind them."

J. R. R. TOLKIEN, *LORD OF THE RINGS*

Like Facebook's sole focus on revenue, your sole focus is on one simple metric—the subscriber. When you go to sleep at night, you should be thinking of attracting subscribers. When you wake up in the morning, you should have subscribers etched in your brain. The Content Inc. model only works if you can build a loyal audience of subscribers over time. Period.

As Andrew Davis states, "Focusing on creating a subscriber database is developing a customer database before you actually have customers to sell to."

Like a subscription to Netflix or (in days past) a newspaper subscription, your goal is to deliver such amazing value through content that your audience is willing to give some piece of personal information up as a value exchange (e-mail address, home address, etc.). The only difference in your situation from the Netflix example is that you are giving your content away for free, so that you can monetize that relationship at a later point.

John Jantsch, founder of Duct Tape Marketing, followed a Content Inc. strategy, including a community blog effort and book series, to grow a multimillion-dollar consulting practice. But John's lightbulb moment came when he added a "sign my guestbook" area to his website in the early 2000s. Instead of just looking at website traffic analytics, John was beginning to build a subscriber database. Those subscribers gave John the ability to launch his consulting network and build a multimillion-dollar platform in the process.

The Tonight Show host Jimmy Fallon is becoming one of the subscription kings of media. After every show, you'll see multiple clips from the show (see Chapter 13 on repurposing) shared around social media to promote (you guessed it) subscriptions. After every short clip, you'll see a humorous clip of Jimmy Fallon asking his audience to subscribe (Figure 14.1).

Figure 14.1 The new "king of late night," Jimmy Fallon, focuses heavily on building digital subscribers.

The following are all the subscription options for *The Tonight Show* and NBC that are shown in the text area below each of Fallon's videos on YouTube:

Subscribe NOW to The Tonight Show Starring Jimmy Fallon: http://bit.ly/1nwT1aN

Watch The Tonight Show Starring Jimmy Fallon Weeknights 11:35/10:35c

Get more Jimmy Fallon:
Follow Jimmy: http://Twitter.com/JimmyFallon
Like Jimmy: https://Facebook.com/JimmyFallon

Get more The Tonight Show Starring Jimmy Fallon:

Follow The Tonight Show: http://Twitter.com/FallonTonight
Like The Tonight Show: https://Facebook.com/FallonTonight
The Tonight Show Tumblr: http://fallontonight.tumblr.com/

Get more NBC:

NBC *YouTube: http://bit.ly/1dM1qBH*
Like NBC: http://Facebook.com/NBC
Follow NBC: http://Twitter.com/NBC
NBC Tumblr: http://nbctv.tumblr.com/
NBC Google+: https://plus.google.com/+NBC/posts

Quick-Quilting Capital of the World

As reported in the *Claim Your Fame* podcast by Andrew Davis

If you're not a quilter, this may be the first time you've heard of the town Hamilton, Missouri—the quick-quilting capital of the world. The moniker was earned thanks to a down-to-earth, engaging quilt shop owner and her custom-made, YouTube video quilting tutorials. Jenny Doan is the cofounder of the Missouri Star Quilt Co., a quilt shop in Hamilton that boasts the largest selection of pre-cut fabrics in the world.

In 2008, Hamilton was hit hard with the turn of the economy. Residents Jenny and Ron Doan had raised their seven children on Ron's income as a machinist for the Kansas City Star. Many residents were getting laid off from their jobs, and Jenny and Ron's kids were becoming concerned about their parents' financial future. To stay busy, Jenny would sew quilts for family and friends. Though she sewed together the fabric pieces to make a beautiful quilt herself, Jenny needed someone who had a long-arm sewing machine to add the batting—the insulation within the quilt fabric. Demand was so great that it could take nine months to a year to secure the batting-filled fabric. That gave Jenny's son, Al, an idea.

Al and his sister Sarah invested $24,000 into a long-arm sewing machine, a dozen bolts of fabric, and a building in Hamilton for the operation. The family worked two years on the business without ever bringing home a paycheck. It was challenging to grow the business in a town of just 1,800 people. Al decided they needed a website. But, as we all know, just because you build it, does not mean they will come.

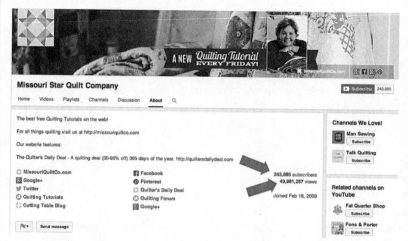

Figure 14.2 The Missouri Star Quilt Company has been able to amass over 200,000 subscribers since 2009.

The Doans knew they had to do something different to attract web visitors and drive more online sales. Al suggested Jenny create quilting video tutorials to post on YouTube. With Jenny's natural and engaging camera personality and Al's amateur behind-the-scenes abilities, the Missouri Star Quilt Co.'s YouTube channel was created (see Figure 14.2).

The channel received 1,000 subscribers in its first year, 10,000 in year two, and today has close to 250,000 subscribers. Jenny's videos have reached as many as a half-million views. The videos have driven new traffic to their website, gaining an average of 2,000 online sales per day and making them the world's largest supplier of pre-cut fabrics. Jenny receives e-mails from individuals all over the world who love watching her videos. From war-torn Iran to South Africa to across the United States, Jenny's fans love her.

Though this in itself is an amazing story, the success does not stop here. As Missouri Star Quilt Co. grew, so did the need for more staff. To date, Jenny and her family now have 120 employees working in Hamilton. They also invested in three other businesses, two local restaurants, and a bakery. Their retail warehouse displays 20,000 bolts of fabric, and they operate five fabric shops on Hamilton's main street.

They also created a "sew-and-stay" retreat center. By year's end, they will add another eight fabric shops to their quilting empire.

The Doans don't necessarily know where the company will go from there. Their focus is on making the best quilts and providing the best products for their customers. In the meantime, they are changing lives and rebuilding a town, one quilt at a time.

THE SUBSCRIBER IMPORTANCE HIERARCHY

As we discussed in Chapter 8, your goal is to build content assets where you have the maximum amount of control. This is especially true for the types of subscribers you attract. While I believe that any fan, follower, or subscriber can be a good thing, they are not equal in value.

For example, let's say that you build your platform on Facebook. Over time, you've been able to attract 50,000 "fans" on that platform.

In November 2014, Facebook made some drastic changes to its platform to hide posts from pages, such as:

- Posts that solely push people to buy a product or install an app
- Posts that push people to enter promotions and sweepstakes with no real context
- Posts that reuse the exact same content from ads

While this makes sense for Facebook's business model to work, at the same time it means that Facebook has the right *not* to show certain posts. Facebook expert Mari Smith recently stated that "bottom line, most Pages can no longer rely on organic reach to gain solid business results on Facebook. You need to have a consistent content strategy . . . to drive traffic to your website and build your email list via ads."

I know some businesses that have seen organic reach on Facebook fall to 1 percent or less. At the same time, Scott Linabarger, former content marketing director at Cleveland Clinic, stated that some posts from the hospital saw up to 60 percent organic reach on Facebook. It really doesn't matter though. You should leverage Facebook however you can, but you need to know that Facebook controls the ultimate reach, not you.

Figure 14.3 All subscribers are not created equal. If you have a choice, e-mail subscribers are the most valuable ultimately because of control.

As you analyze your digital footprint and begin to build your audience, your focus needs to be at the top of this hierarchy (Figure 14.3). Simply put, it comes down to the amount of control you have over the connections.

- **E-mail.** Most control and easiest access. Extremely helpful and relevant e-mails will break through the clutter.
- **Print subscribers.** Incredible amount of control. Communication never instantaneous and feedback difficult. Cost challenges due to print and postal charges.
- **LinkedIn connections.** Full control over what you send to followers and connections, but channel is very congested, so it may be challenging to break through with a consistent message.
- **Twitter followers.** Full control over what you send to followers but messages have an eight-second lifespan, so it may be challenging to reach audience regularly.
- **iTunes subscribers.** Full control over the delivery of audio content, but iTunes doesn't give you access to who subscribes to your content.

- **Medium/Tumblr/Instagram/Pinterest subscribers.** Full control over delivery of content. Users will see your content if they choose to. No ultimate ownership over platform.
- **YouTube subscribers.** Some control over content, but YouTube can decide to hold some of your content back if subscribers aren't engaging with your content (called "subscriber burn").
- **Facebook fans.** Facebook continually modifies its algorithm, which is out of your control. Fans may or may not see your content depending on this algorithm, although quality, helpful, and interesting content has the best chance of breaking through. Promotional content almost always is shut down by Facebook.

While you have more control with certain subscription options, Jeff Rohrs, chief marketing officer at Yext and author of *Audience*, is adamant that no company "owns" its audience: "The reason that the audience is in different places is that no audience is owned. Regardless of whether you're a major television network, pop star, or professional sports team with rabid fans, you simply do not own your audience. They can get up and leave—mentally or physically—at any time."

This is exactly the reason that amazingly helpful and relevant content is the only way to keep our audience connected to us, regardless of which subscription options you choose to leverage.

YOU NEED AN E-MAIL OFFERING

Regardless of whether you are a YouTube star or a pool guy, you need an e-mail offering to attract subscribers. BuzzFeed, the new media entertainment and news site, gained its popularity due to social sharing on Facebook and Twitter. While this is true, and Facebook and Twitter subscribers are important to BuzzFeed, every page on its site has a promotion to gain e-mail subscribers to its daily e-newsletter (Figure 14.4).

As well, business publication *Fast Company* includes a nice little e-mail call to action at the bottom of every article (Figure 14.5).

Let's look at the Content Inc. example of EntrepreneurOnFire.com from John Lee Dumas. His main subscription channel is iTunes. This makes sense since John's key platform comprises audio podcasts. But go to John's website, and the *first* thing you'll see is a call to action for an e-mail subscription (Figure 14.6).

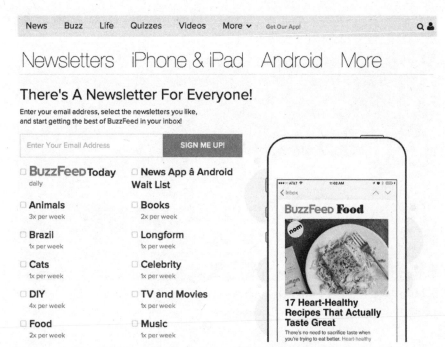

Figure 14.4 Even social media powerhouse BuzzFeed.com focuses on building e-mail subscribers.

Research at the National University of Singapore and the University of Chicago found that participants who tightened their muscles–hands, fingers, calves, or biceps–were able to increase their self-control. Muscle tightening also gives you more willpower.

—*Meredith Lepore is the former editor of the women's career site, The Grindstone.*

This article originally appeared in Levo and is reprinted with permission.

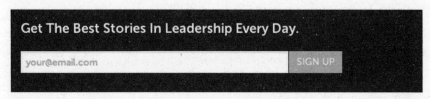

Figure 14.5 At the end of every FastCompany.com article, there is a call-to-action for the company's daily e-mail offering.

Figure 14.6   EntrepreneurOnFire.com shows first-time visitors a full-display promotion to collect e-mail subscribers.

Marketing Automation

As we've discussed, e-mail marketing technology is of critical importance as you build out your audience database. As you begin to get more advanced and consider nurturing content and loyalty content, you may need a more robust system. Enter marketing automation technology.

Before you select any kind of automation technology, be *sure* you actually *need* it. More companies than not invest in marketing automation technology but quickly realize they don't have the staffing resources and investment dollars to keep up with the platform.

When you are ready, consider players such as Act-On Software, Marketo, Oracle Eloqua, Percolate, Pardot (owned by Salesforce.com), HubSpot, and Infusionsoft.

As you employ your Content Inc. strategy, you need some kind of e-mail offering. This could be a:

- Daily e-mail newsletter based on your original blog
- Daily e-mail newsletter curating the best information from the web
- Weekly e-mail newsletter or weekly report offering industry insight
- Report offering a fresh idea to your audience every month

TIPS FOR GAINING SUBSCRIBERS

Think about the last time you clicked on an article on social media and it directed you back to the website. If it's like most sites, the calls to action were all about the products. Perhaps a product demo? Maybe a new product offering?

With a Content Inc. model, every piece of content we send out drives to another piece of content that can be subscribed to (an e-mail offering). At CMI, our best subscription generator is a pop-over (sometimes called a "pop-up") using a tool called Pippity (Figure 14.7).

In the past we served up the pop-over after 15 seconds or on the second page of a first-time user's visit to the site. Recently, we changed this

Figure 14.7 Content Marketing Institute uses a software package called Pippity to show a pop-over to collect e-mail subscriptions.

due to the following testing results; we now serve the pop-over when someone leaves the site. Here are the results of our test:

Standard Pop-Over

Dates served: 2/1–2/15

Impressions: 11,486

Conversions: 356

Conversion rate: 3.10%

Exit-Only Pop-Over

Dates served: 2/16–3/3

Impressions: 41,683

Conversions: 914

Conversion rate: 2.19%

Although the conversion percentage was lower on exit-only, we decided to keep it in place because of the additional conversions (over 100 percent growth in conversions). This is something you should test out yourself.

Other ways to enhance your subscription opportunities include:

- Ask for only an e-mail address, or just a name and e-mail address, for starters. Asking for too much information at first will damage your ability to gain subscribers.
- Promote subscriptions on your website and social platforms.
- Place subscription options in the footer of your e-mail signature line. Do the same for all your employees.
- Leverage SlideShare Pro, where you can upload PowerPoint-type presentations and collect e-mail names (subscriptions) when people download them. (*Note:* SlideShare is owned by LinkedIn.)

You need all your employees and contractors to understand your key metric. Tell them often. Below is a sample note to all our employees about our goals and what we want them to do this week (this note comes from our VP of content, Michele Linn).

Hi everyone,

As I mentioned briefly in Friday's call, the editorial team is trying to be very focused. Our two big goals are:

Goal #1: Building our email list.

Goal #2: Getting subscribers engaged in additional CMI products. (The more someone is engaged, the more likely they are to attend our events and buy from us.)

A few things to note:

1. We like to encourage sign-ups for these three things, as they all require more than email address. This helps the marketing team build out the data for our subscriber base:
   - Chief Content Officer Magazine
   - Webinars
   - SlideShare (*Note:* Someone is subscribed to our weekly newsletter when they download a PDF of the SlideShare)
2. We have two primary gated pieces of content on the site to attract subscribers:
   - Documented content marketing strategy eBook: http://cmi.media/CI-documented=
   - Influencer marketing eBook and toolkit: http://cmi.media/CI-distribution
3. We look a lot at posts that get the most conversions—as well as posts that have lower traffic, but higher conversions—and push people to that content. We will continue to send that list to you on a weekly basis so that you can share those out to your own social networks.

As always, if you have any questions on this—or ideas on how to spread the 4 kinds of content more widely—please let me know anytime.

- Without an audience, your Content Inc. strategy will not work.
- While activity metrics are critical to measure the success of your content, your ultimate goal should always be to get or keep an audience. Laser-focusing on that makes all the difference.
- There are a number of ways to build an audience, but not all subscribers are created equal. If you have a choice, go for e-mail first.
- Web traffic and social media shares are great, but if you are not building an audience, those may be meaningless metrics. Focus on the metrics that help you build an opt-in audience.

Resources

Austin Carr, "Facebook's Plan to Own Your Phone," FastCompany.com, accessed April 28, 2015, http://www.fastcompany.com/3031237/facebook -everywhere.

Facebook for Business, "An Update to News Feed: What It Means for Business," Facebook.com, accessed April 28, 2015, https://www.facebook.com/ business/news/update-to-facebook-news-feed.

Mari Smith, Facebook status update, Facebook.com, January 3, 2015, https:// www.facebook.com/marismith/posts/10152509018550009.

Jeffrey K. Rohrs, "The Proprietary Audience," October 25, 2013, accessed April 28, 2015, http://www.exacttarget.com/blog/the-proprietary-audience-aka -no-audience-is-owned/.

Chapter 15

Building for Findability

The true delight is in the finding out rather than in the knowing.

ISAAC ASIMOV

Matt Cutts, Google's leading search evangelist, recently declared: "I firmly support the idea that people should have a diversified way of reaching their audience. So if you rely only on Google that might not be as strong of an approach compared to having a wide variety of different avenues by which you can reach people and drive them to your website or whatever your objective is."

According to the 2015 Content Marketing Benchmark research from Content Marketing Institute and MarketingProfs, more marketers are focusing on content promotion than ever before. Why? Companies of all sizes are spending vast amounts of money on content creation, only to find out that no one is engaging in that content. Developing ongoing content without a clear strategy for content findability is no plan at all.

SEARCH ENGINE OPTIMIZATION

Getting your content found through search engines is the king of content findability. According to web presence management company Conductor, approximately half of all web traffic comes from organic search (nonpaid results).

For the Content Inc. model to be successful, you need to focus on search engine optimization (SEO) at all times. For a long time, the members of CMI's staff believed that if they understood the basics of SEO and created valuable, shareable content, the content would be found in the organic search rankings. Although respectable traffic was coming to our site from search engines, getting a lot more serious about SEO in the last few years more than doubled search results—and doubled our business in the process. Better yet, the majority of new subscribers come in through search engines rather than any other source. Needless to say, SEO is critical for our survival.

Your "Hit List" of Keywords

Every month CMI reviews a "rolling list" of our top 50 keyword phrases (like "content marketing" or "how to curate content"). For each phrase, we monitor our placement in Google, check how we are doing against competitors, and determine how we are trending from the previous month (are we doing better or worse?). (See Figure 15.1.)

We also look at the results on a historical basis to track how the team is doing on our most important keywords (Figure 15.2).

CMI Editorial - Master Tracker
File Edit View Insert Format Data Tools Add-ons Help   All changes saved in Drive

fx | Google Feb. 2015 Rankings

	A	B Google Monthly Searches	C Notes	D Google Rankings May 2014	L Google Jan. 2015 Rankings	M le Feb. 2015 Ran	N Google March R:	O URL
	UPDATED 1/15/15							
46	content ideas	170	new	10	14	18		14 http://contentmarketinginstitute.com/
47	content job	30	Original	6	3	2		2 http://contentmarketinginstitute.com/
48	content map	480	Original	5	5	3		4 http://contentmarketinginstitute.com/
49	content mapping	390	Original	2	2	2		1 http://contentmarketinginstitute.com/
50	content marketing	40500	Original	1	1	1		1 http://contentmarketinginstitute.com/
51	content marketing agency	1300	Original	2	1	1		1 http://contentmarketinginstitute.com/
52	content marketing best practices	140	Original	1	3	1		2 http://contentmarketinginstitute.com/
53	content marketing blog	480	Original	1	1	1		1 http://contentmarketinginstitute.com/
54	content marketing book	90	Original	1	1	1		1 http://contentmarketinginstitute.com/
55	content marketing calendar	140	Original	4	1	1		1 http://contentmarketinginstitute.com/
56	content marketing guide	110	Original	6	4	6		5 http://contentmarketinginstitute.com/
57	content marketing job	50	Original	2	3	3		1 http://jobs.contentmarketinginstitute.c
58	content marketing jobs	320	Original	2	2	2		1 http://jobs.contentmarketinginstitute.c
59	content marketing news	210	Original	2	4	5		7 http://contentmarketinginstitute.com/
60	content marketing plan	480	Original	1	1	1		1 http://contentmarketinginstitute.com/
61	content marketing process	70	Original	1	1	1		1 http://contentmarketinginstitute.com/
62	content marketing roi	140	Original	1	1	1		1 http://contentmarketinginstitute.com/
63	content marketing strategies	260	Original	1	1	1		1 http://contentmarketinginstitute.com/
64	content marketing strategy	2400	Original	1	1	1		1 http://contentmarketinginstitute.com/
65	content marketing tools	390	new	5	5	7		3 http://contentmarketinginstitute.com/
66	content optimization	390	Original	1	1	1		1 http://contentmarketinginstitute.com/
67	content plan	390	Original	1	1	1		1 http://contentmarketinginstitute.com/
68	content planning	210	Original	2	1	1		1 http://contentmarketinginstitute.com/
69	content producer	590	Original	38	97	>200	>200	none
70	content publisher	110	Original	9	1	1		1 http://contentmarketinginstitute.com/
71	Content publishers	60	New	3	1	1		1 http://contentmarketinginstitute.com/

Figure 15.1 CMI analyzes a rolling set of 50 keywords per month to track search engine optimization performance.

Figure 15.2 Every keyword phrase's performance is tracked monthly in Google and Bing, along with the link to the piece of content that is ranked.

Our goal is to drive subscriptions from every page of content. The CMI staff treats every page like a landing page and monitors top pages for ways to increase traffic to a specific page, as well as increase the conversion of readers to subscribers (Figure 15.3).

	A	B	C
1	Landing Page	October 2014 Sessions	
2	/what-is-content-marketing/	21771	
3	/	19251	
4	/2014/10/2015-b2b-content-marketing-research/	7313	
5	/2014/10/fewer-people-using-content-marketing/	4702	
6	/developing-a-strategy/	4111	
7	/2014/10/content-marketing-roi-tip-sheet/	3893	
8	/2014/10/5-videos-business-cant-live-without/	3817	
9	/2014/10/build-content-marketing-strategy/	3569	
10	/2014/10/boost-website-content-with-social-intelligence/	3556	
11	/2014/10/merril-lynch-uses-content-mapping/	3240	
12	/2014/10/get-more-content-value-from-linkedin/	3221	
13	/2014/10/sticky-note-approach-to-brainstorms/	2886	
14	/blog/	2725	
15	/2014/10/go-agile-adapt-12-principles-to-content-marketing/	2675	
16	/2013/06/essential-content-templates-checklists/	2599	
17	/2010/08/content-marketing-editorial-calendar/	2234	
18	/2014/10/social-media-agencies-and-experts-credibility/	2232	
19	/2013/10/effective-content-marketing-strategy/	2223	
20	/2011/03/blog-post-to-dos/	2100	
21	/mobile-home/	2100	
22	/2014/10/paid-advertising-b2b-content-marketers-share-insights/	1945	
23	/2013/10/2014-b2b-content-marketing-research/	1928	
24	/2008/06/113-expert-and/	1756	
25	/2014/10/content-marketing-strategy-101/	1750	
26	/top-content-marketing-blogs/	1732	
27	/2014/10/2015-b2c-consumer-content-marketing/	1712	
28	/2014/10/listening-communities-marketing-strategy/	1636	
29	/2011/11/how-to-develop-a-wikipedia-page/	1602	
30	/education/ultimate-ebook-100-content-marketing-examples/	1600	
31	/plan/	1553	

Figure 15.3 Every content page is treated like a landing page, and each one is measured on how many subscribers come in through each page.

How do we build a strategy for this concept? Below, CMI's SEO specialist Mike Murray explains how to integrate search in the Content Inc. model.

If half of your traffic comes from organic search, where does the other half come from? Here are a number of tactics you should consider as part of your model.

---

12 Keyword Selection Tips for SEO and Small Business Content Marketing

By Mike Murray, CMI's SEO Specialist

Small business owners and entrepreneurs can ill-afford to operate in the dark when it comes to keyword selection if they want to build an audience from search engine traffic.

Too often, owners take wild stabs with their keyword choices. Sure, they can occasionally guess well. But how often are their efforts a waste of time?

The good news is that you can attract some search engine visitors by constantly creating content even without an SEO strategy. With keywords, you will rank for something because search engine algorithms value content.

You need to be realistic. Every page or blog post won't take you to the first position on Google (or other search engines for that matter). Maybe a keyword phrase with 10,000 searches a month will be out of reach. You can still get more out of SEO with just a bit more effort.

You can reference the following checklist as you consider what keywords to play up in your new content (don't overlook opportunities to also update older articles).

1. **Have I explored keyword research resources?** Check out SerpStat and SEO Chat's free Google Keyword Suggest Tool. Even if you don't advertise on Google, get a Google AdWords account to access the Keyword Planner. Paid tools include Keyword Discovery and

WordTracker. I often use SEMrush, which suggests possible key-words that you may not have considered (it analyzes more than 100 million keywords, including data about competitors). Within a few minutes of using SEMrush, I had an Excel spreadsheet filled with 6,000 keyword ideas from an Inc. 5000 company. You should also look at the keywords that people use at Social Mention.

You can make a list of keyword phrases, but search counts matter. Sometimes you can go after a keyword phrase with 1,000 monthly searches. Quite often, you may want something less competitive. I don't rule out keyword phrases with 50 searches a month.

2. **Is the keyword phrase relevant?** Does the keyword phrase really match your products and services and your target audiences? Keyword specificity is paramount.

   Keep in mind that the keyword searches you discover may include unusual keyword combinations like "soccer uniforms youth." You can see how they rank, but proper sentence structure will force you to switch the order of the words. You can probably use two different spellings in some cases (but avoid doing that on the same page). "Swing set" and "swingset" would be one example.

3. **Are we buying this keyword phrase through paid search?** If you're spending money on paid search (pay per click), the performance data can be helpful. But paying for those clicks won't guarantee organic success for your small business. Only some of the keywords may do well. Depending on the conversions, you may see value in keeping a keyword phrase for both paid and natural search.

4. **Am I already ranking for the keyword phrase?** Are you among the top 10, top 20, top 30, or far out at 99? Use tools like SheerSEO, Web CEO, and Moz to get ranking data. Enterprise SEO Tools: The Marketer's Guide explores different platforms that can help you manage, track, and optimize thousands of keywords (some are expensive, but some packages are affordable). This free report is available at http://cmi.media/CI-seotools.

5. **Will my new page adequately mention the keyword phrase?** Although search engines detect themes or concepts, the outstanding content should still include your most strategic keyword phrases. Rankings will also be heavily influenced by the page title, page header, website age, inbound links, and many other factors.

6. **How much traffic is my website receiving for the keyword phrase?** In your website analytics, start with the words that people use to reach your website and the keyword phrases captured in your internal site search after they arrive. Maybe someone searches for "Cleveland accounting firms," but that may prompt you to look at some options like "accounting firms in Cleveland" or "Cleveland Ohio CPA firms." You can work those phrases into existing content or new pages.

   I always look at multiple keyword phrases on a web page that rank high on search engines. You may find that a single page could support "heating and cooling Dallas" and "Dallas heating cooling." However, both phrases may not appear among the top positions. You may need to create a new page devoted to one of the phrases, which won't need to appear on the original page (giving more weight to a remaining keyword phrase).

7. **Am I refining my set of keywords?** Even after you create your keyword set, you should evaluate it based on your new keyword ideas, industry trends, the competition, your analytics, keywords you see on social media, and other sources. Don't just make a note of words you come across. Think of variations as well.

8. **Is this keyword phrase (or similar phrases) already converting?** You can track keywords through your website analytics and conversion funnels, including e-commerce (connecting keywords and landing pages with product sales). Some businesses gain additional insights with call tracking services such as those offered by Mongoose Metrics, Marchex, and others.

9. **Are there calls to action on the page?** If you want a keyword phrase to pay off for your Content Inc. strategy, make sure the page

has a compelling call to action. Can a visitor call a toll-free number, request a demo, download a guide, or request more information?

10. **Are there related pages that could support an internal link strategy?** A single page can rank well, but sometimes it helps to create several related pages so search engines can determine that you're emphasizing a similar set of keyword phrases. Cross-link the strategic keywords on several of your similar pages or posts.

11. **How will this keyword phrase choice fit into future content?** Your keyword selection options should be based on planned content for the weeks or months ahead, not just the content you already have or are writing today. With a content calendar, consider any number of keyword possibilities well before writing an article or creating a blog post.

12. **Is the keyword phrase in our domain name?** In 2012, Google decided to go after low-quality exact-match domains for websites (meaning their rankings could be affected). I'm sure Google wanted to deal with obnoxious domains like this pretend domain: seocontentmarketingtipsforsmallbusinessmarketers.com. However, for respectable websites, the domain name still seems to have a positive impact on search engine rankings.

GUEST APPEARANCES IN OPC

As noted earlier in the book, OPC is short for "other people's content." The more our thinking gets spread around in OPC, the better chances we will have to attract new people to our site and build subscribers. As you develop better relationships with influencers (see Chapter 16), one of your goals is to find opportunity to help those influencers with their content. That could mean developing a guest blog post for them or guest-starring in a webinar for their audience.

Since 2007, I've written original or repurposed articles for over 200 different websites. At the same time, I've participated in over 30 outside webinars a year. These two activities have been critical to our success. How do I know? In February 2015, users came to the CMI site from over 2,500 different places. Much of that diversity is because we share content on other people's sites.

> In April 2015, Google announced that its algorithm would favor those sites that are "mobile ready." That means, if your website doesn't render well on mobile devices, your content may be penalized by Google.

CREATE MORE LISTS WITH YOUR CONTENT

As much as I'm not a fan of this, lists get found and shared. As a result, more people blog and link to that content, making it easier to be found in search engines. CMI's best-performing content is almost always a numbered list.

Even more impactful is compiling an industry list of influencers. *Forbes* magazine is perhaps the king of this—the magazine develops multiple "best of" reports each month (Figure 15.4).

Presenting today's greatest gathering of young game changers, movers and makers. Our fourth annual celebration is bigger than ever: 600 millennials in 20 fields — no repeats from years past and every one selected by a panel of A-list judges. **Click on the categories below to see the full list, gorgeous photos, surprising trends and videos, and much more.**
— *Edited by Caroline Howard, Michael Noer, and Kate Pierce*

Figure 15.4   Forbes executes a number of "best of" programs, including this one.

CONSIDER STUMBLEUPON

According to analytics blog KISSmetrics, many businesses overlook the value of Stumbleupon as part of their content promotion activities. Readers use Stumbleupon to find or "stumble" onto relevant articles and sites based on their current interests.

Statcounter found that of the top seven most-trafficked sites, Stumbleupon is one of the leaders in driving traffic to those sites. Adding Stumbleupon to your site toolbar would be a solid first step.

GET INVOLVED WITH REDDIT

In February 2015, community site Reddit had over 150 million unique visitors. On Reddit, consumers of every interest share stories, vote, and comment. Depending on your niche area, there may be a few subgroups, called subreddits, where conversations are happening. By being active in these communities, you may receive opportunities to share your expertise—and your articles.

CREATE UNIQUE RESEARCH

It's not even close. More sites share our original research than anything else we do. If this could be an opportunity for you, be sure you plan your research as an ongoing series, like quarterly or annually. That means every time the research is released, you have something new and amazing to talk about.

ANSWER QUESTIONS AT QUORA

Quora is a question-and-answer platform. Most likely, possible subscribers are asking questions that you may be able to answer, again showing your expertise and driving people to your website.

CONTENT SYNDICATION

Syndicating your content means you actively place your articles on other people's sites. In the past, many have thought that search engines like Google penalize your site for duplicate content. Google says this isn't true: "Let's put this to bed once and for all, folks: There's no such thing as a 'duplicate content penalty.'"

Michael Brenner, head of strategy for NewsCred, believes that content syndication is an untapped opportunity. As he shares:

> At SAP, I built an award-winning content marketing hub called SAP Business Innovation and started it with little budget. How do you build a content hub on a small budget? You need an army of volunteer content contributors.
>
> I did this by syndicating content from other experts (mostly employees, to start) with their permission. When I started showing business results and my budgets increased, I added licensed content as well as additional paid original content.

Licensing your content to other sites (syndication) may make sense to give you the added distribution you need. And even though I believe original content creation is the number one option for Content Inc. models to grow, syndicating other people's content may be something to consider until your content factory is in full gear.

Organizations like Newscred and PR Newswire should be considered if this interests you.

LEVERAGE HARO

Help a Reporter Out, or HARO, is a site for journalists and reporters looking for expert content sources. CMI has used HARO for the past few years and received placement in the *New York Times* because of it.

ADD IMAGES TO YOUR TEXT CONTENT

Skyword research has found that business-oriented web pages with images have performed 91 percent better than those pages without images. When in doubt, always add an image to your textual content (Figure 15.5).

Sites like *Huffington Post* and BuzzFeed practice this religiously. Adding images does not have to be an arduous process. Consider the following:

- As you develop your content calendar, hire a graphic designer to develop customized posts.

Figure 15.5   For my podcast *This Old Marketing* with Robert Rose, CMI develops a custom image that is leveraged as part of our social media promotion.

- Subscribe to an online image service like BigStock or Shutterstock. While this is fine, we still recommend having a designer go into the image and customize it enough to make it your own.
- Do it yourself, using a program such as Canva.

MAKE SURE MOST OF YOUR CONTENT IS UNGATED

In the summer of 2014, I conducted a workshop for some leading trade associations. The majority of them were struggling with getting their content found on the web. Why? Because 90 percent of their content was only accessible to members, who had to log in to access the content. This means that 90 percent of their content goes unnoticed by search engines, and users who like the content can't share it on social media.

According to noted author and speaker David Meerman Scott's personal statistics, a white paper or e-book of his will be downloaded at least 20 times more and up to 50 times more without a gate in front of it. You get better results without a lead form in front of downloadable content.

Yes, you want certain content assets with a form in front of them to grow your subscriber lists, but the vast majority of your content needs to be easily accessible to your audience, enhancing both search and social media sharing opportunities.

BRANDSCAPING

Brandscaping, according to author Andrew Davis, is defined as "a collection of brands working together to produce great content" (see Figure 15.6).Think of an example where you have great content, but you need additional marketing exposure. Or possibly someone in your industry has some amazing research that you really want to share with your audience. In these cases, perhaps a partnership can be created.

Test Your Titles like Upworthy

Upworthy, one of the fastest-growing sites on the web, focuses on sharing and curating content that (it believes) uplifts the rest of humanity. In December 2013, over 87 million people visited Upworthy.

What accounts for the extraordinary number of visits? According to Upworthy, "It was because millions of members of the Upworthy community watched the videos we curated and found them important, compelling, and worth sharing with their friends."

How does Upworthy get people to open its e-mails to watch the videos and then share them with friends? The Upworthy staff is meticulous about its headlines. For each article, Upworthy writes a minimum of 25 different headlines. Then the company does various A/B tests with its

Figure 15.6 Two different companies, Traackr and Skyword, partnered together (brandscaping) on an educational e-book.

subscription lists to see which headline led to the most e-mail opens and the most shares. Once Upworthy finds the best performer, the company distributes that winning headline to the entire e-mail database.

PAID CONTENT DISTRIBUTION OPTIONS

Before you gain organic search traction and build a massive audience of subscribers, your content may need a boost to gain readership. It is completely acceptable to engage in paid content distribution techniques to acquire new subscribers. Here are a couple to consider:

- **Pay per click.** Until you can be found in your target keywords on search engines, it may make sense to pay for promotion. Pay per click (PPC) is the idea that you promote your content on search engines and are charged every time someone clicks on your link. PPC charges can range from 5 cents for less popular keyword phrases up to multiple dollars per click for popular searches (like "mesothelioma").

- **Content discovery/recommendation tools.** Services like Outbrain, Taboola, and nRelate form partnerships with media and blogging sites and will promote your content, for a fee, on the sites of your choosing. The investment works exactly the same as for PPC (you are charged every time someone clicks on your story). The biggest difference with content recommendation tools is that the content *has* to be in the form of an interesting story (or the services won't show it). Figure 15.7 shows what a content recommendation section looks like on CNN.com.

Figure 15.7 Many publishers, including CNN, use content discovery engines at the bottom of their articles to promote relevant (and sponsored) content.

SOCIAL MEDIA ADVERTISING

Almost every social website, including Facebook, LinkedIn, Twitter, and Instagram, accepts advertising. Each of these services lets you target very specific audiences with your content. Figure 15.8 presents an example from Facebook promoting a webinar (promoting valuable content is the best way to leverage social advertising).

Figure 15.8 Promoting your content in social media outlets like Facebook can be a great way to target a very specific audience with content.

NEWS RELEASE SERVICES

Services such as PR Newswire and PRWeb will take your press release and distribute it to the media sites of your choosing for additional promotion. Remember, there is no set format. You can be as creative as you can to get attention among the thousands of other releases sent out that day. PR professional Mitch Delaplane had a bit of fun with his press release in 2011 and ended up being promoted on sites, such as TechCrunch, as the "best press release ever" (Figure 15.9).

For more information on promotion options for your content, check out Chad Pollitt's guide to content promotion (http://cmi.media/CI-promotion) and Robert Rose's full report on content discovery tools (http://cmi.media/CI-native).

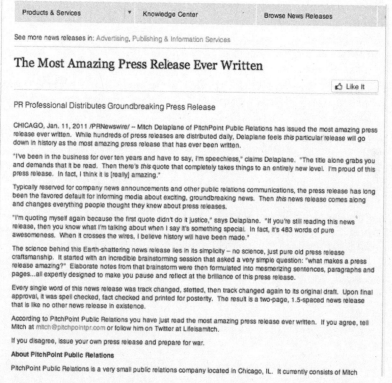

Figure 15.9 Mitch Delaplane's "best press release ever" was picked up by multiple media outlets.

CONTENT INC. INSIGHTS

- While there are many ways for your content to be found, the center of the findability universe is search.
- While setting your content to be found in search engines is not rocket science, most companies don't do the small things needed to be found by search engines. Be sure to create a process for this.
- Advertising your content to build subscribers is a viable option. Look at all available channels to see how you can get your content in front of the right people.

Resources

Eric Enge, "Link Building Is Not Illegal (or Inherently Bad) with Matt Cutts," stonetemple.com, accessed April 28, 2015, https://www.stonetemple.com/link-building-is-not-illegal-or-bad/.

Nathan Safran, "310 Million Visits: Nearly Half of All Web Site Traffic Comes from Natural Search [Data]," conductor.com, accessed April 28, 2015, http://www.conductor.com/blog/2013/06/data-310-million-visits-nearly-half-of-all-web-site-traffic-comes-from-natural-search/.

Kristi Hines, "4 Ways to Increase Traffic with StumbleUpon," KISSmetrics.com, accessed April 28, 2015, https://blog.kissmetrics.com/increase-traffic-with-stumbleupon/.

Google Support, "Duplicate Content," Google.com, accessed April 28, 2015, https://support.google.com/webmasters/answer/66359?hl=en.

Michael Brenner, "Get the Biggest SEO Bang for Your Content Marketing Buck," ContentMarketingInstitute.com, accessed April 28, 2015, http://contentmarketinginstitute.com/2015/03/brenner-seo-content-marketing/.

Upworthy Insider, "What Actually Makes Things Go Viral Will Blow Your Mind," Upworthy.com, accessed April 28, 2015, http://blog.upworthy.com/post/69093440334/what-actually-makes-things-go-viral-will-blow-your.

Alexia Tsotsis, "The Most Amazing Press Release Ever Written," techcrunch.com, accessed April 28, 2015, http://techcrunch.com/2011/01/12/news-about-news/.

Chapter 16

Stealing Audience

Influencer marketing is getting others to share your story,
generate interest, and make your case.

ARDATH ALBEE

The majority of marketing professionals might call this chapter "influencer marketing," but I'd rather just tell it like it is. The goal of building a relationship with an influencer (defined as "the place where the people in your audience are hanging out on the web if they are not on your site") is to steal the influencer's audience and make it yours (I say this in the nicest way possible).

Right now, the people who make up your audience are not just standing around waiting for your content. They are actively involved and engaged in mobile, video, audio, and textual content for informational or entertainment purposes. If you are going to break through, you need to take that attention and direct it toward your content (not an easy task).

This chapter is all about helping you do just that: steal audience!

MAKING THE CASE

This method of tapping into influencers to help amplify your content is otherwise known as "influencer marketing." It's a pretty straightforward concept when you think about it:

- Influencers have a *preestablished audience* that is already receptive to their ideas and recommendations; they are valued by your target audience.
- Influencers have a built-in level of *trust* with their readers. The hope is, these influencers will forge these strong connections on your behalf and help you build credibility.
- They can help you *create the right content* that really meets your consumers' needs, because they have "on-the-ground" experience and perspective.
- By partnering *with them,* you're able to get your content and messaging out in the right way, at the right time, to the right people.

The ultimate goal is to build and expand your own audience.

WHAT'S YOUR GOAL?

Just as you need a strategy for your Content Inc. program, you also need a strategy for your influencer marketing program. Before launching your influencer program, you need to clearly understand and document what you specifically want to accomplish. Said another way: How will your influencer program help you achieve your business goals, and how will it lead to audience building?

Some potential objectives to consider or use as a starting point to build your own list of goals:

- **Brand awareness.** How many people viewed, downloaded, or listened to this piece of content because of the influencer?
- **Engagement.** How resonant is this content, and how often is it shared with others? How is the influencer helping to increase sharing?
- **Lead generation.** How is the influencer helping to convert people into valuable subscribers?
- **Sales.** Did you make money because of this content shared by the influencer? What revenue or ROI can you apply to this program? (See Chapter 22.)
- **Customer retention and loyalty.** How can an influencer help retain a customer?
- **Up-sell or cross-sell.** Is there a way to use an influencer to help someone become more invested in your business?

IDENTIFY INFLUENCER TYPES

The type of influencer you need depends on your specific objective. For example, if your aim is awareness and a broad reach, you may choose a bigger number of influencers to work with who can all produce "bite-sized" pieces of content to increase your share of voice. But if you are looking to retain customers or up-sell, you may want to use other clients as influencers.

How Can You Identify the Right Influencers?

Influencers can come in many different forms. From inside your organization outward, they can take the form of:

- Bloggers
- Customers
- Members of a purchasing group
- Industry experts and analysts
- Business partners
- Internal team members or experts
- Media sites

From these groups you will form your influencer "hit list" (see "Build Your Hit List of Influencers" below).

HOW TO MANAGE THE PROGRAM

Now that you've established what you're trying to achieve with your influencer marketing program and whom you'd ideally like to reach, you will have a better understanding of whether or not you have the right resources in-house to do the work needed. Some things to consider:

- How much capacity does your internal team have for taking on a pilot group of influencers?
- Do you have any tools available in-house (ones you use for social listening, content management, etc.) that you can leverage for an influencer marketing program? See the sidebar "Influencer Listening Tools" for suggestions.

> ### Influencer Listening Tools
>
> - Klout (to find and score influencers)
> - Little Bird (to find influencers)
> - Google Alerts (to identify incoming content based on keywords)
> - Traackr (to find and form influencer relationships)
> - Tap Influence (to find registered influencers open to partnership possibilities)

When you fully understand your internal capabilities, you'll be able to determine what size program you can manage and identify what other resources you'll need to engage to deploy the program that will meet your objectives.

CREATE CONTENT WORTH SHARING

In order to get influencers to work with you, to truly *partner with you*, in amplifying your content, you're going to need something crucial: *compelling and relevant content*. Time and time again, influencers will push back on brands for forcing overly promotional messages into their hard-earned sites, because authenticity is the piece that keeps trust between them and their readers, and no one—not even your brand— is worth jeopardizing that. So, in short, as perfectly stated by Andy Newbom, "Create something for influencers to influence on."

BUILD YOUR HIT LIST OF INFLUENCERS

Does your influencer marketing program ever feel like a spiraling rabbit hole? It's because there are so many potential paths you can take, and the potential pool size of influencers to tap into can feel somewhat overwhelming. Here's what typically runs through an entrepreneur's mind when beginning to launch such a program:

- Whom do we even reach out to?
- How do I know "who's good" and who has powerful influence?
- How do I even manage influencers once I start working with them?

These unknowns can feel daunting for any team, of any size and any level of experience. To help get you started, these are the next *three steps*:

1. Build a small pool of potential partners and learn more about them.
2. Begin your influencer outreach.
3. Test, assess, and optimize.

The first thing to do in building your pool of influencers, after setting your objectives and identifying the influencer "types" with whom you want to work, is to *sit back and listen*. Sounds pretty passive, but taking the time to truly understand what your potential influencer's focal points are will be crucial in understanding how you can work together.

To start, consider building a template that will help you keep track of the top people with whom you'd like to work. It's likely you already have some kind of list, but having a consistent way to keep track of them and assess them is an important place to start.

If you use a tool like Klout or other social ranking tool, you can include that score. Other times, your scoring can be a little bit more "gut based" as you read through the influencers' work. Which brings up a very important part of this process: *read your potential influencers' work!* Read their articles, see how they respond to comments, review their tweets, and really get a sense of what matters most to them. To gauge the level and extent of their influence, you can also see who is responding to their work and following them—all good things to incorporate in your spreadsheet as well (these people could be potential influencers, too).

WAYS TO IDENTIFY POTENTIAL INFLUENCERS

Amanda Maksymiw from Lattice Engines suggests these steps to build your list of influencers:

- Use your listening tools to identify people talking about certain topics based on keywords.
- Ask your customers or others in your industry (never underestimate the power of word of mouth).

- Search on social media platforms, especially LinkedIn.
- Network like crazy. Attend events in different areas—get out of your bubble. Talk to customers, partners and sales.
- Ask peers in your marketing, product development or sales teams.
- Ask other influencers. You'd be surprised as to how many of your top tier influencers work together and recommend each other.
- Get involved in the forums and discussion boards/groups discussing your content. Joining Twitter parties, webinars and even reading through the latest industry reports or blog posts can quickly make you aware of who the key players are in your space.

HOW MANY INFLUENCERS SHOULD I ADD TO MY POOL?

The answer to this question will depend heavily on how you respond to the "How to Manage the Program" section above. But to start, and for efficiency purposes, most people tend to lean toward 5 to 10 influencers as a reasonable and manageable starting point.

BEGIN OUTREACH

Once you've identified a potential pool of influencers and you've spent enough time reading through their work to want to take the next step toward outreach, take a few minutes to consider the following:

- How will you reach out to this person?
- What can you offer that is valuable?
- What exactly are you looking for from this relationship?

This is where all that time spent reviewing the person's work will pay off; sending a generic, impersonal request to a top-tier influencer may end up sounding pretty insulting. And remember, this is a two-way relationship; gone are the days where companies could throw money or samples at bloggers and expect them to fawn over the brand. Influencers have the ability to be much more selective, and they expect to be respected for the talent (and audience) they bring to your projects.

SOCIAL MEDIA 4-1-1

Social Media 4-1-1 is a sharing system first presented by Andrew Davis that enables a company to get greater visibility with social influencers.

I recommend using this as a first-approach method before directly e-mailing an influencer. Here's how it works.

For every six pieces of content shared via social media (such as Twitter):

- Four are pieces of content from your influencer target that are also relevant to your audience. This means that 67 percent of the time you are sharing content that is not yours—and calling attention to content from your influencer group.
- One piece can be your original, educational piece of content.
- One piece can be your sales piece, such as a coupon, product notice, or press release.

While the numbers don't have to be exact, it's the philosophy that makes this work. When you share the content of influencers, they notice. And you should share without asking for anything in return (for a month or so), so that when you do need something someday, the influencers are more likely to say yes.

The key to making this work is consistency. Take your pilot list of 5 to 10 influencers and share each influencer's content at least once a day for a month.

MAKING THE FIRST CONNECTION

There are a few ways you can start to make connections with your target influencers:

- Give them some social media love, either through a reply, retweet, or mention (use the Social Media 4-1-1 plan).
- Provide *thoughtful* comments on their blog posts.
- Connect with them on LinkedIn, introducing yourself and explaining why you'd like to connect.
- Shoot over an e-mail. If you want to go the e-mail route, Figure 16.1 offers an example.

The key for your outreach is not to seem like you're asking for a favor, but rather to suggest a collaboration in some form that takes into account the person's skills first, with your needs secondary.

Hello [Name],

We haven't connected before but I work for [Company X] and I have enjoyed your blogs about [Topic Y]. We'd love to collaborate with you about [Content Idea Z]. We think our audience would love to hear from you.

Figure 16.1 Sample of a possible e-mail sent to an influencer.

NURTURE INFLUENCER RELATIONSHIPS

After you've started making connections with your targeted influencers, you may feel more comfortable asking to work together in different ways, such as:

- Requesting that they cocreate content *with you*
- Requesting custom content created exclusively for your platforms
- Asking influencers to share your content on their platforms

Here are some potential projects to engage your new influencers to work on with you:

1. Ask for a quote for an article.
2. Request to speak at a conference.
3. Ask to join or be a guest on a Twitter chat or webinar.
4. Provide a quote for an e-book.
5. Gather responses on a specific topic for a crowdsourced blog post.
6. Request permission to share or link to their content. (You don't have to request it, but it's polite and will certainly show that you're interested.)
7. Request information or data for a case study.
8. Ask to write a guest blog post or feature in one.
9. Include them in an expert panel at an industry event.
10. Ask to be a guest on a podcast or Google Hangout.

HOW FAR CAN YOUR CONTENT GO?

One thing to consider is the scalability of the content that you are creating together. Just as you execute with your Content Inc. strategy, your influencer program needs legs that extend beyond a single point-in-time campaign (see Chapter 13 on repurposing). For example:

- Consider rounding up monthly guest blog posts into quarterly e-books.
- If you've had a series of influencers host webinars or podcasts, gather those into robust resource guides.
- Put together a collection of quotes or insights from your influencers and consolidate them into best practices articles or roundtable posts.

ASSESS AND OPTIMIZE THE PROGRAM

Although it will take time and effort on your part, eventually you get to a place with your influencers where a true relationship exists. Asking for content sharing will no longer feel like a favor because you put in the effort to show that you truly respect and value their contributions beyond just their audience reach. Now is the time to throw in some goodwill "relationship-building" efforts to further solidify your loyalty. For example, you can invite your influencers to an exclusive event, ask for input on a new product or service before anyone else, crowdsource ideas with them as a "pilot" group, or send them small tokens of appreciation (like a gift card for coffee) or handwritten thank you notes.

These actions will make them feel as valued and unique as you already know they are (and it never hurts to remember their birthdays, too).

MEASURING THE PROGRAM

Here's an idea of how to set up your KPIs (key performance indicators) depending on the objectives you established at the onset of your program:

Objective	Possible Metrics
Brand awareness	Website traffic
	Page views
	Video views
	Document views
	Downloads
	Social chatter
	Referral links
Engagement	Blog comments
	Likes, shares, tweets, +1s, pins
	Forwards
	Inbound links
Lead generation and nurturing	Form completions and downloads
	E-mail subscriptions
	Blog subscriptions
	Conversion rate
Sales	Online sales
	Offline sales
	Manual reporting and anecdotes
Customer retention and loyalty	Percentage of content consumed by existing customers
	Retention and renewal rates
Up-sell or cross-sell	Sales for new products or services

Regardless of what you choose to measure, be on the lookout for areas of potential improvement, especially in the beginning. No program is perfect, and the ability to grow a truly robust influencer marketing program takes a lot of time and effort. By showing more than just your superficial successes, you'll demonstrate the thoughtfulness you put behind growing these working relationships into something meaningful for your company. It's not always pretty and, like any relationship, can mean some "give-and-take" for everyone involved. But in the end, these strong voices, projecting your company messages for you, without solicitation, will have an ROI that far exceeds many of the other programs in your marketing mix.

CASE STUDY: CONTENT MARKETING INSTITUTE

CMI defines an influencer as a blogger, competitor, or media organization that is creating content of interest for our target audience.

To give these influencers visibility, we rate our influencer list quarterly in our "Top 42 Content Marketing Blogs." Initially, this list was made up of influencers we found by tracking keywords (like "content marketing") in Google Alerts, authors in industry trade publications, those that were talking about the topic on Twitter, and other bloggers that we just found interesting. The initial list included 42 influencers.

Getting the Attention of Influencers

Influencers are important people. They generally have real jobs and are extremely active on social networks, spending their time sharing content and blogging. Getting on their radar is not easy. So to get their attention, we gave away content gifts. We did this in a few different ways.

First, we used the Social Media 4-1-1 method as described above. We executed this program for months. The CMI team tracked our "top content marketing blogger" list. We then decided we could get better visibility with influencers by actually ranking them publicly and sharing the rankings with the masses. This was an incredible success.

We hired an outside research expert to put together a methodology of how to rank the top bloggers, looking at areas such as consistency, style, helpfulness, originality, and a few other details. Then each quarter, CMI would publicize the list, showcase the top 10, send out a press release, and make a big deal out of it. Needless to say, the top 10 and the honored top 42 loved the list. Not only did most of this influencer group share the list with their audiences; approximately half of the top 42 influencers placed our widget (with personal rank of that particular influencer) on their home page, linking back to our site. So not only were we building long-term relationships with these influencers, but we were getting credible links and traffic as well.

In addition to the top bloggers list, CMI started to put together large educational e-books showcasing the influencers' work. For example, in 2009 and again in 2011, we launched the *Content Marketing Playbook*. The playbook included over 40 case studies about content marketing, with many coming directly from our influencers. We made sure to note in the playbook which examples came from which influencers.

When we released the playbook and let the influencers know about the publication, the majority of influencers we highlighted in the playbook eagerly shared the content with their audiences. It's important to note that all the information we shared in the publication was either "fair use" material and properly cited or used with the influencer's permission.

Since then, most of the people on our original influencer list have become active contributors in the CMI community. Some started writing blog posts, others participated in our weekly Twitter chats, others became speakers at our events, and still others went on to write books and e-books for us. And maybe the best part, half of our original top 10 influencers are now good friends of mine. Needless to say, it's been an incredible success.

Who says stealing doesn't pay?

CONTENT INC. INSIGHTS

- You need subscribers, and influencers that share your content can help you get those.
- Most businesses that leverage an influencer strategy don't have a defined process behind it. When you execute your influencer strategy, do it with a defined group and cadence of content sharing.
- When starting an influencer strategy, you need to share more influencer content than your own content to make maximum impact.

Chapter 17

Social Media Integration

Social media is not about the exploitation
of technology but service to community.
SIMON MAINWARING

For a time, social media and content creation may have seemed inter-changeable, but they are actually quite different. Though there can be quite a bit of overlap, the easiest way to think about their relationship is that content is needed to drive social media, while social media is most essential during two key content marketing processes:

- Listening to the people in your audience to understand what they care about, so you can create content that they will find engaging and relevant
- Distributing content (from your business, as well as from others— i.e., the Social Media 4-1-1 approach)

In short, you really can't have one without the other.

If you are just getting serious about your social media distribu-tion efforts, it's best to start small. Consider the top social platforms (Twitter, LinkedIn, Facebook, and YouTube), and see where the largest concentration of your target audience members are congregating.

FOCUS

B2B companies are traditionally hesitant about, say, Pinterest;
yet if you really double down and focus on Pinterest as a key strategy,
I'm absolutely sure you can make that work. It's just [a question of]
where are you going to direct your resources best [for] having
a real potential to engage with the community better.

TODD WHEATLAND, HEAD OF STRATEGY, KING CONTENT

Choose the channels where you can build and engage with a genuine community, and focus your attention on those. Study what others are doing in this space so you can learn what people respond to the most favorably. And by "others," I don't mean your competition but, rather, anyone who may be taking your audience's attention away from your social media content (such as your influencer group). Ask yourself how you can be more useful or entertaining than other content providers.

TEST

While it makes sense to choose the primary channels you will focus on, the landscape is changing quickly, and it's important to experiment to keep your social media content efforts fresh and current. As Airbnb's chief marketing officer Jonathan Mildenhall told us during Content Marketing World 2013, "If you don't have room to fail, you don't have a way to grow."

It doesn't make sense to start using a platform simply because it's become trendy or because your competitors have a presence there. But don't let fear of failure stop you from trying something new. Follow these recommendations to guide you in your decisions:

- *Don't* sign up for an account without having a plan for what you will do there.
- *Do* prioritize the channels you want to experiment with, and spend a dedicated amount of time to test out what works—and learn from what doesn't. You may discover something new about your audience, or you may learn that it's not a priority channel for your business.

CUSTOMIZE

So, a Facebook post should be very different than [one on] Pinterest, or Twitter, or LinkedIn, but a lot of times it's just "Ugh, just put it all out, because you've got the tool so you do it and you hit send so it goes to all your channels."

MICHAEL WEISS, SPEAKER AND CONTENT MARKETING STRATEGIST

The easiest way to turn off your community members is to broadcast the same message across multiple channels. Instead, determine the kind of content that interests the members of your community in a way that is useful to them. Plan ahead to make sure you are leveraging your content assets in multiple ways but are still communicating it differently on your preferred distribution channels.

SOCIAL CHANNELS TO CONSIDER

Here's a quick overview and my recommendation on resources to check out for each major social media channel. Remember, you should leverage social media to develop audiences, but you do not get direct access to them. That's the domain of the platform, such as Facebook or YouTube. You should be using social media to ultimately drive people back to content offers so you can grow your e-mail subscription lists.

Facebook

According to Pew Research Center, 71 percent of adult Internet users and 58 percent of the entire population are on Facebook. That means Facebook matters. Most likely, at least a portion of your audience is leveraging Facebook.

As we discussed in Chapter 14, Facebook continually changes its algorithms to show the most interesting and engaging content to users. This means that promoting yourself on Facebook won't work.

Britt Klontz, digital content strategist at Distilled, recommends these two Facebook initiatives:

- *Provide exclusive access: One of the best ways to continually engage fans and create new "likes" is by providing exclusive access, as long as whatever you're providing access to is rich and meaningful. #PepsiExclusive does this with events, but you can also provide exclusive access to deals or even to fun or particularly helpful pieces of content. You might, for example, write an extensive guide for a process or procedure you know your audience will be interested in, host it on a microsite, and provide an access code to your fans. This way, they'll feel rewarded with excellent—and free!—content just for returning to your page.*

- *Make good use of hashtags: While hashtags can be effective across the board when it comes to social media, they're especially effective for brands that already have cult followings on Facebook. Nutella, for example, incorporates a #spreadthehappy hashtag throughout all of its Facebook content. This tag appears often in "vs" competitions (i.e., "New York bagel or New Orleans baguette?"), and is used to invite fans to share their own photos, videos, and recipes. Again, the hashtag makes searching easy, and it engages fans in a way that encourages their own creativity.*

Best resources: Moz offers an excellent beginner's guide to Facebook (http://moz.com/beginners-guide-to-social-media/facebook), while JonLoomer.com is the absolute best place for more advanced Facebook strategies.

Twitter

Twitter has become the official broadcasting tool of the web. How do you make your story stand out on Twitter? Here are some tips to follow:

- **Tell a story through your tweets.** Present a consistent voice to tell the story of your industry and your brand. Each post should be compelling in its own right, but be sure to take a consistent voice into consideration.
- **Make use of hashtags.** Including one to three relevant hashtags with your tweet makes it simple for people to find your content. (For example, we at CMI use #cmworld for our annual event.) Creating

an original hashtag and linking it to a specific campaign is an even better use of the tactic.

- **Use it as a testing ground.** Tweet your original content, and keep tabs on which pieces of content get more shares. Use this information to direct your future content efforts.
- **Cover industry events.** Tweet live coverage of events that are significant for your audience to offer insights in real time. That way, your brand can act as the eyes and ears for individuals who can't make it to the event.

Best resource: Twitter Power 3.0 from Joel Comm.

A new app called Periscope has been growing rapidly in popularity since the beginning of 2015. Periscope, owned by Twitter, is an easy way to live-stream an event or interview, and then it works well with Twitter to let your followers know the event is taking place.

LinkedIn

LinkedIn has become so much more than a company Rolodex. It is perhaps the most powerful business publishing platform on the web. Since launching its "influencer" program where niche celebrities were able to publish content exclusively on LinkedIn, the company has now opened up publishing to every user—for free (Figure 17.1).

Here are some tips if you intend to publish:

- Understand what audience you'd like to target on LinkedIn and publish content there to attract that audience to your subscription offerings.
- Take full advantage of your profile by embedding your SlideShare presentations and YouTube videos and link to all your content resources.
- Do an audit of your team's profile to make sure each employee is representing the company properly.

Best resource: Maximizing LinkedIn for Sales and Social Media by Neal Schaffer.

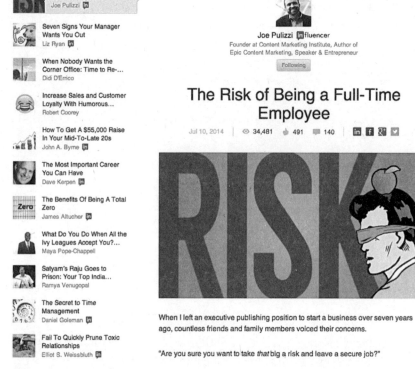

Figure 17.1 Anyone with a LinkedIn account can now publish original articles on the platform.

SlideShare

SlideShare is best known as the YouTube for PowerPoint presentations. But since LinkedIn purchased the company, SlideShare has added full video content to its arsenal. Over 60 million professionals visit the site each month looking for high-quality presentations.

SlideShare's PRO feature (now free) is able to collect e-mail subscriptions while someone is viewing the presentation. This has now become CMI's third-best subscription generator.

Best resource: The Marketer's Guide to SlideShare by Todd Wheatland.

Instagram

Purchased by Facebook in early 2014 for $1 billion, Instagram is still the most dominant image-sharing social media site. Here are two ideas to leverage Instagram:

- **Share unique, behind-the-scenes, and personal content.** Get personal with your audience; give followers an insider view of the inner workings of your organization. A behind-the-scenes feel comes with an exclusivity factor.
- **Turn followers into sources of content.** Ask your followers for pictures that represent your brand, and reward the best contributors with recognition. Offer them a sense of ownership to strengthen the relationship.

Best resource: The Power of Visual Storytelling by Ekaterina Walter.

Pinterest

Pinterest is an extremely popular photo-sharing site, where you can actively manage your own photos and share images and videos from others. It's been extremely popular in the retail space to date. Interested in seeing if Pinterest can work for you? Here's some ideas that will help:

- **Decide if the platform fits your audience before jumping in.** As an interest-driven community, Pinterest is geared toward 18- to 34-year-old women, but it's beginning to expand. If a good portion of your audience lands in this category, it's a good fit.
- **It's more than just images.** Videos are powerful (and pinnable). If you have a strong repertoire of video content, use Pinterest to drive traffic back to your website or YouTube channel.
- **Show your customers some love.** Strengthen relationships, highlight success stories, and drive more traffic by creating a board showing off the achievements of your customers. It's a great way to illustrate your work without much braggadocio.
- **Share your reading list.** Share book recommendations that are relevant to your audience to establish a stronger bond. Leveraging books that you've actually read helps demonstrate your brand's commitment to constant improvement.

- **Show your company personality.** Instead of a lone product image or a posed staff picture, show your product or team in action for an image with more personality. Action shots help the people in your audience imagine themselves as a customer or client.

  Best resource: Pinterest Power by Jason Miles and Karen Lacey.

Google+

In March 2015 Google announced that it was splitting Google+ into photos and streams. Some believe that this marks Google's move away from Google+ into something completely different. Regardless, many businesses have found that Google+ can be one of the most powerful social media networks for active engagement.

For example, Copyblogger Media recently decided to kill its Facebook page entirely and focus on communicating with its audience via Google+.

Regardless, you need to be aware of the constant changes in Google+ (it's been this way from the beginning, as Google hasn't quite found the right fit yet).

Best resource: Pay attention to Mashable.com for the latest changes in Google+.

YouTube

I've listed YouTube here because it is indeed a social media network, but I believe the best opportunities in YouTube are as a platform, as we've seen with Matthew Patrick and Claus Pilgaard. If you choose to share content on YouTube outside the platform model, consider the following:

- YouTube is the number two search engine in the world, so developing content specifically for search findability is something you need to focus on.
- Whatever content you decide to publish on YouTube, do it consistently, just as you would on any other platform. The majority of companies publish without any particular schedule, which never works in building an audience.

Best resource: YouTube Marketing Power by Jason Miles.

Vine

Vine is a video-sharing service where you can record snippets up to six seconds long. As of August 2014, over 100 million people watch Vine videos each month.

Like YouTube, Vine is big business for Content Inc. models. Husband and wife Michael Alvarado and Carissa Alvarado are the folk-pop band *Us the Duo*. They have amassed more than 4.5 million followers and over 600 million loop plays of their vines, which they converted into a record deal with Republic Records, an international tour, and a recently released second album (Figure 17.2).

Best resource: The Beginner's Guide to Vine on Mashable (http://mashable.com/2013/12/11/vine-beginners-guide/).

Figure 17.2   Like YouTube, Vine is big business for Content Inc. models. The husband and wife team of Michael and Carissa Alvarado, are the pop band Us The Duo. They have amassed more than 4.7 million followers and over 700 million loop plays of their vines, which they converted into a record deal with Republic Records, went on to an international tour, and recently released their second album.

Tumblr

As of this printing, Tumblr now hosts approximately 500 million blogs, making it an industry powerhouse. Here are some tips to making Tumblr work for you:

- **Use your tags.** Tag content to help with searchability. Include descriptive tags on each piece of content to give your page much stronger visibility.
- **Post snippets of content.** Snag an eye-catching quote from a popular post on your blog, include the link and tags, and share the preview. Other snippets (like pictures) work well to offer a preview of your content before the viewer makes the jump.
- **Reblog, comment, and "like" often.** Use these features to share content from other Tumblr users. That way, you reduce some of the burden of content creation while still getting the attention of influencers. You can also create relationships that may result in more people sharing your original content.
- **Link back to your page.** Attach a link to your Tumblr on every piece of content you post. If content goes viral, users can trace it easily back to your page. Without that link, your content may spiral off, giving you very little ability to track sharing.
- **Focus your content.** Make sure your content fits a tight niche to help you dominate search results and focus in on the top ways your audience finds you.

Best resource: "Quick Guide" (Tumblr http://quickguide.tumblr .com/).

Medium

In 2012, Twitter cofounder Evan Williams launched a publishing site called Medium. Medium's objective is for individuals anywhere to be able to share their perspective with others in a meaningful way. It is, perhaps, the best place to create content and get ongoing community feedback within the content itself.

Personally, I love everything about Medium, from the user experience to the community interaction . . . except . . . you have little control over your audience. That said, if you are looking for an audience to share a

M

6. DESIGN FOR HABITS

Meaningful relationships and increased engagement are created by designing content and products that fit into a user's existing and underserved behavior.

NOTES

Love this point. So often we see things that are feature led and then companies find a reason or need to simply bolt users on to. User-centric thinking is critical from the get-go so that UX is robust, resilient and resonant with the user.

Leave a note for jim babb

BUILT FOR COMMUTERS

Much of WNYC's audience spends time underground commuting so they designed an app that pre-downloads the right amount of content for the trip.

Figure 17.3 Medium makes it possible to view comments in line with the content, instead of at the bottom like most blogs do.

particular point of view, and gain rapid feedback from that audience, Medium is a solid solution (Figure 17.3).

Best resource: The Marketer's Guide to Medium from KISSMetrics (https://blog.kissmetrics.com/marketers-guide-to-medium/).

Yik Yak and Snapchat

I've never used Yik Yak or Snapchat, but I've read enough articles to know that both services are going to be around for a while. Both social media sites give the users anonymity (if they wish). As more and more millennials move away from Facebook (this *is* happening), kids and young adults are finding a home on these two sites. If you target younger audiences with your content niche, you'll need to check for opportunities. If I had to put my money on the next big app, it would be Snapchat.

THE KEY ELEMENTS OF A SOCIAL MEDIA CONTENT PLAN

As mentioned above, for best results, you need a dedicated plan for every channel on which you intend to distribute social media content. Just because you *can* share something on every channel there is, doesn't mean that you should.

Percentage of Content Marketers Who Use Social Platforms to Distribute Content

	B2B North America	B2C North America	Nonprofit North America	B2B and B2C Austrailia	B2B and B2C UK
LinkedIn	91%	71%	53%	86%	85%
Twitter	85%	80%	69%	79%	89%
Facebook	81%	89%	91%	79%	75%
YouTube	73%	72%	65%	74%	65%
Google+	55%	55%	27%	47%	55%
SlideShare	40%	19%	5%	26%	33%
Pinterest	34%	18%	24%	29%	42%
Instagram	22%	32%	17%	30%	20%
Vimeo	22%	16%	15%	20%	25%
Flickr	16%	18%	22%	15%	21%
StumbleUpon	15%	13%	3%	14%	18%
Foursquare	14%	16%	10%	9%	17%
Tumblr	14%	18%	8%	10%	19%
Vine	14%	13%	5%	13%	17%

Figure 17.4   Most businesses leverage an average of five to six social media channels to distribute their content.

Source: 2014 Content Marketing Institute annual research: http://contentmarketinginstitute.com/research.

To start, it may be helpful to look at how most marketers are distributing their content in social media channels. The big three of LinkedIn, Twitter, and Facebook continue to dominate worldwide, with contenders such as Pinterest, SlideShare, and Instagram on the rise (Figure 17.4).

To create a basic social media plan, answer these questions for every channel you are considering.

What Is the Goal of This Channel?

You need a reason to be on every channel on which you decide to publish content. "To gain followers" is not a viable reason, in and of itself, but "to gain followers on Facebook to drive traffic back to our website to enlist subscribers" is. The important part here is that your content on the channel serves as a method to convert viewers into taking the next step in your Content Inc. process—i.e., move them from Facebook follower to website viewer, e-mail subscriber, event attendee, or however you monetize the platform.

What Is the Desired Action?

Similar to the point above, figure out what you want someone to do in each channel. Share? Comment? Visit your website? Register for something?

What Is the Specific Type of Content the Audience Wants to Get in This Channel?

Customize the content you distribute on each channel. Consider what messages are appropriate for each channel and create a message you think will resonate with that specific audience. Think about the kind of informational needs people in this channel have and how you can help. Will you primarily publish text, images, or video?

What Is the Right Tone for This Channel?

As you consider the topics and content formats in each channel, it's critical to determine what the overall tone for the channel should be. Friendly? Fun? Conversational? Professional?

What Is the Ideal Velocity?

It's a smart idea to understand how often you want to publish content in each channel. How many posts do you want to publish per day or week? What time of day is best? You'll have different cadences depending on if you are sending or responding to tweets, updating your Facebook status, or publishing a new SlideShare, for example. Our team found that posting on Facebook once or twice a day, monitoring Twitter all day, and spending time each day on LinkedIn works best for CMI. But every company is different, so you want to spend some time determining the schedule that's likely to work best for you and your customers.

Key tip: Let your goals dictate the decisions you make in regard to social media content. For example, since the goal of your Content Inc. plan should be to increase e-mail subscribers, would it really make sense to broadcast all your blog posts on Facebook and Twitter? What reason would readers have to subscribe to your e-mail program if they can get the same information on the social channels they already visit regularly? Think about how you can tweak and repurpose the content you share on your social networks, as it applies both to your goals for the channel and to your overarching business objectives.

AN EXAMPLE FROM CMI

As CMI has grown over the past eight years, so, too, has our social media presence. At the beginning, we admit to being a bit haphazard with our approach; but over the years we have developed a more strategic plan and tailored our content marketing processes accordingly.

Here is how our marketing director, Cathy McPhillips, and community manager, Monina Wagner, approach some of our key channels in terms of both content and distribution:

Twitter

We're active on Twitter every day, sharing thoughts from our community, as well as promoting our own content. However, our favorite thing we do on Twitter is our weekly #CMWorld chats (every Tuesday at noon ET). It's something we started in the summer of 2013 as a way to promote the topics and speakers from our annual Content Marketing World event, but it was so useful that our community asked us to continue the chats throughout the year. Twitter, both during the chats and at other times, has helped us develop a community of influencers and a trusted network. This community has guided many of our efforts in regard to our daily blog posts and even some sessions and tracks for Content Marketing World.

LinkedIn

Our LinkedIn strategy focuses on discussing industry trends with the members of our CMI LinkedIn group. We have noticed that this group tends to like content specific to careers and to content marketing strategies (see Figure 17.5). We've also used it to bounce around ideas we are considering for either our magazine or our live events. It has helped us gauge interest and needs and fine-tune some of our efforts, as a result. Also, by actively moderating posts within this community, our group members trust that the content appearing in our group feed has been vetted by the Content Marketing Institute, which helps maintain our position as a trusted content marketing resource.

Facebook

This is the channel where we like to share the fun side of CMI (after all, isn't that what Facebook is all about?). We use it to discuss news,

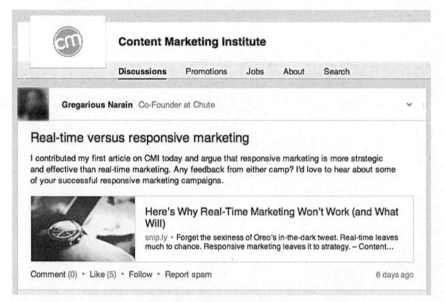

Content Marketing Institute

Discussions   Promotions   Jobs   About   Search

Gregarious Narain Co-Founder at Chute

Real-time versus responsive marketing

I contributed my first article on CMI today and argue that responsive marketing is more strategic and effective than real-time marketing. Any feedback from either camp? I'd love to hear about some of your successful responsive marketing campaigns.

Here's Why Real-Time Marketing Won't Work (and What Will)

snip.ly • Forget the sexiness of Oreo's in-the-dark tweet. Real-time leaves much to chance. Responsive marketing leaves it to strategy. – Content...

Comment (0) • Like (5) • Follow • Report spam   6 days ago

Figure 17.5   LinkedIn's recent content promotion changes have enabled businesses to get more attention for their original content.

events, and a new content marketing example each week, as well as to share exciting news and announcements on things that are happening within CMI. We have a fun team, and this gives us all an opportunity to showcase our personalities. Our weekly coverage of content marketing examples has allowed us to share some great work by brands, which has given our audience a chance to see the work of others and think, "We could do that too." We also try to inspire our audience with weekly motivational graphic posts (another great way to repurpose older blog posts and articles) (see Figure 17.6).

SlideShare

We aim to publish three or four new SlideShare presentations per month. It has been interesting to track which kinds of presentations get the most views and leads, and we make sure to mix up our presentations to align with our content marketing strategy and still generate interest and buzz. Since most of CMI's content is ungated, publishing presentations on SlideShare give our community access to view and reference nearly

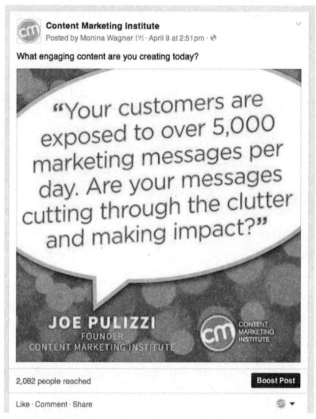

Figure 17.6 CMI takes quotes from senior staff, presents them visually, and shares them on Facebook weekly.

everything we produce—all we ask in return is an e-mail address if our customer wants to download the content (this is an important e-mail subscription generator for CMI). The longer-form content we share here has increased our subscribers, since these presentations are better suited for downloading and referencing or printing, while our short-form and livelier presentations have a higher tendency to get social shares and to draw in new followers.

CONTENT INC. INSIGHTS

- You don't have to be active in every social channel. At the start, choose the best two or three (where your audience is hanging out) and put resources behind them.
- Yes, we want to build out our digital footprint and audience on social channels, but remember the goal is to build our e-mail subscription audience as much as possible.
- Most businesses don't plan their content distribution on social media. It just happens whenever they get to it. Treat your social channels as importantly as any other communication channel.

Resources

Britt Klontz, "How to Keep Facebook Viable as a Content Marketing Platform," ContentMarketingInstitute.com, accessed April 28, 2015, http://content marketinginstitute.com/2014/05/keep-facebook-viable-content-marketing -platform/.

Maeve Duggan, Nicole Ellison, Cliff Lampe, Amanda Lenhart, and Mary Madden, "Demographics of Key Social Networking Platforms." PewInternet .org, accessed April 28, 2015, http://www.pewinternet.org/2015/01/09/ demographics-of-key-social-networking-platforms-2/.

Seth Fiegerman, "Why Google+ Is Splitting into Photos and Streams," Mashable.com, accessed April 28, 2015, http://mashable.com/2015/03/02/ google-plus-changes/.

Craig Smith, "25 Amazing Vine Statistics," expandedramblings.com, accessed April 28, 2015, http://expandedramblings.com/index.php/vine-statistics/.

Jon Swartz, "Twitter co-founder Evan Williams has plans for Medium," usatoday.com, accessed April 28, 2015, http://www.usatoday.com/story/ tech/2014/12/19/evan-williams-medium-co-founder-twitter-instagram/ 20320963/.

Jim Babb, "9 Ways the Most Innovative Media Organizations Are Growing," medium.com, accessed April 28, 2015, https://medium.com/@jimbabb/ 9-ways-the-most-innovative-media-organizations-are-growing-5ac50d 7457d5.

Business Insider, "The 30 Most Popular Vine Stars in the World," business insider.com, accessed April 28, 2015, http://www.businessinsider.com/most -popular-vine-stars-2014-12#22-us-the-duo-9.

Part 6

Diversification

Career diversification ain't a bad thing.
VIN DIESEL

You built the model and are reaping the rewards with new subscribers and audience loyalty. Now is the time to diversify your portfolio and stake your claim as the leading voice in the industry.

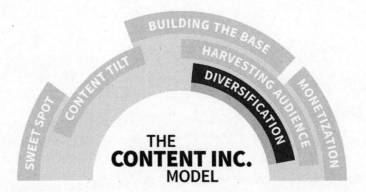

Chapter 18

The Three
and Three Model

We learn wisdom: First, by reflection, which is noblest; second, by imitation,
which is easiest; and third by experience, which is the bitterest.
CONFUCIUS

Now that your audience is growing, it's time to take your Content Inc.
strategy to the next level. In Content Inc. interviews we find trends,
consistencies, and surprising repetition in the patterns that define success. I call this the "three and three" model. The first three are personal.

IT'S PERSONAL: PLANNING THE FIRST THREE

In *Jeopardy* style:

The answer: A blog, a book, and speaking.

The question: What are the three most critical strategies an entrepreneur can do to build a thriving personal brand?

From personal experience, building a blog, writing books, and
spreading my message through public speaking have been the three
most impactful strategies for growing my personal brand. All three
have led to the most amazing business opportunities.

But it's not just me. Jay Baer, Ann Handley, Marcus Sheridan, Michelle Phan, Ann Reardon, and other successful thought leaders from around the world such as Michael Hyatt and Tony Robbins have used this strategy. Each of these successful entrepreneurs leverages the same formula. Let's break it down.

- **The blog.** A place on the web where you distribute your differentiated story on a consistent basis and which is shared by your audience to gain wider reach. Most Content Inc. strategies use this as the main platform.
- **The book.** The greatest business card on the planet. The book is your story in physical form. If someone asks you what you are all about, you hand the person the book.
- **Speaking.** The blog and the book lead to public speaking opportunities. Conference providers from around the world will reach out to you to gain your insight and expertise in the area you now own. Think of it this way—you will get paid to get your message in front of an entirely new audience (talk about stealing audience!).

Now that we have covered building your blog platform, here's how to execute the next two: the book and public speaking.

8 TIPS FOR EXECUTING A BOOK

In 2010, over 2 million books were published around the world (over 300,000 in the United States). Just a handful of people made money from the book itself. So here's the deal: done correctly, you make money from other things you sell in your Content Inc. program, not from the book directly. The goal for a book is to help expand your business opportunities.

Creating a book that makes an impact on your industry and business is anything but easy. Nevertheless, there are some tips I've picked up along the way (in publishing four books) that will make a difference in helping get your book off the ground:

1. Do a "Deep-Dive" Content Audit

You may already have a treasure trove of material that can be repurposed, or at minimum you have content that can be collected to form the initial workings of some key chapters. Be sure you do the work up front to see what you have to start with.

Key point: Don't overlook this step. Most individuals start from ground zero with writing a book. If properly done, a content inventory will give you a head start.

2. Mine the Blog

For all four of my books, including this one, a lot of the material, ideas, and content originated from existing blog posts. If you have six months of blogs, you might already have half a book. Now writing a book is not an easy endeavor, but you may have a lot of the raw content already at your disposal to develop a book.

Key point: The "blog-to-book" strategy can be amazingly effective. As you create content for your blog, keep your book in mind and start to build the chapters as you go, using the blog as the conduit.

3. Cocreate

Do you have key, noncompetitive partners that target the same prospects and customers as you? If so, consider reaching out to them about partnering on the book concept. Also, once you start promoting, you have two different networks to reach out to.

In a phone conversation with Newt Barrett in 2007, I learned that Newt was writing a book on content marketing, same as I was. After a few additional calls, we decided that partnering made more sense, and in 2008, *Get Content Get Customers* was born as a joint project.

Key point: You don't have to do this alone. Most likely, you have many partners who will benefit by getting your message out to the public (and they may have the content assets to help).

4. Get It Funded

My first book *Get Content Get Customers* was self-published before McGraw-Hill purchased the rights. Much of the up-front investment for the book was covered through selling bulk shipments to partner companies. This enabled us to cover much of the up-front costs of the book.

Jeff Rohrs, former VP of marketing at Salesforce.com and now chief marketing officer for Yext, was working on a book, entitled *Audience.*

He recognized quickly that the topics in the book were ones that his employer deeply cared about. Because of this, Salesforce assisted Jeff in bringing the book to life.

Key point: Most likely, there are players in your industry that care about the book you are producing. If it makes sense, approaching them early could help you fund your project.

> If you decide to publish the book yourself, try services like Amazon's CreateSpace or Lightning Source. Both services do on-demand printing. If you are willing to pay a publisher, check out a service like Advantage Media. It's pricier than doing it yourself, but the company handles everything in the process for you, including the ongoing marketing if needed.

5. Identify Your Mission—What You Want Readers to Get from Your Book

Be very clear about what you want your readers to get out of the book. Write it down and keep it posted on your wall as you work on the book. Many writers focus on what they are trying to say, instead of pinpointing the main focus of interest for the reader.

Key point: Go small to go big. Focus on a content niche with your book where you position yourself as the leading expert in your niche.

6. Include the Influencers

If possible, include key examples from industry influencers, as well as partners, as long as it's good content. The more people you include in your stories, the more opportunities for outside sharing.

Key point: Repeat after me . . . I should not write the entire book by myself. You'd be surprised about the number of people out there that would love to be included in your book and give you the rights to use their content (notice the number of guest articles in this book). Also, if you include others in the book, they are more likely to share it with their friends and colleagues.

7. Consider a Ghostwriter

Believe it or not, many of the books from the authors you love have been written by someone else. I know, hard to believe, right? But it's true. The best ghostwriters out there start at about $50,000 and then go up from there. If you simply can't make the internal time or don't have the resources to get it done, consider it.

Key point: You may not have the skills or the time to make a book happen. There are some amazing people out there who can help.

8. Get Editorial Help

Authors should not edit their own writing. If you want to create a professional piece you are proud of, you need to identify reviewers and editors that will give you honest feedback about the content and the style of the book.

Key point: One editor to review the book as you develop it and one editor to review the final manuscript are the bare minimum.

Elements of a Book Proposal

- **Title page.** Include an image and contact information.
- **Concept brief.** Highlight the problem and why the book's content will be valuable.
- **Concept summary.** Give a compelling overview of the book. Include the key takeaways that readers will learn.
- **Chapter outline sample.** Make this as complete as possible.
- **About the author.** Provide a detailed look at your life and tell why you are qualified to write this book.
- **Author's backstory.** Explain how you got to this point in life.
- **Book marketing section.** Include *all* your marketing assets. How many connections do you have on which channels? E-mail addresses? Upcoming speaking engagements? Any partnerships with trade associations? This is the most critical section. The publisher will want to know how many copies you can sell.
- **Audience section.** Show who the audience for the book is and why this book will fill a content gap.

> - **The competition.** List the books that most closely compare with your competitive set.
> - **Introduction to the book.** Include this if possible.
>
>   Overall, the proposal should be between 10 and 15 pages.

A book is not just a "nice to have," it's a game changer. A published book opens up more opportunities than you could ever imagine. Now is the time to put your big idea in motion.

TOP WAYS TO GET SPEAKING GIGS

It was the middle of 2008. At the time, I was still working on the blog platform and building a loyal audience. Newt Barrett and I had just released our self-published book (through Lightning Source), *Get Content Get Customers*. It was then that I received an intriguing e-mail from Belgium.

In the e-mail a large Belgian publishing company told me it was hosting a large customer event in Brussels and wanted to know if I was available to speak at the event. The company offered to fly me over, all expenses paid plus a small stipend. How did this happen? The blog and the book.

What I now know is that *it's next to impossible to truly be a thought leader in your industry without a killer blog, a thoughtful book, and a speech that rocks.* Yes, the first two are critical, but it's as a regular speaker where you hit the lottery. When you get regular speaking engagements, people talk about you, spread your message, and want to actively do business with you. It's where the magic happens.

> Many conference producers won't even consider you as a speaker unless you have a published book.

If you think public speaking can make a difference in your Content Inc. model, here are the top ways to get speaking engagements.

Back to the Blog: Your Proof of Expertise

If people asked you for proof of your expertise, what would you show them? Awards, perhaps? Maybe testimonials?

While those are fine and dandy, they are secondary in today's world of absolutely everything being available on the web. As a conference producer looking to choose the best speakers for our event, the first place I go is to the prospective speaker's blog. A *consistently delivered blog* is proof of both dedication to and passion for the industry. Also, if done properly, the blog very quickly shows your area of expertise. *That means if you blog about all sorts of topics, it will hurt you.* Get focused on what makes you a leading expert in your field.

A Video Example

For the Content Marketing World event, we received over 500 speaking submissions in 2015. I discounted almost 200 immediately because they didn't have a link to a prior speaking event or a compilation of speaking engagements.

Most conference planners won't sign on speakers without at least seeing them speak in some capacity. That means if the speaker selection committee hasn't seen you speak, and you don't have a proper example of your speaking skills in action, *you won't get the speaking engagement.*

If you've never done any speaking, make a video. Even an edited video will suffice so people can see you in front of a camera.

Andrew Davis has a website (at http://www.akadrewdavis.com/) dedicated just to his speaking. It includes multiple videos; there is even one that specifies what he believes makes a great speech and another that tells you how he can help you promote your event.

Get a Hook

You need something to stand out and separate yourself from the pack. Why should anyone choose you? Why are you special? Here are some ideas:

- **Get a color.** Orange is my color. I wear some form of orange to every event . . . shirt, suit, shoes, pocket square, etc. I have an entire ward-

Figure 18.1 Facebook expert Mari Smith leveraged her passion for one color to assist in her notoriety.

robe dedicated to the color, and I have set that expectation with my audience.

Social media expert Mari Smith uses turquoise as her color (Figure 18.1). She even decorates the stage before she begins her talk. If color is not your thing, try a certain theme or costume.

- **The elevator pitch.** Can you very quickly state what you speak about? Is it on "networking for shy people" or "how financial companies can grow without advertising"? Don't ever say you can speak on anything . . . that means you will speak on nothing. Refine the pitch that encompasses your niche.

Focus on the Hit List

So many public speaking wannabes talk about wanting to speak more often. When I ask, "What are the top events you'd like to speak at?" you'd think I'd asked them to recite the *Apostle's Creed*.

If you don't have a clear vision of where you want to speak, then you don't want it bad enough. Follow these steps:

- **Create your event bucket list.** Have a list of at least 10 events that your target customer attends. Then find out when speaking submissions are due for each event. Develop a calendar for it.
- **Contact each one, using the proper channels.** (Do not send an e-mail outside the form . . . event organizers hate that.) Convey a clear vision for your speech (where it could be placed, why it's a good fit, how long it will be). Include a link to your video. Event planners dislike uncertainty the most, so make sure you are specific and take out all the guesswork.
- **Share your terms up front.** If you require travel expenses paid, say that now to avoid conflict later. You'll be cutting yourself out of some events, but if that's your deal, that's your deal.

THE NEXT THREE: ALL BUSINESS

Now we turn our attention to the second "three" of our model. In contrast to the first three, which are personal, the next three—digital, print, and in person—are business (see Figure 18.2).

Take a look at some media brands that you may have heard of:

- **ESPN.** Multiple properties in digital, a print magazine, and multiple in-person events.

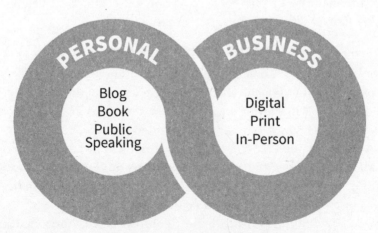

Figure 18.2 The three and three model, visually represented.

- **Forbes.** Multiple properties in digital, a print magazine, and multiple in-person events.
- **Inc.** Multiple properties in digital, a print magazine, and multiple in-person events.

As a publisher, I have always believed in the three legs of the publishing stool—print, digital, and in person. Those are the three key channels, and to be the true informational expert for your niche (like those listed above), you need all three. That's why we launched a print magazine and an in-person event in conjunction with our key platform (the blog).

As you begin to learn more about the behavior of your audience, you'll see patterns showing that the more you can get the people in your audience to engage in your content in different ways, the more likely they will be to buy from you.

CMI's main revenue driver is an event, Content Marketing World. It's imperative that we communicate in a way that maximizes the chances for our audience to attend the event in person.

After Content Marketing World 2014, we asked attendees what channels they access from CMI. What we found was astounding: 80 percent of our paid attendees consistently engage in at least three channels (Figure 18.3).

This is exactly why it's imperative at the diversification stage of the Content Inc. model to begin building out properties in each channel. Since the majority of this book covers digital channels in detail, let's quickly look at print and in-person events.

THE PRINT OPPORTUNITY

According to 2015 Content Marketing Institute and MarketingProfs research, only about one in three marketers uses the printed channel as part of a content marketing strategy. Marketers today are so focused on digital channels that they've all but forgotten the power of print.

Now am I saying that you should be looking at print as an opportunity right now to get and keep audience attention? Yes, that's exactly what I'm saying. *I believe there has never been a bigger opportunity for brands in the printed channel than right now.*

While I would not want to be in the broad-based, horizontal print game (à la *USA Today*), highly niche, highly targeted publications are

Attendees Also Engage with CMI:

CCO Magazine	
Weekly eMail Newsletter	
Blog or Daily eMails	
PNR: This Old Marketing Podcast	
Online Training	
Webinars	
#CMWorld Twitter Chat	
Consulting/Advisory Services	
Content Marketing Master Class	
None of the Above	

0   10   20   30   40   50   60   70   80

Figure 18.3   CMI finds that those that spend money to go to our events engage in multiple other content initiatives throughout the year.

flourishing as a marketing tool. For example, *ThinkMoney* magazine from TD Ameritrade sees about 90 percent of its customers take direct action on a product it sells through its print magazine. The magazine is a true collision of amazing design and provocative information. It's the type of content that is anticipated by its trader audience. And better yet, since traders are in front of computers all day long, they look forward to the opportunity to disconnect and discover.

And the best finding: subscribers who regularly read the magazine trade *five times* more than those who do not. Now that's a magazine that will always get budget approval.

Is Print Dead?

Digital prognosticators say that most print media will be gone in the next decade. I think anyone who makes those types of comments does not understand history. Just type into Google "the death of TV," and you'll see hundreds of articles predicting the end of television. One could make the argument that right now is the golden age of television, with amazing shows like *House of Cards, The Walking Dead,* and *Game of Thrones* leading the way.

The evolution of the Internet doesn't kill off these channels . . . *it makes us look at them differently* because they are used differently by consumers.

And just recently, online housing rental service Airbnb launched a customer magazine called *Pineapple* (the universal symbol for "welcome"). As well, digital car service Uber launched a magazine for its drivers called *Momentum.* When the most innovative companies on the planet are now looking at print, it's time to take notice.

Here are a few reasons to starting thinking print.

It Grabs Attention

Have you noticed how many fewer magazines and print newsletters you get in the mail these days? I don't know about you, but I definitely pay more attention to my print mail. There's just less mail, so more attention is paid to each piece (I actually get excited when *Inc.* magazine arrives at the office). Opportunity? With traditional magazines like *Newsweek, SmartMoney,* and others ceasing publication, there is a clear opportunity for brands to fill the gap.

Customers Still Need to Know What Questions to Ask

We love the Internet because consumers can find answers to almost anything. But where do we go to think about what questions we should be asking? I talked to a publisher recently who said: "The web is where we go to get answers but print is where we go to ask questions."

The print vehicle is still the best medium on the planet for thinking outside the box and asking yourself tough questions based on what you read—it's "lean back" versus "lean forward." If you want to challenge your customers, print is a viable option.

Print Still Excites People

I talked to a journalist who said it's harder and harder to get people to agree to an interview for an online story. But mention that it will be a printed feature and executives rearrange their schedules. The printed word is still perceived as more credible to many people than anything on the web. It goes to the old adage, "If someone invested enough to print and mail it, it must be important."

We've seen this firsthand with our magazine, *Chief Content Officer*. Contributors love being featured on the website, but they crave having their article in the printed magazine. It's amazing how different the perception is of the print versus online channel when it comes to editorial contribution. This goes as well for consumers.

Print Lets People Unplug

More and more, people are actively choosing to unplug, or disconnect themselves from digital media. I'm finding myself turning off my phone and e-mail more to engage with printed material. Today I relish the opportunities when I can't be reached for comment.

If I'm right, many of your customers (especially busy executives) are feeling the same way. Your print communication may be just what they need.

SOCIAL CONNECTIONS NEED
IN-PERSON EVENTS

I attended an executive meeting at Penton in the mid-2000s, where the subject of the meeting was what to do with our events portfolio. There was concern that because more of our audience was communicating online and, increasingly, through social media, there would be less of a need for conferences and events.

Boy, were we wrong!

In-person events and conferences continue to grow. As more people connect socially, we are seeing an increased need for those people to meet face-to-face.

Some questions to consider:

• Does your content niche have a dedicated event?
• If the answer is yes, could there be an opportunity to develop a small event for just one particular portion of your audience.

Let's look at CMI's event portfolio:

- Content Marketing World is the largest industry event. We have multiple tracks for marketers and business owners of all types. It attracts 4,000 delegates.
- Intelligent Content Conference is our West Coast event that only targets more technically savvy marketers and content strategists. It attracts 400 delegates.
- CMI Executive Forum is an invitation-only event for senior executives who are concerned about content marketing. It attracts 40 delegates.

Michael Stelzner added an event to his Content Inc. portfolio in 2012. Brian Clark added one in 2014. Rand Fishkin has been running his event, entitled Mozcon, for years.

The conference you design can be small, midsize, or large, but there is most likely a deep need for your audience to meet and network, strengthening your industry leadership at the same time.

Digital Events

As much as I believe in the power of in-person events, you may want to consider launching a digital event to test the waters. Webinars and virtual trade show technology from companies like ON24 and GoToWebinar are relatively inexpensive and logistically much easier to produce.

• • •

The greatest new and old media companies around the world started out leveraging one channel. As they have grown, each one has built out the digital, in-person, and print channels to wrap its readers in "content love." Your opportunity is to do this from an individual and business perspective to ultimately drive your Content Inc. model.

CONTENT INC. INSIGHTS

- As you begin to diversify your platform, be sure to look beyond digital for hidden opportunities. The greatest media brands in the world leverage not only digital, but in-person and print components as well.
- The most successful Content Inc. entrepreneurs focus on a blog, a book, and public speaking. All three of these in combination will help take your Content Inc. strategy to the next level.

Resources

Neha Jewalikar, "Are Social Media and Content Marketing the Same?," radius.com, accessed April 28, 2015, http://radius.com/2014/10/27/content-marketing -social-media-interview-joe-pulizzi-cmi/.

Statistica, "Facts on Trade Show Marketing in the United States," statistica .com, accessed April 28, 2015, http://www.statista.com/topics/1498/trade -show-marketing/.

Chapter 19

Building Out Extensions

Without continual growth and progress, such words as improvement,
achievement, and success have no meaning.
BENJAMIN FRANKLIN

Andy Schneider (the Chicken Whisperer) initially built his platform by doing in-person meetups (monthly gatherings with his audience in Atlanta) and home shows. That transformed into his very popular radio show, *Backyard Poultry with the Chicken Whisperer*, now over five years old. Andy then published the book *The Chicken Whisperer's Guide to Keeping Chickens*, followed by the print magazine, titled *The Chicken Whisperer Magazine*, sent to 60,000 subscribers.

Scott McCafferty and Mike Emich launched WTWH Media with one platform, Design World Online, as the go-to online product resource for mechanical engineers. Shortly after, *Design World* magazine (print) was launched. WTWH then launched both a customer event and an industry event for mechanical engineers.

And this was just the beginning. Scott and Mike have now launched additional platforms into several associated industries such as renewable energy, fluid power, and medical design (Figure 19.1). Today, with more than 1 million registered users, WTWH has gone from nothing to an $11 million business in less than 10 years.

embedded devices, mechatronics, robotics and real-time electronic parts sourcing and data sheet searching.

World brings interactive online tools, resources, social media engagement, podcasts, webinars, video, and tutorials to professionals worldwide.

Fluid Power World
Fluid Power World is written by engineers for engineers engaged in designing machines and or equipment in Off-Highway, Oil & Gas, Mining, Packaging, Industrial Applications, Agriculture, Construction, Forestry, Medical and Material Handling. Fluid Power World covers pneumatics, mobile hydraulics and industrial hydraulics.

Medical Design & Outsourcing
Medical Design & Outsourcing will explore and educate on the technical advancements in the design, development, and contract manufacturing aspects of medical devices and equipment.

1.6MM Registered Users   **1.8MM** Visitors*   **5.1MM** Page Views*   **810K** Followers**

*monthly
**Total of social media account followers
Summary of digital network

Figure 19.1   WTWH Media reaches over 1 million design engineers. It did this through the help of multiple acquisitions.

CHOOSING THE RIGHT EXTENSIONS

There are two different ways to launch additional platform extensions:

- **Adding channels within the same platform.** For example, Matthew Patrick and his Game Theory brand are in the midst of launching additional shows to target different audiences, all on the YouTube platform. Darren Rowse from Digital Photography School launched a subsite called Snappin Deals, as part of the current website platform.
- **Extending with current brand into new platforms.** This is the Andy Schneider example of taking the in-person platform and launching a radio show, a book, and a magazine.

The standard Content Inc. model is going to already have an online platform (a website or blog) and an e-newsletter offering to build the subscription list. From that, the most common brand extensions within the model are:

- Books
- Podcasts
- Events
- Magazines

Content Marketing Institute has launched brand extensions into all four platform types. Let's take a quick look at each one.

Books

Chapter 18 told you why developing a book is critical to building your personal brand and optimizing all possible business opportunities. At CMI, we assist the members of our staff in creating books in their core expertise area (Figure 19.2). For example, in addition to my own books (such as *Epic Content Marketing*), Robert Rose, our chief strategy officer, recently released his new book, *Experiences: The 7th Era of Marketing*. And we also partner with industry influencers. As examples, we helped underwrite and promote influencer books such as *Brandscaping* by Andrew Davis and *The Marketer's Guide to SlideShare* by Todd Wheatland.

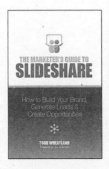

Figure 19.2   Just a sampling of some of the recent printed books launched through CMI.

Podcasts

CMI launched its first podcast in November 2013 called *PNR's This Old Marketing*, where Robert Rose and I cover the content marketing news of the week. This was a natural extension since CMI didn't have a news offering, and we believed our audience needed this kind of information. Each episode is repurposed into a blog post with show notes later in the week, as well as e-book compilations as subscriber giveaways.

On the basis of the success of *This Old Marketing*, CMI launched a podcast network that includes additional podcasts such as Andrew Davis's *Claim Your Fame* and Pamela Muldoon's *Content Marketing 360*.

Podcasts: Getting Started

It's easier than ever to get started with podcasting. Here's what you need:

- **A professional microphone to record your podcasts.** I recommend the Audio-Technica AT2020USB (cost approximately $100).
- **A way to record.** PC users can leverage Audacity for free. Mac users can use GarageBand. Both software programs will edit your podcasts.
- **A way to publish and syndicate your podcasts.** We use Liberated Syndicate (https://www.libsyn.com/), which hosts all our podcasts and automatically feeds them to iTunes and Stitcher.

Events

In September 2010, CMI announced that it was planning Content Marketing World, our flagship event, in September 2011. The key that made this work was a luncheon meeting that took place in November 2010. We organized the lunch with marketing and governmental leaders in Cleveland, Ohio, to announce the event and, we hoped, gain their support. At that event, we secured our platinum sponsor.

Initially we reserved hotel meeting space to accommodate 150 people. By the event date, we had 660 people attending the event, taking over much of the hotel space.

The event concept worked for the following reasons:

- We included influencers early in the process.
- We gave plenty of time for our audience to budget time and expenses for the event.
- We offered the people in our audience tools to attend the event, such as a complete document on how they could justify the event to their boss.
- We budgeted for a small event but secured a location that we could grow into if the need arose.
- We planned far in advance. As it was our first event, we had to learn all the ins and outs of event planning, and so the time was necessary.
- We hired a reputable and experienced event planner.

In five years, that little event idea has grown into 4,000 delegates from 50 different countries and is now the largest recurring business event in downtown Cleveland.

Magazines

Chief Content Officer (CCO) magazine (Figure 19.3) was launched in January 2011. As of September 2015, *CCO* has delivered 23 issues to 20,000 marketers for each issue. *CCO* is now critical to our overall strategy since the content of the magazine and the content of the original platform (the blog) are now fully integrated.

The original idea for *CCO* was to reach chief marketing officers and other senior marketers that had budgetary responsibility for content mar-

Figure 19.3   *Chief Content Officer* magazine.

keting. Our strategy was simple. Get the magazine into their hands, and they would begin to see content marketing as a valuable go-to-market strategy and start funding content resources within the enterprise.

Understanding the budgeting behind what makes a magazine work is critical. Areas to consider include:

- **Project management.** The fee for someone to oversee the production of the magazine.
- **Editorial.** Raw content costs (including outside contributors), managing editorial costs, and proofreading fees.
- **Design.** Someone to lay out the graphics for the publication.
- **Photos and illustrations.** Investment in any photo shoots or custom graphic creation.
- **Database fees.** Charges to make sure your audience list is postal ready.
- **Printing.** Cost to print the publication.
- **Postage.** Post office fees to deliver each issue.
- **Shipping.** Any bulk shipping fees from the printer or to your office location.
- **Commissions.** If your magazine is supported though advertising revenue, you'll need to pay a commission to the salesperson. Commission rates are generally 8–10 percent for one of your staff and up to 20–25 percent to hire a freelance salesperson who covers all his or her own costs.

Our general folio (page count) is between 40 and 64 pages. Your cost will depend on the number of total pages, number of editorial pages, and total print count, but you should prepare to spend at least $40,000 an issue. To subsidize this, we include sponsor advertisers in the publication to defray those costs entirely.

Although there are other extension options such as webinar programs, video series, and mobile apps, consider looking at these top four first: books, podcasts, events, and magazines.

Content Velocity

When Jon Loomer started his Content Inc. model, he produced 350 posts in the first year. In the second year, he decreased his output to 250 posts. By the third year, he was at 100 original pieces of content.

The point? As Jon built his audience and began to diversify into other content offerings, he realized he didn't have to create as much content to get the maximum amount of impact. Although this is different depending on the platform you are building, more content isn't always the best use of your resources.

CONTENT INC. INSIGHTS

- Once you've built the base, start to contemplate the best opportunities for diversification.
- One of the hottest Content Inc. extensions today is around podcasting. With the technology barriers coming down rapidly for podcasting accessibility, we have only seen the start of the podcasting revolution.

Chapter 20

Acquiring Content Assets

Buy land, they're not making it anymore.
MARK TWAIN

I recently sat in a marketing meeting with one of the largest producers of consumer goods in the world. The discussion centered on building audiences through content in various markets. In some of the markets, the company already had a solid content platform built. In others, there was nothing on the horizon.

The plan being discussed was an acquisition strategy of multiple properties where the organization would approach and, if terms were worked out, buy blogging sites and media properties that already had a built-in audience and content platform.

Sometimes it makes sense to build. Sometimes it makes sense to buy.

TWO THINGS

Blogging sites and media companies have two things that we want and need.

The first is the capability to tell stories. They have the people and processes to churn out amazing content on a consistent basis.

The second, and maybe more important, is that blogs and media sites come with built-in audiences.

Although merger and acquisition strategies have been happening ever since the first media company was launched, nonmedia companies are starting to get into this game recently. Photography supplies store Adorama put a buying group together when *JPG* magazine was going out of business. The group got access not only to JPG's Content Inc. platform and content, but also to JPG's 300,000 subscribers (which just happen to be Adorama's prospects and customers).

L'Oreal, the global makeup conglomerate, purchased Makeup.com from Live Current Media for over $1 million back in 2010. Marketing automation company HubSpot wanted to add an agency blog to match its marketing and sales blogs, so it approached Agency Post and acquired the blog instead of starting fresh (Figure 20.1). In mid-2015, the SurfStitch Group, a leading online retailer in Australia, purchased two small media companies in the surfing industry, further positioning SurfStitch as the clear content leader in the category.

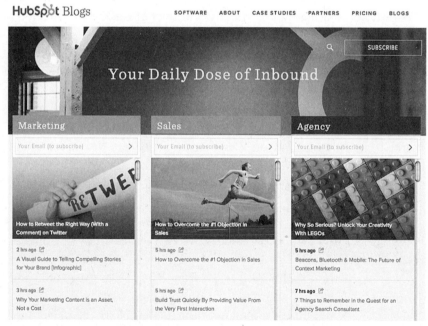

Figure 20.1 Marketing automation company HubSpot decided to acquire an outside blog, Agency Post, to fill its agency blog channel.

Scott McCafferty and Mike Emich founded WTWH Media, LLC, in 2006 after running a boutique media rep firm. Nine months previous, Scott attended sales meetings with six different publishing operations. At those meetings, Scott noticed a consistent trend: when he brought up online advertising solutions, every publisher told him to stay focused on selling print pages. Scott knew he needed to make a change.

Scott and Mike went ahead and developed a comprehensive business plan with close to 50 pages detailing projections and assumptions. Within that nearly 10-year-old plan, there were two critical factors that remain true today. They believed readers would take control of their information channels and marketers would require measurable results from their investments.

As the business grew, Scott often referred to business advice he received from David Murdock, chairman and CEO of Dole Food Company. In a social meeting with Mr. Murdock, Scott asked him how he bought and sold companies. Murdock stated that he simply made a list of the industries in which he wanted to acquire a business and a list of companies he wanted to purchase. He then would call each owner and ask if he or she wanted to sell. Some would say yes; some would say no.

Applying Mr. Murdock's advice, Scott made lists of websites in technologies that WTWH covered. He then e-mailed the owners asking if they would consider selling. Over an eight-year period, WTWH has identified and negotiated five transactions applying this principle. Along the way, he recognized a certain mix of common ingredients within each transaction.

- Typically, the sites were community based with an active user group.
- They were owned and operated by a single operator who viewed the business as a hobby.

Today, WTWH Media, LLC, is a four-time Inc. 5000 honoree with close to 50 team members headquartered in Cleveland, Ohio. The company manages close to 40-plus technology-based websites, five print publications, and a series of vertical events and provides marketing services in the design engineering, renewable energy, fluid power, and medical markets. In 2015, the company forecasts close to $11 million in sales.

As you build out your Content Inc. strategy to grow your industry dominance, acquisition strategies are a natural path to follow.

THE PROCESS OF ACQUIRING A CONTENT PLATFORM

CMI purchased multiple properties to add to its platform, including a West Coast conference called Intelligent Content Conference and an awards program dubbed (fittingly) the Content Marketing Awards. We made the decision that purchasing these platforms made more sense than creating them from scratch and then competing with these properties.

To acquire new platforms, follow these seven steps.

Step 1. Determine Your Goal

Like any good business decision, start by determining the reasons it might possibly make sense to purchase an existing content platform. Your business objectives for a purchase might include:

- To cover a geographic area that your business is currently absent from with an in-person component. The ultimate goal would be to reach more customers for cross-selling, up-selling, and decreasing your customer turnover rate in that region.
- To insert your brand into the conversation around a topic you are not well known for. Let's say you manufacture a certain type of steel, and you've identified some use in the oil and gas industry. It may then make sense to look at smaller oil and gas blog sites or events and immediately become a credible part of the industry lexicon.
- To accomplish subscription objectives. Most likely, the platform will come with a built-in audience for you to nurture, grow, or leverage for cross-selling.
- To purchase the content assets themselves and the associated search engine optimization and sharing benefits with them.

Step 2. Clearly Identify the Audience

For this to work, you need a clear understanding of the audience gap you are trying to fill. For example, CMI targets senior-level marketers at large organizations for our magazine, *Chief Content Officer*. We target marketing, PR, social media, and SEO managers and directors (the "doers") at mid-market and larger enterprises for Content Marketing World (our event).

Step 3. Make Your Short List of Platforms

After you identify your objective and your audience, start making a list of relevant platforms that will help you meet your goals. The key is to avoid setting any limitations at this point. You can list events, blog sites, media sites, association sites, and maybe even some sites directly from your influencer list.

When you are making the list, it's handy to put it all into a spreadsheet containing relevant subscriber information such as:

- Origination date.
- Current number of subscribers.
- Known revenue sources (list each of them).
- Ownership structure (for example, independent blogger or media company).

For a conference or trade show, here is a list of assets we look for when purchasing an event:

- Number of attendees (past two years) with percentage of growth (or loss).
- Number of exhibitors (past two years) with percentage of growth (or loss).
- Number of media partners (past two years).
- General regional location.
- Registration cost (rate card).
- Marquee value (this is a subjective rate determining the cache for the event—a five-point scale should work just fine).
- Possibility for setting up a media platform around the event (again, something on a five-point scale is sufficient). The idea here is that there may be potential to build the event into a fully functional media platform with online content, web events, and more.

Step 4. Approach the Best Opportunity

There are two approaches I recommend, and I've seen both of them work. You can reach out to your top pick and see where the conversation goes. The issue is that you are putting all your eggs in one basket. A better option may be to approach your top three picks all at once and convey your intentions (i.e., that you are interested in purchasing their website, event, etc.).

You'll likely be amazed at the reactions you receive. Some of the operators will never have imagined that they'd be approached on a purchase. Others (probably those with a media background) will already have an exact idea of their exit strategy and what they are looking for.

The key at this point is to get discussions started so you can gauge where potential interest may lie. Worst-case scenario when approaching a possible seller that isn't interested in selling is that you now have the potential to grow a relationship from this first contact. Simply put, you never know when intentions might change, and now you have an inside track if they do.

> Andrew Davis believes that the best opportunities for acquisition are amazing content creators that lack any kind of business model. The good news? Today every industry has many of these.

Step 5. Determine the Purchase Value

There is a standard measure to smaller web properties and events (we will get to that in a second), but this first part is critical: *figure out what the owner wants.* Just like you do with your influencers, it's your job to find out what the platform owner's goals and aspirations are. Maybe it's just monetary (though this is unlikely). Perhaps the owner is looking for a new opportunity, or he or she desperately wants out of the business (many blog site owners or event owners never imagine that their project might get larger than what they can manage or might grow in a different direction than what they intended).

As I said, there is a proper valuation process for smaller web properties and events. To do this, you both need to sign a mutual nondisclosure agreement for protection—on both sides. Then you want to request the business's profit and loss statement for the previous two years, at least. You may also need to see documentation on current sponsorship agreements and other contracts the company holds to confirm that its P&L statement can be verified. (*Important note:* Legal specifics can vary widely, so please consult your legal representation before you approach any opportunity.)

For website purchases, some deals are done on a "per-subscriber" basis, some on a net profit basis. In one example I personally worked on, a media deal was based on paying $1 per subscriber. In another, it was five times earnings, paid out over a two-year period. Smaller conferences generally go for around five times net profit (for example, if the annual profit of the conference is $100,000, you would pay $500,000 for the property).

Let's look at a small conference example:

Attendees: 250

Exhibitors: 20

Revenue: $340,000

Expenses: $270,000

Net profit: $70,000

General value of the business: $70,000 × 5 = $350,000

There is a bit more that goes into it, but the estimated general value of this event would be around $350,000.

Step 6. Make Your Offer

Before you make a formal offer, you want to make sure that your price is in the right ball park and that the owner agrees to the basics of your terms. If you have that agreement, you'll need the event owner to sign a formal letter of intent (LOI). The LOI basically means that both sides agree to continue the conversation and take the relationship to the next level of the process; it's the business acquisition equivalent of getting engaged—while it's not a meaningful or legally binding act in and of itself, it serves as an official statement of your intentions. (*Note:* Please consult legal representation on creating an LOI.)

Step 7. Enter Final Negotiations

Now, before you sign anything, consider these final questions:

- What e-mail and print lists are available? What permissions do you have to send to the company?
- What assets are available? Videos? Blog posts? SlideShares? Conducting a full audit of the company's assets might be necessary.
- What are the social channels in use?
- Who are the prime influencers in this space that we should connect with? Request contact details and areas of expertise (if needed).
- What vendors does the company work with? Whom would it recommend?

Over the following 30 to 60 days, you would be working on a formal asset purchase agreement and reviewing all the documentation to make sure all facts, figures, and discussions are accurate and verifiable. From there, contracts are signed, followed by corks being popped on your celebratory bottles of champagne (optional, but a nice touch).

CONTENT INC. INSIGHTS

- You have a real decision to make as you develop your plan for extensions . . . should you build or buy?
- Buying becomes expensive without a plan. If you can determine the properties you want and build relationships with those owners over time, the better the chance for an acquisition and a lower price.

Resources

James Dillon, "Should You Buy or Grow a Pineapple for Your Audience?," ContentMarketingInstitute.com, accessed April 28, 2015, http://contentmarketinginstitute.com/2015/02/buy-or-grow-pineapple-audience/.

Andrew Alleman, "L'Oreal Buys Makeup.com for 7 Figures," domainnamewire.com, accessed April 28, 2015, http://domainnamewire.com/2010/03/04/loreal-buys-makeup-com-for-7-figures/.

Part 7

Monetization

I will tell you the secret to getting rich on Wall Street.
You try to be greedy when others are fearful.
And you try to be fearful when others are greedy.
WARREN BUFFETT

You've created a relationship with a loyal audience. You've built the base and have diversified into multiple channel extensions. Now is the time to reap the rewards.

THE
CONTENT INC.
MODEL

Chapter 21

Waiting for Revenue

Ma'am, I don't doubt the steak was overcooked,
but did you have to eat it all before you complained about it?

DAN FROM THE MOVIE *WAITING...*

As Brian Clark discusses in the Foreword of this book, Content Inc. models can better monetize the program when they get to their MVA, or minimum viable audience. As he explains: "An MVA is the point when your audience starts growing itself through social sharing and word-of-mouth. Even better, it's also when you start getting the feedback that tells you what product or service your audience actually wants to buy."

Successful Content Inc. companies don't just get to an MVA point or level-of-subscribers point and then make a decision to sell a product. All along the way, these savvy entrepreneurs are leveraging creative thinking to sustain the business model while it is being developed and is growing.

This chapter reveals how I did it upon launching our Content Inc. model.

IN SEARCH OF ... MONEY

In March 2007 when I left an executive position with excellent benefits to start a new company, I launched without a sustainable income

237

source. So while I began to build the Content Inc. approach for myself, I started consulting for media companies and associations.

One association in particular, a small nonprofit focused on mechanical engineers, needed to develop strategies for generating new revenue streams from its publishing portfolio. The advertising revenue from its magazines was slowly deteriorating. At the same time, the association had major challenges trying to increase digital revenue from sales of online banners and buttons. Adding to the challenge was the fear at the association that without increased sales, major layoffs were in the works.

After a few hours analyzing the association's media information and conducting staff interviews with its sales and marketing teams, I found four key issues:

- The sales team was accustomed to and focused on selling print advertising. Selling online products was completely foreign to these sales and marketing professionals.
- The association's core advertisers were just dipping their toes into buying online advertising to promote their products and services.
- There was no digital sales strategy for the association. Simply put, the salespeople were winging it.
- Traffic on the website was still nascent. It was a major challenge to sell digital products because the association's website didn't have enough eyeballs on the content (yet).

It looked like a long road ahead. Normally this would be fine, but my contact said we simply didn't have the time to wait for the traffic to increase. We needed new revenue now to survive.

From this desperation, we developed the limited-inventory model.

If you understand the life of a print advertising salesperson, there is always inventory. You can always add another form (more pages) to a magazine to accommodate an ad. The magazine publisher will gladly add more pages if new revenue is on the way. Sure, we have sales targets and anticipated folios (the page count of the magazine), but we can always sell more ads.

This is exactly how the salespeople were selling digital. They were selling unlimited space availability to a finite group of online readers . . . and no one was buying.

We developed a new limited-inventory model that looked something like this:

- We didn't call it advertising. We called it sponsorship.
- We limited the number of available sponsors per month—from unlimited (in theory) to six sponsors.
- The sponsors received a logo at the bottom of every page and were listed as "Association Partners."
- Each sponsor split the inventory six ways, meaning that each sponsor received a digital advertisement that was promoted to one-sixth of all the site visitors.
- We significantly increased the cost of the sponsorships, versus what the former display advertising cost.
- We offered category exclusivity for a 50 percent increase in investment.

At first, the members of the sales team detested the idea. They believed that limiting the products they could sell would hurt their livelihoods. In addition, they didn't like the "six-sponsor" concept because it could shut out some advertisers, and if that happened, the association could take a credibility hit for not being open to all supporters.

Fortunately (or not), we didn't have a choice. We had less than three months to turn it around, or people were going to lose their jobs.

The next week, we sent out an e-mail simultaneously to the promo list (all possible advertisers) about the opportunity. Once the e-mail was sent, the salespeople called their best customers and talked through the opportunities, basically saying "When they're gone, they're gone . . . but I want to give you first crack at the opportunity."

Inside a week's time we had confirmations for the next six months. Yes, we sold out of inventory. From a revenue perspective, it was already a 500 percent increase in digital revenue from the previous year.

From that moment on, all digital products were sold on a limited-inventory basis, including webinars, e-book and white paper sponsorships, and specialized directory listings.

THE BENEFACTOR MODEL

Why is this story relevant? As we've discussed, the Content Inc. model, the informational annuity that it is, takes time and patience to work. If you are in a situation similar to mine, you probably need a source of income until you build your audience and find your ultimate product.

And this is the position I was in just a few months after that association consulting engagement.

My wife, an accomplished social worker, left her job a few years before I started the business to stay home with our two boys, then ages three and five. We needed an income to survive. Sure, we cut our expenses down to the limit, but we still had a mortgage, a car payment, and two kids to feed. The consulting would have worked fine on its own, but since we were investing so much into our future product (a content marketing matching service), there wasn't enough to support the family. By 2009, we were bleeding cash as an organization.

The core matching service wasn't growing at my anticipated projections. In other words, the financial model was flawed. The more I scrutinized the model, the more negative my thoughts grew. After multiple conversations with my wife, I was very close to closing down the business and going back to find a job.

And it was then that I remembered the limited-inventory model.

MAKING THE PIVOT

After weeks of thinking about whether to double down or jump ship, I went back and analyzed the audience we had developed (see the section in Chapter 7 on listening posts).

- What were the biggest pain points?
- What were people asking to buy?
- Was there some low-hanging fruit in revenue opportunities that we were missing?

Only a very small percentage of our audience members were interested in finding content vendors. The majority were in need of education, training, and tools to help them succeed at content marketing. It was no wonder we were seeing massive requests for consulting and speaking . . . their need wasn't vendor selection; it was education and training. This insight was a game changer!

We decided to change the revenue model around sponsorship and events (more on that in the next chapter). The problem: we still needed revenue now.

Enter our limited-inventory model—the benefactor package. I immediately began calling and e-mailing our best supporters, offering them an opportunity to fund our new direction. This included opportunities for just 10 companies, where each "benefactor" received 10 percent of our site promotion and the opportunity to include content on our site (sponsored content).

Within a few weeks we were sold out. This strategy enabled us to fund our pivot and keep going. The following year, we made the Inc. 500 as one of the fastest-growing small companies in North America.

We still sell the benefactor package today, and no sponsorship slot has ever been open for more than a few hours. I've listed the full details below with the idea that you could develop something similar for your key supporters.

CMI's Benefactor Package
(as outlined in the 2015 CMI Media Kit)

- *Become a benefactor of CMI: $35,000 USD LIMITED availability—Only offered to TEN companies annually*
- *Access to author educational blog posts on CMI online*
- *Submitted posts MUST adhere to CMI's editorial guidelines: http://contentmarketinginstitute.com/blog/blog-guidelines/*
- *CMI has the right to decline any blog post that does not meet its editorial guidelines/standards*
- *If desired, sponsor can work with a CMI content/account manager (exclusive benefactor benefit) to help shape content topics, direction and adherence to CMI's guidelines/standards*
- *Sponsor has the option (at an additional cost) to approach CMI's custom content team to author a blog post, with collaboration from the sponsor*
- *12 months of online banner display advertising (10% of all advertiser impressions via 250 × 250 creative unit)*
- *Ad inclusion in weekly CMI enewsletters and daily blog alerts (minimum 40 per year)*
- *Branding on footer of every CMI website page*
- *First chance at special partnerships and opportunities*

GENERATING REVENUE UNTIL THE PRODUCT IS IDENTIFIED

If you are like most Content Inc. entrepreneurs, you need to identify revenue opportunities throughout the process to keep paying the bills. CMI did it through the benefactor model. Digital Photography School did it through affiliate sales. *Game Theory* did it through YouTube advertising. Moz did it through consulting. Copyblogger Media did it through royalties from partner product sales.

Today all these companies are multimillion-dollar enterprises growing at some of the fastest rates around.

In the next chapter, we'll go through all the opportunities for you to build and sell products on top of the platform. Until you get to that point, think creatively about how to keep paying the bills like other successful Content Inc. entrepreneurs.

SO WHEN SHOULD I START MONETIZING THE PLATFORM?

I have the opportunity to meet with entrepreneurs on an ongoing basis. In many of these conversations, the question often arises about when they should start monetizing their products or services. My answer is always this: "Today!"

For Content Inc. to work, you don't have to go through each of the five stages and then think about revenue. You need to be thinking about making money from your platform from day one. For CMI to work, I sold the dream of what it was going to be to our benefactor sponsors. It was that revenue that enabled us to build out the platform.

Ardath Albee, author of multiple books including *Digital Relevance*, believes that the best place to start a content approach is with your most important relationships. The same holds true for your Content Inc. monetization model. If you've been working your influencer channels properly, those same people should be your first options for locating revenue opportunities.

CONTENT INC. INSIGHTS

- It will take time to find the right monetization model for your business. In the meantime, begin to experiment with different ways to make money from your content asset.
- You don't need a lot of support to get started, just the right support. Focus on a few companies that are passionate about your content to help offset expenses.

Resource

Ardath Albee, *Digital Relevance*, Palgrave Macmillan, 2015.

Chapter 22

Building
the Revenue Model

A successful man is one who can lay a firm foundation
with the bricks others have thrown at him.

DAVID BRINKLEY

According to *Entrepreneur* magazine, the majority of people make money in very few ways. Individuals who collect a salary from a business generally have one or maybe two sources of income (their paycheck and possibly an investment account). Perhaps you know many people in this situation. They go to the same job every day, work to pay off their bills, and don't have much left over for savings or investment after each month.

Millionaires, on the other hand, have multiple sources of revenue coming in, whether that's through multiple businesses (and multiple products and services within those businesses), real estate transactions, countless investments, or more.

That's exactly the type of thinking that surrounds entrepreneurs who engage in a Content Inc. strategy.

YouTuber Rob Scallon describes it this way:

I'm always trying to think up new ways to diversify and have more streams of revenue. My band recently had a song licensed for a national TV ad, which was really exciting. I would love to do [more] licensing. I would love to do merchandise too . . . there are a whole lot of different revenue streams around my YouTube channel that I do take advantage of and I do get excitement out of.

Whether you are an entrepreneur in a start-up environment or running a Content Inc. program in a large organization, you should always be thinking of how many ways you can monetize the asset of content you are consistently creating.

REVENUE RIPPLES

Doug Kessler, cofounder of Velocity Partners, introduced a concept on Todd Wheatland's *The Pivot* podcast that he refers to as "ripples" within a content marketing program. For the most part, marketers measure content programs by increasing sales, saving costs, or creating more loyal customers. These are the obvious objectives, with their associated metrics. But Kessler believes that there may be a more important metric, the one that he called "ripples."

Ripples are the unexpected benefits that come from a Content Inc. approach . . . like an invitation to speak at an event, someone spreading the word about your expertise, or other unanticipated benefits of becoming a leading expert in your field.

When it comes to revenue for your Content Inc. program, it's all ripples. When we begin a Content Inc. approach, we are most likely unsure what the revenue possibilities could be. For example, River Pools & Spas had no idea that its Content Inc. revenue line would be through manufacturing. Matthew Patrick didn't think for one day that YouTube would call him up for his expertise.

We need to go through the process to get there . . . but when we do, the benefits are powerful.

CASE STUDY: CHEF MICHAEL SYMON

Michael Symon is perhaps the best-known celebrity chef from Cleveland, Ohio. Michael's entrepreneurial journey started in a fairly typical way (for a restaurant owner) with a restaurant in Cleveland and one in New York. He was slowly growing, adding more restaurants, but it wasn't until Michael appeared on *Iron Chef America* in 2007 that everything changed. From there, he continually starred on Food Network shows, culminating in a lead spot on *The Chew*, a daily, syndicated talk show on ABC.

Michael is seen by millions a day now on various network shows, but the key is that he's converted that into an audience of over a million social media fans in just a few short years.

Michael's restaurant business is thriving, including launching gathering spots like Bar Symon and amazing burger joints like B Spot. As of today, Michael is involved in dozens of profitable restaurant ventures, but it's his ancillary activities that are most worth noting. Michael has built a platform from which he now derives additional revenues including:

- Books—*Michael Symon Live to Cook* and *The Chew: What's for Dinner?*
- Licensing of specialty food items to Aramark (which runs Quicken Loans Arena, home of the Cleveland Cavaliers)
- Paid spokesperson for Vitamix and Calphalon and official partnerships with companies such as Lay's Potato Chips
- Official Michael Symon cookware from Weston
- His own brand of signature knives

The list goes on. What works for Chef Symon and other celebrities that build a Content Inc. platform is deriving multiple revenue streams from the content. A shortsighted business model may only look at the added attention to generate more restaurant sales. Michael Symon has taken his audience and generated dozens of different ways to make money.

CONTENT INC. REVENUE EXAMPLES

Here are some Content Inc. examples and how they monetize their audience.

The Content Marketing Institute, the content marketing educational website, makes money from its platform in the following ways:

- Attendees paying to attend live events
- Sponsors paying to exhibit at live events
- Readers investing in online training
- Sponsorship of live online webinars
- In-person corporate workshops
- Ongoing consulting retainers
- Book purchases
- Podcast sponsorships
- E-mail newsletter sponsorships
- Sponsorship of direct e-mail promotions
- Paid speaking opportunities for CMI staff
- Online website sponsorships

Michele Phan, the YouTube makeup star, generates revenue from:

- YouTube advertising royalties
- Book royalties
- Paid appearances
- Music label she launched, called Shift Music Group
- Partnership with L'Oreal on a makeup line called "em"
- "MyGlam"—a beauty products subscription site she cofounded
- YouTube talent network she launched

Andy Schneider, the Chicken Whisperer, monetizes his platform through:

- Event sponsors such as Kalmbach Feeds
- Paid magazine subscriptions
- Magazine advertisers
- Podcast sponsors
- Paid appearances
- Book royalties
- Website sponsors

Darren Rowse at Digital Photography School grows his platform with:

- Affiliate programs (paid royalties from promotion on-site)
- Purchased e-books and tutorials
- Paid online training programs
- Online advertising
- Brand extension sites such as Snappin Deals

Brian Clark at Copyblogger Media monetizes his platform through:

- Software subscription products such as Rainmaker Platform
- Hosting services such as Synthesis
- Paid sponsors for Copyblogger Media events
- Registration fees for event attendees

Over the years, Brian has leveraged dozens of additional products and affiliate programs that have paved the way for his current fast-growing products lines.

WAYS TO MONETIZE YOUR CONTENT

Marc Andreessen, multibillionaire and cofounder of Netscape, is one of the largest technology investors on the planet. As of March 2015, he has made 33 investments through his venture capital company, Andreessen Horowitz. If Andreessen lets his money do the talking for him, he's making a big bet on content platforms. With investments in companies such as Reddit (the online community site), PandoDaily (news and information site), and BusinessInsider (news and information site), Andreessen believes the future of media has never been stronger.

Except for one thing. Andreessen believes the business model for media companies needs to be expanded beyond just advertising: "The news business should be run like a business."

Those leveraging a Content Inc. model can make money in a variety of ways from their content. In Andreessen's words: "This isn't a pick one model and stick with it prospect; news [or *Content Inc.*] businesses should mix and match as relevant."

Let's review the different ways to monetize your Content Inc. platform.

Advertising and Sponsorship

Advertising revenues are still the go-to business model for most media companies. Simply put, a company wants access to your audience and pays you to give it that access, which may come in the form of a banner advertisement, a print ad in your magazine, or a booth sponsorship at your event.

Baking queen Ann Reardon makes the majority of her revenues from collecting YouTube advertising royalties while she diversifies her revenue streams. Some YouTubers, like Daniel Middleton, who runs *The Diamond Minecart*, a Minecraft video series with 4.3 million subscribers, has deployed his own outside mobile app for viewing in the hope of someday cutting YouTube out of the royalty equation and selling to sponsors directly.

If you are getting into the advertising-sponsorship game, the best model is to sell packages directly to prospective advertisers. For example, CMI's weekly podcast, *This Old Marketing*, sells to one sponsor for each episode, which covers the cost of producing the show and throws off a nice bit of profit.

While there is nothing wrong with collecting advertising revenue, it's important as a Content Inc. business to not get seduced into this one form of revenue creation. Just like a diversified stock portfolio, we would never put all our assets into one stock.

An Opportunity with Native Advertising

Sharethrough defines native advertising as a form of paid media where the ad experience follows the natural form and function of the user experience in which it is placed. In simple terms, the advertisement looks like the content. This could be paid content that looks like an article on a media site, or it might be a post on LinkedIn that looks exactly like all the other updates from the people you follow.

There is probably no term that is getting greater play in the marketing space right now than native advertising. Even the largest media brands in the world, like the *New York Times* and *Wall Street Journal*, are trying to figure out how to generate revenues from sponsored content.

There could be a great opportunity for you to "dip your toe" into the sponsored content game, but it's imperative to understand all the moving parts.

Native advertising is growing as a part of the larger advertising sector for a few reasons:

1. Media brands (including Content Inc. models like yours) and social platforms (like LinkedIn and Facebook) are aggressively offering native advertising products.
2. Brands now spend approximately 25 to 30 percent of their budget on content marketing initiatives. Brands have started to make this a priority, so native advertising is seen as a viable opportunity.
3. When done right, it can work. For example, the majority of BuzzFeed's revenues are through native advertising, and this strategy has been so successful that the company has been able to generate revenues at a substantial premium over traditional online advertising.
4. There is a renewed passion in the advertising community around native. This "new advertising" (even though it's not new at all) has given hope to media buyers around the world that something can perform better than a banner ad.

Examples of Native Advertising

If we take a very broad approach to native advertising, it may look like:

- Paid search units like you'd find on Google or Bing (see Figure 22.1)
- Promoted listings you find on Twitter (Figure 22.2)
- Sponsored content updates you find on LinkedIn (Figure 22.3)
- Content recommendation engines you find on Fast Company (Figure 22.4)
- An SAP-sponsored post on the Forbes website (Figure 22.5)
- A 6-second vine for HP honoring Valentine's Day, created by Folk-pop group Us the Duo (Figure 22.6).

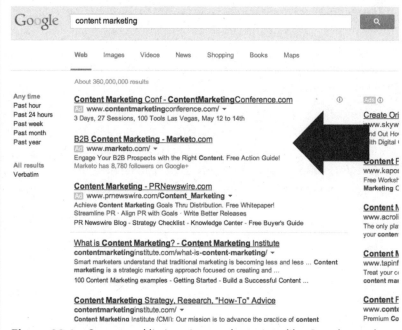

Figure 22.1 Sponsored listings in search engines like Google are the original digital native advertising.

Figure 22.2 Sponsored tweet example on Twitter.

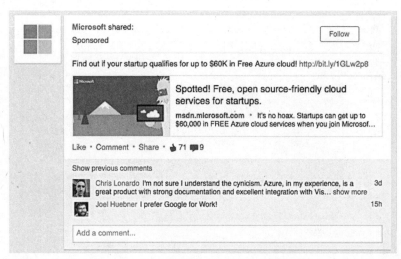

Figure 22.3 Sponsored content example on LinkedIn.

Figure 22.4 Content recommendation example that you find on sites like Fast Company and CNN.

Figure 22.5 SAP pays for the opportunity to publish content that looks like editorial content as part of the Forbes BrandVoice program.

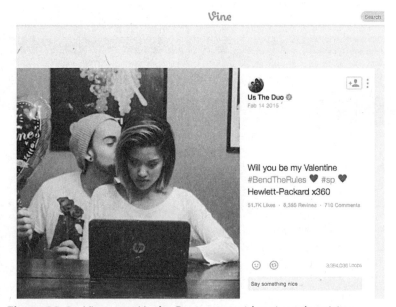

Figure 22.6 Vine stars Us the Duo run a paid native advertising program on behalf of HP.

What Are the Benefits of Native Advertising?

If you approach a company that has direct access to its entire audience through e-mail or another connection, it probably will have no need for native advertising (or any advertising for that matter). Most organizations are not in that position, which is why native advertising can be valuable (they are trying to steal audience, as we showed you in Chapter 16).

Other considerations:

- **On the smaller mobile screen,** the stream itself is the entire user experience. More and more, display advertising is not available. In the future, advertising options on mobile may only be native advertising. If a potential sponsor wants to reach your audience via mobile, native advertising is a possible revenue stream.
- **Traditional banner ads generally do not perform well.** According to *Adweek*, the average click-through for traditional banners is 0.12 percent. That means you are more likely to get hit by a bolt of lightning than click on a banner ad.
- **Rent-to-own strategy.** Native advertising can be a core strategy for sponsors to borrow your credibility and then transfer that good faith over to their own brand. At the same time, they are trying to make your audience their own. You need to be careful here as well.

The Best Way to Use Native Advertising

If you pursue native advertising as part of your Content Inc. strategy, consider the following:

- **It cannot sell.** The content needs to be educational, informative, helpful, or interesting. If it's just about your sponsor's products and services, it probably won't cut the mustard. In addition, most media brands have quality teams to ensure that the content is good enough. They can also assist you in producing the content (for a fee). Remember, bad content on your site can destroy the credibility of your brand. That's exactly why the *New York Times* has a division that only creates sponsored content for brands. The *Times* will not allow brands to create the content themselves for fear that they won't get it right.

- **Clear labels.** As of this printing, the FTC is not going to get involved with any guidelines, in the hope that the industry will police itself. I believe that will happen—and is even happening now. Using terms like *sponsored, promoted,* or even *advertorial* is appropriate. Just make sure it's clear to visitors that the content is a paid placement. Use your common sense.

Why Native Advertising Might Be Neither

Content Marketing Institute chief strategist Robert Rose believes that native advertising, in the purist sense of the term, is neither native nor advertising.

Rose on why it's not native:

> With few exceptions, my aim is to create content that stands out so well that you can't help but notice the ironic, inherent pitch in there. I'm leveraging the fact that it's in context with the brand to draw a certain reaction from the audience. So . . . the less "native" content is—and the more I can creatively leverage both brands in context with each other—the more powerful it can be.

Rose on why it's not advertising:

> The point is that if we are going to successfully utilize contextually placed content to achieve a marketing result, we have to think about it differently than we would an advertisement. . . . We, as marketers, must rethink what kinds of goals we want to achieve with contextually placed content. It is, quite simply, different than our goals with advertising.

Overall, some are concerned about the way that the lines between editorial and advertising are blurred with native advertising. In all likelihood, those concerns will continue to linger as native advertising continues to grow.

Regardless, as you grow out your content platform, native advertising is a possible tactic to diversify your revenues and support the platform.

Subscriptions

The second oldest way to generate money from content is through subscriptions, such as a magazine or newspaper subscription. Over the years, these have morphed into digital subscriptions, like paying for access to the *New York Times* online.

Because so much content today is available for free to consumers, content subscription programs may be the hardest to monetize of all your options. That said, John Lee Dumas created a very successful community subscription called Fire Nation Elite, which includes regular coaching conference calls and exclusive content (Figure 22.7).

Figure 22.7   John Lee Dumas at EntrepreneurOnFire.com launched a paid subscription program for VIP members

Premium Content

The majority of Content Inc. models serve up premium content, like e-books and exclusive reports, for free to gain more subscribers or more information about subscribers (called "progressive profiling"). Some, like Digital Photography School, develop e-books and specialty reports

Figure 22.8 Digital Photography School sells premium e-books as part of its monetization strategy.

for direct sale (Figure 22.8). DPS's premium content sales have become the core of the company's monetization strategy.

Conferences and Events

As more and more people begin to form relationships online, it has created an unexpected need for these people to actually meet in person. The event and conference business has never been more robust. Both Content Marketing Institute and Social Media Examiner drive their revenue models through events. For example, Content Marketing World alone is a $6 million event, with about 30 percent of that coming from sponsorship sales and the rest from paid attendees (Figure 22.9).

Cross-Media (Books, Magazines, Webinars, Podcasts, Etc.)

Once you develop a content platform, you can monetize that content through a full suite of content products (both paid and sponsored) such as book offerings, video programs, print or digital magazines, webinar programs, and podcasts.

Comedian and podcast celebrity Marc Maron has built one of the largest podcast audiences in the world with his flagship, *WTF with Marc Maron*. At the same time, he's launched a bestselling book, *Attempting Normal*, and a CD series called *This Has to Be Funny*, as well as a successful video series on Netflix called *Maron*. Maron also performs at comedy clubs around the country. (*Note:* Maron has an

CMWorld 2015

Content Marketing World is the one event where you can learn and network with the best and the brightest in the content marketing industry.

You will leave with all the materials you need to take a content marketing strategy back to your team – and – to implement a content marketing plan that will grow your business and inspire your audience.

Figure 22.9   CMI monetizes its Content Inc. model primarily through events like Content Marketing World.

impressive subscription model where superfans can get early access to all the podcasts as well as complete access to his content archives; for more about this, check out http://cmi.media/CI-WTF.)

Crowdfunding

With services like Kickstarter on the rise, it's easier than ever to ask your community to help fund your Content Inc. model. Seth Price decided to launch his own Content Inc. platform with a podcast. In the absence of funding, he went to Kickstarter to try to raise $5,000. Seven days and 69 backers later, Seth had his funds and was off to the races (Figure 22.10).

Micropayments

Although I personally have not seen this work, Marc Andreessen believes that collecting micropayments through Bitcoin is a viable option for Content Inc. models. Coinbase, an online wallet system for

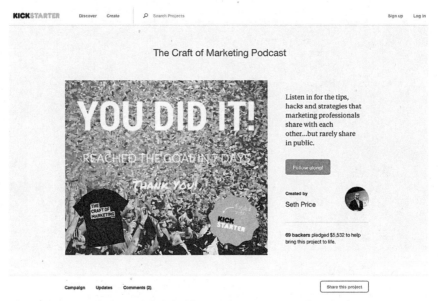

Figure 22.10 Seth Price funded his podcast in seven days by leveraging Kickstarter.

Bitcoin, is one easy way to set up your site to collect micropayments using the online currency model.

Philanthropy

Pro Publica (http://www.propublica.org/) is a nonprofit organization that uses its funding to develop investigative journalism that it deems is important for the public to hear. Founded by Paul Steiger, former managing editor of the *Wall Street Journal*, Pro Publica employs 45 journalists and received its major funding from the Sandler Corporation, which committed funding for multiple years upon Pro Publica's launch in June 2008. Pro Publica also accepts ongoing donations from anyone that believes in the organization's cause.

Products

According to Anne Janzer, author of *Subscription Marketing*, selling products from a content site, while being the most intensive in research and development, has the biggest revenue upside.

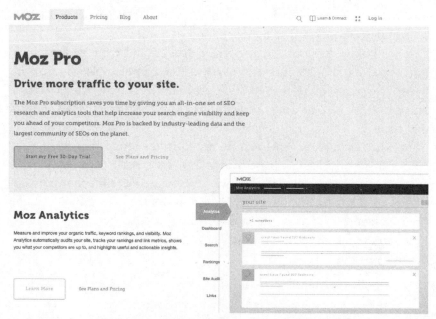

Figure 22.11   Moz has built a $30 million-plus business by selling an analytics and SEO measurement product.

As an example, look at Copyblogger Media. It sells content and search software as its core sales driver. Moz, which launched as an SEO blog, has grown into a $30 million–plus business off the back of its search analytics product (Figure 22.11).

WHAT IF YOU ALREADY SELL SOMETHING?

If you're a mature company with multiple products or services, you monetize your content by answering this question: "What is the difference between those that subscribe to my content and those that do not?"

Let's look again at River Pools & Spas. Before launching its Content Inc. approach, the company installed fiberglass pools. By monitoring the engagement of its blog content, River Pools found that those audience members that engage in at least 30 pages of content and request a sales appointment will buy 80 percent of the time. The industry average for sales appointments is 10 percent. So in this particular case, there is an 800 percent increase in the likelihood of a sale.

River Pools also looks at particular articles and their performance. In using a marketing automation system (the company uses HubSpot), River Pools has found that its blog post entitled "How Much Does a Fiberglass Pool Cost?" has resulted in over $2 million in sales. How's that for a return on investment?

Another example is American Express. It has found that its content platform, Open Forum, delivers as many new credit card sign-ups as anything else it does digitally. How? Once someone joins the site (subscribes to the content), the company monitors that person and, at the right moment, delivers credit card offers.

If you are trying to find the impact of your content, here are a number of questions to consider:

- Are subscribers more likely to buy?
- Are subscribers more likely to buy new products?
- Do subscribers stay longer as customers?
- Do subscribers talk more about us on social (word of mouth)?
- Do subscribers close faster than nonsubscribers?
- Do subscribers buy more on average than nonsubscribers?

Any one of these can justify the investment behind a Content Inc. approach.

The most recent Content Marketing Benchmarks report from Content Marketing Institute and MarketingProfs offers a look at the top organizational goals for business-to-business marketers in North America (Figure 22.12). Ongoing, engaging content leads to a number of benefits that will help grow your business. Your challenge is to find the benefit that justifies the program.

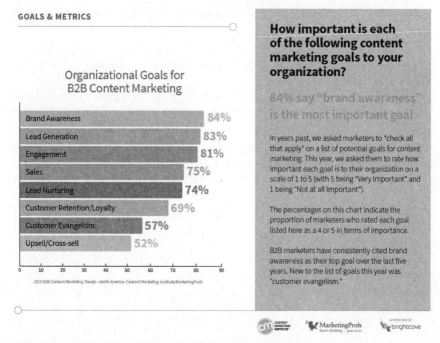

Figure 22.12 Businesses have many objectives for employing content marketing strategies.

CONTENT INC. INSIGHTS

- There are many ways to make money from your content and subscribers.
- Sometimes the best revenue opportunities are unexpected. It's important to not get so tied up with your main revenue generation source that you might miss a better opportunity.
- Some of the best Content Inc. models employ multiple ways to make money from their audiences.

Resources

Pamela Muldoon, "How Doug Kessler Went from Limos to Crap to Content Marketing Success," ContentMarketingInstitute.com, accessed April 28, 2015, http://contentmarketinginstitute.com/2015/03/kessler-b2b-content-marketing-podcast/.

Grant Cardone, "The Seven Secrets of Self-Made Millionaires," Entrepreneur.com, accessed April 28, 2015, http://www.entrepreneur.com/article/222718.

Rob Scallon, interview by Clare McDermott, February 2015.

Joe Crea, "Michael Symon Signature Knives Can Be Part of Your Kitchen Tools Later This Year," Cleveland.com, accessed April 28, 2015, http://www.cleveland.com/dining/index.ssf/2015/02/michael_symon_signature_knives.html.

"Michael Symon," Wikipedia, accessed April 28, 2015, http://en.wikipedia.org/wiki/Michael_Symon.

Ivan Walsh, "Case Study: How Copyblogger Shifted from Blog Publishing to Product Development," ivanwalsh.com, accessed April 28, 2015, http://www.ivanwalsh.com/case-study/copyblogger/.

Marc Andreessen, "Why I'm Bullish on the News," Politico.com, accessed April 28, 2015, http://www.politico.com/magazine/story/2014/05/marc-andreesen-why-im-bullish-on-the-news-105921.html.

CrunchBase, "Mark Andreessen," Crunchbase.com, accessed April 28, 2015, https://www.crunchbase.com/person/marc-andreessen.

Marc Andreessen, "The Future of the News Business," a16z.com, accessed April 28, 2015, http://a16z.com/2014/02/25/future-of-news-business/.

Stuart Dredge, "YouTube Star The Diamond Minecart Launches App for His Minecraft Videos," theguardian.com, accessed April 28, 2015, http://www.theguardian.com/technology/2014/nov/28/youtube-minecraft-the-diamond-minecart-app.

IAB, "Native Advertising Report," iab.net, http://www.iab.net/nativeadvertising.

Hexagram, "State of Native Advertising Report," hexagram.com, accessed April 28, 2015, http://stateofnativeadvertising.hexagram.com/.

Terri Thornton, "Native Advertising Shows Great Potential, but Blurs Editorial Lines," pbs.org, accessed April 28, http://www.pbs.org/mediashift/2013/04/native-advertising-shows-great-potential-but-blurs-editorial-lines092/.

Benjy Boxer, "What Buzzfeed's Data Tells Us About the Price of Native Advertisements," Forbes.com, accessed April 28, 2015, http://www.forbes.com/sites/benjaminboxer/2013/09/10/what-buzzfeeds-data-tells-about-the-pricing-of-native-advertisements/.

David Amerland, "How Native Advertising Is Going to Change Marketing in 2014," socialmediatoday.com, accessed April 28, 2015, http://www

.socialmediatoday.com/content/how-native-advertising-going-change
-marketing-2014-video.

Mitch Joel, "We Need a Better Definition of 'Native Advertising,'" hbr.org, accessed April 28, 2015, https://hbr.org/2013/02/we-need-a-better-definition -of/.

Adweek, "The 4 Major Digital Ad Formats Face Off," adweek.com, accessed April 28, 2015, http://www.adweek.com/news/advertising-branding/4-major -digital-ad-formats-face-161667.

Michael Winkleman, "Branded Content Trends in 2014," commpro.biz, accessed April 28, 2015, http://www.commpro.biz/marketing/branding/ branded-content-trends-2014/.

Seth Price, "The Craft of Marketing Podcast," Kickstarter.com, accessed April 28, 2015, https://www.kickstarter.com/projects/sethprice/the-craft-of -marketing-podcast.

Part 8

Next-Level Content Inc.

Knowledge has to be improved, challenged,
and increased constantly, or it vanishes.
PETER DRUCKER

You found the sweet spot, identified the content tilt, built the base, attracted an audience, and identified your monetization strategy. What can you do to keep the momentum going?

Chapter 23

Putting It All Together

Never look back unless you are planning to go that way.
HENRY DAVID THOREAU

The year was 2001. Joy Cho, a recent Syracuse graduate with a bachelor of fine arts in communications design, moved to New York to find a job and start her career in design. Joy was able to land an opportunity at a boutique advertising agency in New York, where she was a graphic designer and worked with a number of clients.

SETTING THE GOAL

After working a couple of design jobs in New York, Joy moved to Philadelphia to be closer to her then boyfriend (now husband). While looking for her next job, she started freelancing and began her blog, *Oh Joy!* Although a hobby at the time, her blog attracted readers and thus resulted in a freelance client who came to her through the aesthetic she developed and shared on her blog. Soon her plans to get a new full-time job turned into the decision to start her own design studio as a full-time freelancer. Although Joy loved her design work (for the most part), it was hard for her to see that she could make a decent living from it. There was the constant "hustle" of having to find and maintain clients to pay the bills. On having this discussion with her brother-in-law (also a freelance graphic design) about the ability to support herself, he said,

"Who says you can't? You can absolutely make a good living doing what you love; you just have to believe it."

It was then that she began to write down her (lofty) financial goals (which she continues to do to this day). The simple act of writing them down helped to provide her with the motivation to keep doing great work and gave her the goal to make a decent living at doing what she loved.

THE SWEET SPOT

Joy had skills in graphic design. She was trained in communications design and had a keen sense for what worked and what didn't around design and fashion (the knowledge area). At the same time, Joy was passionate about design variety. She dreaded working on the same old banner ads or client briefs. Every day Joy wanted to work on something different (the passion), and this variety led her to a new opportunity. Her sweet spot was a melding of design and fashion and variety (Figure 23.1).

THE CONTENT TILT

Joy had the gift of extreme authenticity. She loved sharing her thoughts and ideas and knew she could find just the right balance of how much

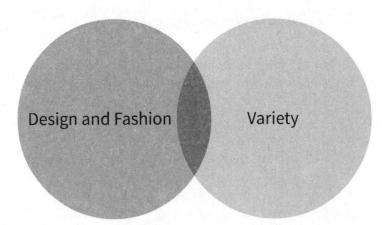

Figure 23.1 Joy Cho's life passion of variety and her knowledge area around design and fashion made up her sweet spot.

sharing would feel right to her. In an interview with *Glamour* magazine, she revealed that she secretly admires people who "walk to the beat of their own drum and don't care what people think." She wasn't always that way, but over time, she saw how important it is to do what you love and not worry so much about what others think.

What Joy found was that this sharing method was extremely attractive to a certain audience that was passionate about design and fashion. As Michael Grothaus of Fast Company writes, "In spite of the public appetite for expertise, there's a value in being approachable." The people who made up Joy's audience didn't want to hear from "the expert"; they wanted to hear from someone who didn't sound like she knew it all and was interested in how we can all, together, find the truth. It was this authenticity combined with her sweet spot that created her content tilt (see Figure 23.2).

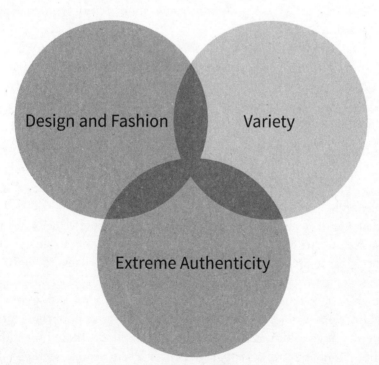

Figure 23.2 Joy's content tilt was her extreme authenticity. Mixed with her sweet spot, that became a powerful combination.

BUILDING THE BASE

In transitioning between jobs, Joy decided to launch a blog (September 7, 2005), *Oh Joy!* In her initial post, she announced the things you might read about on her blog:

1. *Being a freelance designer & all things related to shopping, home stuff, and visually cool things.*
2. *Being newly engaged, in love, & in the process of planning a wedding.*
3. *Being the owner of three cats. Mind you, I did not get three cats on my own . . . they are the result of the merging of assets between Me and my New Fiancé . . . one + two = three.*
4. *Being friends with Beth without whom this blog would not be possible. She also deserves credit for the name of my blog.*
5. *Being a fan of food and eating . . . all the time. You'll wonder how a small Asian girl could think about food so much. But really, it's possible.*
6. *Lastly, being a huge nerd. This is something I have come to accept in my recent years of adulthood. I am a dork/nerd and there is nothing anyone can do about it. Once you pass your mid-twenties, the level of dorkiness within you is pretty much set.*

In that first month, Joy posted 35 times and stayed true to her mission. Her posts were deeply personal, focusing on a variety of fashion and design tips (and included cats), and integrated first-rate photography and design skills.

From October on, Joy continued with her publishing velocity, posting sometimes up to three times a day. She was receiving so many client inquiries through her website that she never went back to work for another company. Within a year, Joy was confident that she could launch her own design studio off the back of the blog as her primary platform.

As Joy's platform grew, she adopted a collaborative publishing model where she hired additional bloggers to add to the depth and breadth of the site's content. She kept that model for a few years and then, after having her first baby, decided to go back to posting on her own from the desire to blog a bit more personally again.

HARVESTING AUDIENCE

Joy was actively building a loyal audience as more and more people signed up to Joy's daily e-mail newsletter. As she continued to meet the needs of her audience Joy set an official editorial calendar and workflow to publish three times daily. As social media began to grow in importance, she broadened her digital footprint to build additional audiences on Instagram, Pinterest, and Twitter. In 2008, *Time* magazine named *Oh Joy!* one of the top 100 design blogs on the planet. Figure 23.3 presents a snapshot of her blog.

DIVERSIFICATION

The three legs of the personal branding stool are now in full force for Joy, who has published three books (*Blog Inc.*, *Creative Inc.*, and her newest title, *Oh Joy! 60 Ways to Create & Give Joy*) and has keynoted

Figure 23.3   Early on, Joy recognized the need to build an audience through e-mail.

at a variety of design and marketing events, even sharing the stage with Martha Stewart. Joy has a robust following, to put it mildly:

- **Instagram.** Over 200,000 followers.
- **Twitter.** Over 70,000 followers.
- **YouTube.** Even lower-performing videos on Joy's YouTube page see thousands of views, and she's now amassed 20,000 subscribers on the platform.
- **Pinterest.** One of the most pinned designers on the platform, Joy has over 13 million followers.

MONETIZATION

Joy's studio business is thriving; she's consulted on design projects for some of the largest brands in the world.

In addition, Joy has designed and coproduced products for such brands as Target and Microsoft, and she has developed stationery lines, wallpaper, bedding, diaper bags, and even computer accessories. She also recently debuted a line of Band-Aids from Johnson & Johnson, which are almost certain to sell out in a similar fashion to her Target line.

Joy also accepts advertising on her site through sponsored content (or native advertising). Joy only works with brands she believes in and works with each of the brands to make sure the content works for her audience's needs.

Joy's revenues are diverse, from direct client engagement revenues to product sales to sponsorship to licensing deals. Even though Joy's platform has been around since 2005, it looks as though the sky's the limit, and the best is yet to come for Joy Cho.

THE COMPLETE PACKAGE

Like all the Content Inc. examples described in this book, Joy's Content Inc. success can be broken down into six distinct steps. The same was true for Matthew Patrick, Darren Rowse, Ann Reardon, and yours truly. Joy found her sweet spot, became a truly differentiated voice through her extreme authenticity, built the base through the blog, began acquiring a loyal audience, diversified through books and social media, and now monetizes her platform with dozens of product lines, licensing deals, and consulting opportunities.

And as for Joy's financial goals . . . Joy continues to write down lofty and, in her words, "insane" annual financial goals at the start of each year. Each and every year, she has surpassed what she's written down.

MORE CONTENT INC. CASES TO INSPIRE

Lucas Cruikshank

Cruikshank created the first YouTube channel to reach 1 million subscribers through his "Fred" character (a fictional six-year-old with anger management issues). He parlayed that success into a series of Nickelodeon hits. He's currently on his second Content Inc. model, now going by just the name "Lucas," which has quickly garnered well over a million subscribers (see https://www.youtube.com/user/lucas).

David Seah

After developing a loyal following for his blogging platform around design, David began to monetize his Content Inc. strategy through productivity tools. While the majority of his business is still consulting, tools such as the Emergent Task Planner and the Concrete Goal Tracker have gone from just a few sales a week to thousands a month via Amazon.com. David believes that pretty soon he'll be able to retire on this very unexpected business (see http://davidseah.com/).

Razor Social

Ian Cleary has single-handedly built the go-to resource for social media tools at RazorSocial.com. While there were many sites that talked about social media tools from time to time, Ian recognized the need to make sense of all the social tools that were available. His directory has become a treasure trove of resources for marketers, and the site now garners hundreds of thousands of visitors per month (see http://razorsocial.com/).

Gary Vaynerchuck

Gary's *Wine Library TV* was one of the early Content Inc. models to gain national appeal. With his daily videos covering wine for the "everyday" person, Gary turned his small family liquor store into a multimillion-dollar franchise. Soon after, Gary launched Vayner Media, one of the top social media consultancies, which now employs over 400 people and works with some of the largest brands on the planet (see http://vaynermedia.com/).

Greg Ng
Greg launched a frozen-food review site, Freezerburns, back in 2008. Since then, with over 1,000 frozen-food reviews and 700-plus videos later, Greg easily reaches 75,000 views per episode. "Freezerburns was the result of careful planning and identifying of a profitable, untapped niche," says Ng (see http://www.freezerburns.com/).

LEGO
Everyone knows the story of LEGO's storytelling empire, capped off by the unexpected success of *The LEGO Movie*. But very few realize that LEGO started *Brick Kicks* magazine (now *LEGO Club* magazine; see http://www.lego.com/en-us/club/) in 1987. (I received the first issue.)

Red Bull Media House
A separate entity from Red Bull, Red Bull Media House produces *Red Bulletin* magazine (in print and digital), distributing it to over 6 million subscribers. In addition, Red Bull licenses video and photography to traditional media companies, which turned Red Bull Media House into a stand-alone profit center. According to sources at Red Bull, the content assets owned under Red Bull Media House will actually produce more revenue than Red Bull earns from selling beverages (see http://www.redbullmediahouse.com/).

RockandRollCocktail.com
Jason Miller might be best known for his content marketing role at social media powerhouse LinkedIn, but it's his photography model that is working for Content Inc. lovers. Jason has photographed some of the greatest acts of all time, including Patti Smith and the Smashing Pumpkins. After every show, Jason shares key photos out to his Facebook audience and has built a cult following. Jason's content tilt of

marketing infused with rock 'n' roll has set Jason apart from the pack (see http://rocknrollcocktail.com/blog/).

The Good Life Project

Launched by serial entrepreneur Jonathan Fields, the Good Life Project has become a movement around doing good and not just doing things. Jonathan produces a weekly web show and highlights people working on amazing projects around the world. The three-legged-stool model is alive and well with Jonathan, who's developed a bestselling book and powerful speaking platform, in addition to the digital platform (see http://www.goodlifeproject.com/about/).

Fold Factory

Trish Witkowski, CEO of Fold Factory, has become a celebrity in the direct mailing industry through her regular video show, *The 60-Second Super Cool Fold of the Week*, where she details amazing examples of print direct mail. According to Andrew Davis, "Her 250-plus videos have yielded over 800,000 views and more than 3,100 subscribers. In addition, Trish has become a spokesperson for a number of brands, tours the world as a speaker, and conducts workshops." Trish's Content Inc. initiative has been directly responsible for over $500,000 in new revenue (see her website at https://www.youtube.com/user/foldfactory).

Marriott

In late 2014, Marriott announced the development of Marriott Content Studio, which aims to become the leading media information company in the travel industry. Like LEGO and Red Bull before it, who have built substantial content platforms in their respective fields, Marriott believes that becoming a leading voice in travel is not relegated to just selling hotel rooms.

STACK Media

As high school teammates, Nick Palazzo and Chad Zimmerman realized that they had major challenges finding workout information specific to high school players. Building on that realization, they launched STACK Media and covered regular workouts from pros like Peyton Manning and LeBron James that high school athletes could emulate. Nick and Chad have turned STACK into a top 10 sports video distribution site, garnering 15 million monthly unique visitors and partnerships with over 13,000 schools (see http://www.stack.com/).

PewDiePie
Sweden's Felix Arvid Ulf Kjellberg, aka PewDiePie, is the most subscribed YouTube personality on the planet. Since inception, PewDiePie's videos on indie games have garnered more than 8 billion views (see https://www.youtube.com/user/PewDiePie).

EvanTubeHD
What if I told you one of the most successful entrepreneurs on YouTube is just nine years old? Evan from EvanTubeHD.com consistently reviews toys on his YouTube channel, amassing over one million subscribers and a staggering one billion views in just a few years. According to ESPN, Evan generated $1.3 million in revenue last year. Wow (see https://www.youtube.com/user/evantubehd).

Glossier
Emily Weiss, founder and CEO of Glossier, began the company as a simple blog. 200,000 followers on Instagram and 60,000 Facebook fans later, Glossier has become one of the leading online retailers for skin care products. The business is thriving, with Emily recently raising $8.4 million from Thrive Capital and other investors (see https://www.glossier.com/).

ONE WORD: *PATIENCE*
If you've made it this far, I'm going to ask you to go one step further:
  Be patient.
There are only nine months between when I believed I was a complete failure and when I started something that looked to have the promise of success. As I think back, it would have been so easy to give up and go find a "real" job.
I can't even imagine that. I love my career, the time I have with my family, the flexibility of my schedule, and how I wake up every morn-

ing inspired to work on a project. If I hadn't been patient, none of this would be possible right now.

I launched the business in April 2007. It wasn't until the end of 2010 that I felt we were on to something. The next three years we made the Inc. 500 list of the fastest-growing private companies in the United States. Today we have a $10 million business, and I'm still able to pick my kids up from school. It wasn't easy, but having patience made all this possible. It takes time to build a loyal audience. It takes time to find the right revenue model for your Content Inc. business.

But there is no doubt in my mind that this is the absolute best way to launch a business. Yes, it's different . . . some may say it's strange . . . but it's a better strategy than just hoping that a new product idea will take hold. Be like David, who fought the urge to fight just like everyone else had against Goliath (and lost). Take a different route and put the odds in your favor.

GETTING STUCK

As you progress through this model, there will be moments where you feel the model isn't working quite to your expectations. That makes sense. Content Inc., as a way of launching a business, is a new muscle for most people. We've been used to communicating through mass media for so many years, and now we are trying to figure out how to deliver value to our customers outside of our products and services.

If you are struggling with your program, come back and review this chapter. You may be struggling because of one of these reasons:

- **Selfish content marketing.** Create content that solves customers' pain points. Stop talking about your products and services so much. If you do, make it about your customers.
- **You stop.** The biggest reason why content marketing fails is because it either stops or isn't consistent. Remember, the content you deliver is like a promise to your customers. The biggest reason why the examples in this book succeeded was because the people never stopped producing amazing and compelling content.
- **Activity instead of audience.** Having people share and engage with your content here and there doesn't mean much unless you are

building an audience. One of the biggest mistakes companies make is not planning, in advance, to acquire an audience through content creation and distribution.

- **No point of view.** In order to position yourself as an expert in your industry, you need a point of view. Take a stance. Walking the fence is boring and, more importantly, usually doesn't work.
- **No process.** I see it every day. *Scenario:* Marketing campaign . . . ads to be placed . . . then someone asks about the blog or white paper . . . people scurry about . . . someone runs out to get the content. Plan up front to create, repurpose, and distribute content.
- **Where's the call to action?** Each piece of content should have a call to action or behavior you'd like to see. What would happen if you asked "why" to each piece of content you create? By doing this, you'll be compelled to either know the call to action or kill the content (for lack of purpose).
- **Channel silo.** Are you paying attention to one channel at the expense of all the others? We want to have one main platform, like a blog, but you'll miss the true power of content marketing by not leveraging all available channels as you expand your model. Think like a media company. The greatest media companies of all time focus on all three legs of the stool—digital content, print content, and in-person content.
- **Forgetting employees.** Employee expertise is the most underutilized content marketing asset. Your employees give your brand life. Leverage them in the creation and distribution process. Start with the 5 percent that get it. Show success stories and move on to the rest of your employee base.

   Tip: Don't force your employees into a process they won't do. Gather the raw content from employees however you can.
- **One word: *editing*.** Editing may be the most underrated piece of the content marketing process. Sometimes we as entrepreneurs don't understand that the first draft of a piece of content is called a good start. Enter the editor. Get one or hire one.

What's holding you back from your Content Inc. model?

MOVING FORWARD

Yes, there will be challenges. There will be times that you're not sure you are on the right path. That is natural for any entrepreneur or small business owner. But here's the truth: Until now, it was cost prohibitive for entrepreneurs to build a loyal audience. Until now, the communication channels were not available. Until now, the audience wasn't willing to connect.

Until now.

By reading and following the Content Inc. method in this book, you have an opportunity to make a difference in your life, with your family, with your career path, and in the world. My hope is that you seize that opportunity today and never look back.

CONTENT INC. INSIGHTS

- The Content Inc. model is successful because of six distinct and important steps. What steps are you missing in your model?
- What's holding you back? Whatever it is, pinpoint the problem and move forward. Content Inc. is an amazing opportunity for any entrepreneur striving to make a difference in the world.

Resources

Emily Ryles, "Joy Cho of Oh Joy!," theeverygirl.com, accessed April 28, 2015, http://theeverygirl.com/joy-cho-of-oh-joy.

Jane Buckingham, "5 Career Questions with Oh Joy!," Glamour.com, accessed April 28, 2015, http://www.glamour.com/inspired/2014/03/job-advice -from-oh-joy-blogger-joy-cho.

Stephanie at Design Sponge, "Biz Ladies Profiles: Joy Cho of Oh Joy!," design sponge.com, accessed April 28, 2015, http://www.designsponge.com/ 2013/02/biz-ladies-profile-joy-cho-of-oh-joy.html.

Joy Cho, *Oh Joy! Blog*, accessed April 28, 2015, http://ohjoy.blogs.com/.

Michael Grothaus, "The Secrets of Writing Smart, Long-Form Articles That Go Absolutely Viral," FastCompany.com, accessed April 28, 2015, http:// www.fastcompany.com/3042312/most-creative-people/the-secrets-of -writing-smart-longform-articles-that-go-absolutely-viral.

Time Staff, "30 Most Influential People on the Internet," Time.com, accessed April 28, 2015, http://time.com/3732203/the-30-most-influential-people -on-the-internet/.

"Lucas Cruikshank," Wikipedia, accessed April 28, 2015, http://en.wikipedia .org/wiki/Lucas_Cruikshank.

David Seah, interview by Clare McDermott, February 2015.

David Griner, "After 1,000 Meals, Here's What Made the Frozen Food Review King Call It Quits," adweek.com, accessed April 28, 2015, http://www .adweek.com/adfreak/after-1000-meals-heres-what-made-frozen-food -review-king-call-it-quits-159850.

Marriott News Center, "Marriott International's Content Studio Rapidly Expands Presence," Marriott.com, accessed April 28, 2015, http://news .marriott.com/2014/12/marriott-internationals-content-studio-rapidly -expands-presence-with-additional-content-development-.html.

"PewDiePie," Wikipedia, accessed April 28, 2015, http://en.wikipedia.org/wiki/ PewDiePie.

Kim Mai-Cutler, "Glossier CEO on Building a Skincare, Cosmetics Empire Online at Disrupt NY," Techcrunch.com, accessed on June 11, 2015, http:// techcrunch.com/2015/04/16/glossier-2/.

Tracey Harrington McCoy, "The Most Popular Kid You've Never Heard Of," Newsweek.com, accessed on June 11, 2015, http://www.newsweek.com/ 2013/11/01/most-popular-kid-youve-never-heard-243854.html.

Chapter 24

Join the Movement

The revolution is not an apple that falls when it is ripe.
You have to make it fall.

CHE GUEVARA

When I started writing this book, I quickly realized how much need there really is around the subject of Content Inc. In addition, as a Content Inc. believer myself, how could I "just" write a book and not include a number of additional resources. Simply put, I needed to eat my own dog food.

So here's my list of important and useful resources to help support your Content Inc. initiative:

• **The Content Inc. website.** Content Inc. has an official website as part of the Content Marketing Institute ecosystem. You can access all the site content at http://www.content-inc.com. Be sure to sign up to receive the e-newsletter updates, where you'll see our free webinars and upcoming events, as well as some epic content.

• **The Content Inc. podcast.** Every Monday and Tuesday I release short podcast episodes, which are always less than 15 minutes long. I try to keep them very actionable . . . and depending on how fast you run, three episodes equals about a 5-kilometer run. To sign up via iTunes or Stitcher, go to http://cmi.media/CI-podcast.

- **The Content Inc. Summit.** As part of Content Marketing World, every September in Cleveland, Ohio, we hold a one-day event dedicated to the Content Inc. model. The event takes place toward the front half of the month (and always depends on when Labor Day falls in the United States). For more information on that event, go to http://cmi.media/CI-summit.

NEXT-GENERATION CONTENT INC.

As you progress in your Content Inc. journey, you'll get to the point where you'll need even more resources and insights to keep growing. Here are some resources that will help:

- *Epic Content Marketing.* My third book will help you build in a segmentation and engagement cycle as you develop your product and service offerings.
- *Experiences: The 7th Era of Marketing* **by Robert Rose and Carla Johnson.** As your business grows, creating even more amazing experiences through content is imperative. Robert and Carla will show you how.
- *Digital Relevance* **by Ardath Albee.** Ardath is a leading expert on nurturing leads and integrating content into your business. Before you purchase any technology platforms for your marketing automation, read this book (http://cmi.media/CI-ardath).
- *Smartcuts* **by Shane Snow.** Shane covers a number of Content Inc. examples in his book that looks at, not shortcuts to developing audiences, but smarter strategies (hence, Smartcuts).
- *Everybody Writes* **by Ann Handley.** *Content Inc.* (the book) is not designed to help you learn how to effectively write, but Ann's book is. If you need writing help, get this book.
- *Art of the Start 2.0* **by Guy Kawasaki.** When I launched my business, *Art of the Start* was the first book I read, and it made an immediate impact. Guy has updated the book, and it's simply fantastic (http://cmi.media/CI-ArtStart).
- *UnSelling* and *UnMarketing* **by Scott Stratten.** Scott uses the worst social media case studies in the world to teach businesses how to

create an authentic presence on the web without using hard selling or marketing tactics (http://cmi.media/CI-stratten).

In addition to the hundreds of resources found in this book, there are some additional sites you'll want to check out to help you in your efforts:

- *Sorry for Marketing* **blog.** Jay Acunzo's fantastic blog, heavy on content creation and analysis (http://cmi.media/CI-sorry).
- *Orbit Media* **blog.** When I have a website question, I usually go to Andy Crestodina's blog for help (http://cmi.media/CI-orbit).
- **Convince & Convert.** Yes, it has great helpful content, but if you want to see how a great Content Inc. model works, just see what Jay Baer does (http://cmi.media/CI-convince).
- *TopRank Online Marketing* **blog.** Lee Odden has developed his own Content Inc. platform at TopRank, where he and his team discuss the most pressing marketing challenges on the planet (http://cmi.media/CI-toprank).

FINAL THOUGHTS

Even though it's not as easy as it used to be (because there are more people contacting me—a good problem), I still try to respond to as many tweets and e-mails as I can. You can find me on Twitter @JoePulizzi and on e-mail at joe@zsquaredmedia.com. Although I've cut my speaking back a bit, I still do a number of keynotes throughout the year. If you are interested in finding out more about having me speak at your event, you can get all the details at JoePulizzi.com.

Thank you for taking the time to read this book. I truly hope it was a valuable experience for you.

Now go out and make life happen. Be epic!

Acknowledgments

To the CMI staff, the most amazing people on the planet. You are a special and talented group of people. Shenanigans!

A very special thanks to Clare McDermott, who conducted most of the interviews for the book, to Michele Linn, who assisted in the development of the content, and to Joseph Kalinowski for the creative direction (to you, I will always be Chuke).

To Jim McDermott, my mentor and initial editor of this book. I'm here because of you.

To my parents, Terry and Tony, for always being there for me, no matter what I was doing.

To my Coolio friends in West Park. The best friends anyone could ever ask for.

To my boys, Adam and Joshua. Never settle. Don't be normal. Follow your passion. I'm so proud of both of you.

To Pam. My best friend. With you, every day is better than the last. I love you.

Phil 4:13

CMI's Contributor/ Blogging Guidelines

Thanks for your interest in contributing to the Content Marketing Institute. Below you will find details on the types of posts we look for and specifics about our editorial process.

Our editorial mission is to advance the practice of content marketing. While the core of our blog has been how-to posts, we have broadened our editorial focus and will now consider *useful* posts that truly aim to move this industry forward.

OUR AUDIENCE

While we educate anyone who uses content marketing, our ideal reader is marketers at large- and midsize B2B and B2C organizations.

SUBMISSION CRITERIA

We have a limited number of publishing slots available to guest contributors, and we will only accept posts that satisfy the following criteria:

- Posts need to *advance the practice of content marketing*. We will only accept posts that provide new insights for content marketers (i.e., we are not looking for posts with rehashed ideas).
- Posts need to be *useful*. While posts do not need to be a step-by-step how-to, they need to include a specific takeaway or key thought.

- Posts need to be *logical and interesting to read.*
- Posts need to be *specific to content marketers.*

These are the specific types of post we look for.

How-to Posts

We look for detailed posts that very clearly outline how to do something; templates, checklists, and step-by-step approaches work well. Examples include:

- "How to Put Together an Editorial Calendar for Content Marketing" (http://cmi.media/CI-editcal)
- "7 NEW Things to Do After You've Written a New Blog Post" (http://cmi.media/CI-blogpost)
- "An Easy Planning Worksheet That Will Jump-Start Your Content Marketing Productivity" (http://cmi.media/CI-worksheet)

"Thought Leadership" Posts

Content marketing is an industry that has been evolving quickly, and we want to be evaluating trends and figuring out what is coming next. Are there conversations you think we need to have to move the industry forward? Is there something going on that you want to call out that is not true or not working? What are the current trends? Examples include:

- "Content Marketing: The Fallacy That More Content Is Better" (http://cmi.media/CI-morecontent)
- "Oracle Acquires Eloqua: Will Content Marketing Be Impacted?" (http://cmi.media/CI-eloqua)
- "6 Ways the Content Marketing Backlash Is Getting It Wrong" (http://cmi.media/CI-backlash)

Content Marketing Career Posts

While content marketing has been evolving as a discipline, so too have the careers of many of our readers. We are looking for posts that share personal experiences or concrete ideas on what marketers need to be considering as they plan their careers. Examples include:

- "Content Marketing Best Practices: 5 Tips for the Modern CMO" (http://cmi.media/CI-modernCMO)
- "Content Marketing for Career Development" (http://cmi.media/CI -careerdev)

Content Marketing Tools and Technologies Posts

We will consider posts that profile specific content marketing tools and technologies when:

- The tool is free (e.g., Twitter, LinkedIn, Facebook).
- The author is not someone directly associated with or compensated by the technology vendor.
- The post does not discuss competitive benefits.

CMI occasionally covers paid tools in our Technology Landscape series or in posts that include a roundup of tools.

To increase the likelihood that your post will be accepted, consider these suggestions:

- Whenever possible, include real-life examples and/or case studies to demonstrate the concepts described.
  Example: "4 Ways to Use PR in Your Content Marketing Efforts [Case Study]" (http://cmi.media/CI-PR)
- Use of videos, photos, charts, screenshots, and other visual content is strongly encouraged. Feel free to embed new types of content platforms as well.
  Example: "Epic Content Marketers: 20 More Women Who Rock" (http://cmi.media/CI-womenrock)
- Articles should include detailed instruction or specific recommendations that will help marketers incorporate your advice into their content marketing processes.
  Example: "The Essential Guide to Meta Descriptions That Will Get You Found Online" (http://cmi.media/CI-meta)

In addition, we do not accept submissions that fall into the following categories:

- Posts with unclear focal points or those that are not clearly organized or formatted to grab reader attention. We encourage writers to use *subheadings, bulleted lists, and bold fonts to highlight key concepts and action items.*
- Articles created as blatant link-bait, with little original insight or practical discussion provided within the post copy.
- Op-ed–style posts that discuss why an issue is important without discussing how, specifically, it can be leveraged by content marketers.
- Posts that have already been published elsewhere.
- White papers and other promotional content that is meant to tout the benefits of one specific product or service over others.
- Posts that focus on content marketing basics (such as writing to a specific audience, finding time or ideas for content, etc.) or those that give only a general overview of complex topics (such as content creation, SEO, or making your content "social").

Due to the volume of submissions, we do not respond to guest post inquiries that include a request for a link exchange. These posts are not accepted.

WHY WRITE FOR CMI?

As you likely know, sharing your expertise with an engaged audience of content marketing professionals is a great way to improve your industry profile.

Many of our bloggers have told us they can directly trace new business to their posts on CMI (and sometimes posts they have written more than a year ago!).

Additionally, we have people contact us looking for work or asking to get involved in Content Marketing World. The best way to work with us is to become an active blogger who contributes solid, detailed posts. This is the pool of people we look to when we have opportunities.

OUR EDITORIAL PROCESS

Each post we receive is first reviewed for acceptance criteria. It may take a few days before our team can respond to new submissions. We receive many submissions, so we appreciate your patience throughout our review and production process.

If your submission fits our criteria and is likely to be a good fit for the CMI audience, we will contact you within seven business days of receipt to confirm our intent to review your post for publication.

Please note: Because of the volume of submissions, if your post is not a fit, we are unable to provide detailed feedback.

For posts being considered, average turnaround time for review is 10 business days, though the timeline may be shorter or longer, depending on the current volume of submissions under review.

Once a post has been accepted for publication, it is generally scheduled to run within a two-week time span. While we cannot always honor specific publication date requests, our editorial team will do its best to accommodate the needs of our contributors.

PROMOTION AND SOCIAL MEDIA DISTRIBUTION

CMI will promote all posts via Twitter, LinkedIn, Facebook, and other relevant social platforms. All authors are encouraged to promote their posts through their own networks, as well.

REPUBLISHING AND REPURPOSING YOUR CMI POSTS

While we can only consider original, unpublished materials for publication, we are happy to allow our published authors to repurpose their posts elsewhere, with the following stipulations:

- There should be a two-week window between the time your article goes live on CMI and the time it is published on another site.
- All subsequent publication of your article must cite the Content Marketing Institute as the original source and provide a link to the article on CMI.
- All CMI posts that are to be used in content curation efforts must adhere to standards of fair use of online content for content curation (http://cmi.media/CI-fairuse).

WHAT TO SEND WITH YOUR ARTICLE SUBMISSION

- **Your bio.** Bio should be approximately 60 words and should include your Twitter handle, as well as any other relevant links you wish to display (e.g., your blog, Facebook page, website URL, etc.).
- **Your headshot.** We use a site called Gravatar (http://cmi.media/CI -gravatar) to manage our authors' headshots. New contributors should create an account there and upload a headshot. Once this is done, we'll need the *e-mail address that was used to register the account*, so we can associate your headshot with the author profile we will use in your posts.
- **A thematically related cover image.** We also ask authors to include a high-resolution image that we can run as a "cover" image for each post. This can be a photo, a chart, a screenshot, or a piece of theme art that represents the article topic in a compelling visual way. Images can be taken from the web or a stock photo service, as long as they are royalty-free (or in the public domain or available as part of Creative Commons), or you hold the copyright. If the image requires creator credit, please provide the necessary sourcing information, so that we can be sure to attribute it properly.

If you would like to submit a post or article idea, or have any questions, please contact us at blog@contentinstitute.com. New contributors may also wish to submit links to additional writing samples that may aid in our decision-making process.

An Inside Look into CMI's Publishing Process

By Michele Linn, Content Marketing Institute's Vice President of Content

In 2010, I was lucky enough to join Joe on his journey when he launched Content Marketing Institute. Looking back at that (crazy) time, we got *a lot* done with a super-small team, but much of the process was ad hoc and trial and error.

Fast-forward to 2015 when we have launched another blog (and will soon be adding another). These days, the process is no longer a nice-to-have, but it's a necessity. It's not a matter of not having enough people on the team (as we do), but *because* there are more people, it's even more critical to have processes documented so things are getting done consistently and we don't drown in e-mails in which we're figuring out who needs to do what.

The information below, replete with checklists, is CMI's general process for our blog posts. No doubt this process will evolve between the time I am writing this and the time *Content Inc.* is published, but this offers a general framework so you can learn from our mistakes (although, truly, there is sometimes no better way).

SETTING UP THE TEAM

Before we dig into our blog processes, it's useful to walk through the kinds of people you need on your editorial team. For CMI, this includes:

- Lisa Dougherty, who manages the editorial calendar and all communications with our blog contributors
- Ann Gynn, who edits all the posts for logic, flow, and structure
- Yatri Roleston, who uploads and proofreads all our posts into WordPress

Ann, Yatri, and Lisa Higgs help across all the blogs, while Lisa Dougherty is focused on CMI.

Tip: When you have a high-volume blog that accepts contributors, look for a blog manager who has good communication, diplomacy, and business etiquette—and most importantly, someone you can trust implicitly to get the job done. This person needs the skills to be able to foster positive relationships with outside and internal members as well as strong project management skills, a thirst for knowledge, and a process-oriented mindset.

In previous evolutions of the blog, we had one person, first I was the one and then Jodi Harris, who managed the calendar, contributor relationships, and all the editing. However, as we increased the number of posts—and wanted to offer the best possible experience to our contributors as they are core of our community—we broke this into two roles: one who manages the calendar and contributors and one who handles the editing.

For a high-frequency blog like CMI, I far favor the structure we have now:

- It's very helpful to bounce ideas off each other, including what we should run, what titles work best, etc.
- It's a much more sustainable model that allows for people to take time off as needed—and it's something that we can more easily manage if staffing were to change.

Tip: It's worth every penny to have a strong copyeditor review everything before it is published. Even if you have other editors on the team, it helps to have a fresh perspective on the live version of the piece and someone whose sole focus is to proofread.

That said, if you are starting out and don't have a rigorous posting schedule, you may be able to get away with having two people on the team: a managing editor who reviews and schedules all posts (and writes as needed) and a copyeditor who checks everything before publication.

This is similar to the model we use for Intelligent Content (one of our brand extensions). Marcia Riefer Johnston is the managing editor of the Intelligent Content blog. She is a writer, editor, and member of the community who engages in conversations and asks great questions that serve as fodder for the blog. We publish two posts per week on the Intelligent Content blog, which is a much lower frequency than for the CMI blog, so Marcia's role is a combination of Lisa Dougherty's and Ann Gynn's. Lisa Higgs proofreads all posts, and I review all the content at a high level to make sure it is in line with CMI's overall editorial strategy (as I also do for CMI).

Tip: While managing editors have critical skills, if you need an editor who can also write (as is the case for the blogs we have launched), it's very useful to hire someone with skills—and relationships—in your industry. Not only can this person sniff out good stories, but she can also find the best writers in the space (and call in favors if needed).

GENERAL BLOG PROCESS

The CMI blog receives far more submissions than we can accept. In many ways, this is a great problem to have, but in other ways, it's a lot of communication to manage for content we don't end up using. As such, our process for working with all contributors has evolved as we have tried to really focus our time on publishing the best possible content while also respecting all the people who are generous with their time and contributions.

Here are the general steps we follow:

We review all posts to see if they are a fit with the mission of the CMI blog. Lisa Dougherty is our point of contact for all who submit posts, and she responds to all inquiries.

Tip: If you have a blog to which contributors can submit content, it's useful to have blog guidelines that you can easily share. Additionally, make it clear, as CMI does, if you only accept posts that are complete;

we don't consider pitches because the full text an author creates is often what differentiates a go versus a no-go post.

If we quickly know the post is not a fit, the author is notified.

If the post has potential, it is entered into our editorial tracker/calendar (more on this below). We have also created a central repository for all submissions using Dropbox so all posts can be easily accessed by all editorial team members. I, as CMI's vice president of content, am the first line of defense and review all feasible submissions to ensure a global and practical fit. From there, one of three things happens:

- The author of a post that is not a fit is notified by Lisa.
- An "on-the-fence" post is reviewed by Ann. Lisa follows up with the author to let him or her know more time may be needed.
- A definite-fit post is edited by Ann. We often expedite editing on submissions that are well written and follow CMI blog guidelines, as well those from regular contributors.

Tip: Create template responses for common submission scenarios that can be customized and e-mailed by the editorial team. These can save a tremendous amount of time (and they are especially useful when your primary outreach contact is out of the office).

After a blog post submission is considered viable, Lisa will then schedule it on the editorial calendar. On the line of its run date, she includes author name, headline, image type (custom or CMI stock image), general status, and upload status.

Managing our bloggers has become an increasing priority for us, and something we want to invest the time into. CMI relies heavily on influencers, as they write for our blog, speak at our events, participate in our Twitter chats, speak at our webinars—and more. It's also common that they spread the word about CMI. Because of this, our bloggers are the key influencers for CMI—and the industry as a whole—so we want them to have the best possible experience.

BLOG PUBLICATION CHECKLISTS

While checklists have their limitations, they are exceptionally useful in the publication process. Here are a few of the checklists for every blog post we publish.

Tip: It can be helpful to set up templates for posts that have recurring elements. For instance, our podcast show notes have standard sections and links. The author uses this template to create the show notes each week, which saves time for both the author and the editorial team (and the output is more consistent).

The Editorial Team's Checklist

These questions are checked off before the blog post has been finalized:

Editorial Checklist

- Are there any errors or inconsistencies? Does the post follow a logical conclusion?
- Does the post include actionable next steps? Will a reader know what to do after reading this?
- Does the post include things that make it easy to skim?
  - Are headers descriptive?
  - Are key points in bold?
  - Are there places where bulleted lists make sense?
  - Can we add screenshots to help illustrate or walk through key points?
- Is the headline effective?
- Has the post been fact-checked?
- Does the post include relevant internal (CMI) links to give readers more info (and help with SEO)?
- Are there too many external links? Do the links provide an example, add relevant detail, or provide source info for stats—not used purely for link-back or other promotional purposes?
- Is there a "cover image" that serves as the main image for the post—or does one need to be created?
- Does the post include a relevant call to action? (We have a running list of CTAs that the editorial team can use for reference. It's a mix of events, offers, and most popular and useful content.)
- Is there a previous post where we should add a link to the new post?
- Is there an excerpt for that post that is 255 characters max that can be used for e-mail and social sharing?

- Is there a metadescription that is 156 characters at most? This will be displayed in the search engine results.

     Tip: Keep a list of top-performing posts to which you want to continually link in other things you publish. We keep this list in our editorial tracker.
- Add "Click to Tweet" if appropriate. This is an easy way to prepopulate tweets that cover key points in a post.

Tip: Create a basic style guide for your team (even if it is a team of one). Decide on which professional style guide you want to generally rely (CMI uses AP style) and then develop a custom addendum (document) that stipulates your brand's variations or special cases that deviate from the primary guide. CMI's style guide is in Google Docs, to which the editorial team—and whole company—has access.

Once posts go through the editing process, they sometimes need to be returned to the author for clarification on some questions or additional information. In these cases, the post may be reviewed multiple times.

Publication Checklists

Once the blog post has been finalized, Yatri loads it into our content management system, WordPress. Here are our publication checklists:

General

- Set up the author profile if he or she is a first-time CMI author.
- Set the publication date and time.
- Select the appropriate categories, which are the main topics of your blog. (For instance, CMI categories include things such as content marketing strategy, visual design, and measurement.)
- Select the author
- Add the cover/main image. (*Note:* We also use Yoast's SEO plug-in so we can upload images at the right size for social.)
- Add all images and label accordingly for SEO optimization.

Tip: All the assets are uploaded to Dropbox for the editorial team to access. Each author has his or her own folder, and all assets are labeled consistently with author name_title_name reviewed_date of version.

Checklist for Text Elements

- Subheads should be H2.
- CMI links should open in same tab.
- Outside links should open into a new tab.
- CTAs should be italics, not bold.
- Under CTA, add "Cover image via . . ." and a link to the source, if available.
- Add "more" tag to beginning of post (usually 4 lines/2 paragraphs down in the article. This keeps the entire post from appearing on the CMI home page—only a snippet of the post will show unless visitors click "Read More").
- Maintain 1 line of space between an H2 subhead and the copy below it. Also add 1 line of space between the copy and a bulleted list. (If you do this in Word, it should transfer automatically when flowed into WordPress.)

SEO Considerations

- Include the permalink: 4–5 words with dashes; words someone may use in a long-tail search query.
- Include the excerpt: 235 characters max for social.
- Write the metadescription: 156 characters max for the SERP.
- Upload images: limit to 3–5 words with dashes. Words in images can be similar to the headline but not identical; change up the order and augment with a new word that reflects the image.

Preview Checklist

- Check all links.
- Make sure everything is displaying properly and all images are rendering clearly.
- Make sure formatting is consistent and correct (e.g., subheads are H2; bullet points are aligned properly; images aren't running into text anywhere, etc.).
- Read and verify links in author's bio.
- Make sure author's bio picture is showing up.
- Make sure there is "Cover image illustration by . . ." credit.

Once posts are loaded into WordPress, Yatri connects with CMI's e-mail team so it can load the daily e-mail.

A LOOK AT OUR EDITORIAL TRACKER/CALENDAR

We have been using Google spreadsheets as the basis for our editorial calendar/tracker for years (although we are looking into a number of new tools presently). Like everything else, this spreadsheet has evolved, and we keep our critical calendars and list in this one place. This is the "bible" for our editorial team. These are the tabs included:

- **Schedule of upcoming posts.** This is also where we track notes such as permalinks we need to use.
- **Posts in process.** This tab is a running list of every post we are working on, segregated by which team member is working on the post. (For instance, I have the section for posts I need to review. I know to look here instead of having to have Lisa e-mail me each time a post arrives.)
- **Priority keywords.** These are the keywords we want to rank for as well as details on each.
- **Editorial agenda.** The team updates this tab with anything we want to discuss during our weekly check-in calls.
- **Top posts and pages.** These are the posts that perform the best that we want to promote more heavily via social or within our editorial.
- **SEO best practices.** These are reminders to the team on things such as images, metadescriptions, and anything related to SEO.
- **Brick content.** This tab tracks any big content we have coming out.
- **Archived blog posts.** A list of all the blog posts that have run for reference (we simply move the published posts from the "Schedule of upcoming posts" tab here).
- **Important links.** These are things we refer to regularly that are handy to have in one spot.
- **Calls to action.** This is a running list of calls to action we can use in our blog posts.
- **Key topics.** These are the primary categories we use for our blog posts.

COMMUNICATIONS WITH AUTHORS

Once posts are scheduled, Lisa reaches out to authors with a preview of their posts. This includes:

- Final draft of the post
- Publication date
- Easy ideas on how to share the post via social channels

This step is useful, not only because it helps increase the sharing of the post, but because it also ensures there are no surprises with the final post.

Tip: Lisa does not seek final approval from the authors; however, by sending the authors the final draft and including the publication date, the authors know they should review the post and address any concerns before that date.

Authors are also notified when they receive the first comment to their live post. Lisa is notified of all comments, and our assistant, Kim Borden, moderates all comments so we can quickly remove any spam.

Tip: While our social team has its own system for content promotion, the editorial team socially shares all posts as well. Authors have noticed this—and have been very appreciative.

COMING FULL CIRCLE

Of course, we measure what we are doing so we can provide more content that works—and less of what does not.

While I often dig into Google Analytics, we look at the posts more systematically on a monthly basis. The data we track include:

- Publication date
- Title
- Author
- Tweets
- LinkedIn shares
- Facebook likes
- Other social shares
- Total social shares

- E-mail conversions from that page
- Page views

Many top-performing posts have high social shares as well as e-mail conversions, but this is not always the case.

Once we have a list of top posts, we share those with the CMI team members via our private LinkedIn group and encourage them to share these in their social networks (with prewritten tweets from our community manager, Mo Wagner), and Lisa individually reaches out to authors who have top-performing posts—and those we want to work with again.

While I think about process more than I ever imagined I would, it's core to creating consistent, high-quality content. It's also the guardrails and structure we need so we have time to think creatively.

Index

Page numbers in italics refer to figures.

About the Author

Joe Pulizzi is an entrepreneur, speaker, author, podcaster, father, and lover of all things orange. He's the founder of multiple start-ups, including the Content Marketing Institute (CMI), the leading content marketing educational resource for enterprise brands, recognized as the fastest-growing business media company by *Inc.* magazine in 2014. CMI is responsible for producing Content Marketing World, the largest content marketing event in the world (held every September in Cleveland, Ohio), as well as the leading content marketing magazine, *Chief Content Officer*. He began using the term *content marketing* back in 2001. CMI also offers advisory services for innovative organizations such as HP, AT&T, Petco, LinkedIn, SAP, the Gates Foundation, and many others.

Joe is the winner of the 2014 John Caldwell Lifetime Achievement Award from the Content Council. Joe's third book, *Epic Content Marketing: How to Tell a Different Story, Break Through the Clutter, and Win More Customers by Marketing Less*, was named one of the Five Must-Read Business Books of the Year by *Fortune Magazine*. Joe has also coauthored two other books, *Get Content Get Customers* and *Managing Content Marketing*. Joe has spoken at more than 400 locations in 15 countries advancing the practice of content marketing. He's delivered keynote speeches for events and organizations including SXSW, NAMM, *Fortune Magazine*'s Leadership Summit, Disney, Cisco Systems, Oracle Eloqua, DuPont, SAP, HP, and Dell.

Joe not only writes one of the most influential content marketing blogs in the world; he writes a column for Entrepreneur.com and LinkedIn. You can also hear Joe on his podcasts, *This Old Marketing* and *Content Inc*, the companion podcast to this book. If you ever meet him in person, he'll be wearing orange. Joe lives in Cleveland, Ohio with his wife and two boys. You can find Joe on Twitter @JoePulizzi.